GENDER AND DISCOURSE: THE POWER OF TALK

edited by

Alexandra Dundas Todd

Sue Fisher

Volume XXX in the Series
ADVANCES IN DISCOURSE PROCESSES
Roy O. Freedle, Editor

ABLEX PUBLISHING CORPORATION
NORWOOD, NEW JERSEY

Printed in the United States of America

Library of Congress Cataloging-in-Publication Data

Gender and discourse.

  (Advances in discourse processes series ; 30)
  Bibliography: p.
  Includes index.
  1. Feminism. 2. Discourse analysis.   3. Social structure.   4. So-
ciolinguistics. I. Todd, Alexandra Dundas.   II. Fisher, Sue, 1936–
III. Series: Advances in discourse processes ; v. 30.
HQ1154.G38 1988   305.4'2   87-33703
ISBN 0-89391-482-7
ISBN 0-89391-491-6 (pbk.)

Ablex Publishing Corporation
355 Chestnut Street
Norwood, New Jersey 07648

Contents

IV: Cultural Discourse

Preface to the Series

Roy O. Freedle
Series Editor

This series of volumes provides a forum for the cross-fertilization of ideas from a diverse number of disciplines, all of which share a common interest in discourse—be it prose comprehension and recall, dialogue analysis, text grammar construction, computer simulation of natural language, cross-cultural comparisons of communicative competence, or other related topics. The problems posed by multisentence contexts and the methods required to investigate them, while not always unique to discourse, are still sufficiently distinct as to benefit from the organized mode of scientific interaction made possible by this series.

Scholars working in the discourse area from the perspective of sociolinguistics, psycholinguistics, ethnomethodology and the sociology of language, educational psychology (e.g., teacher-student interaction), the philosophy of language, computational linguistics, and related subareas are invited to submit manuscripts of monograph or book length to the series editor. Edited collections of original papers resulting from conferences will also be considered.

Volumes in the Series

The Authors

Susan E. Bell is an assistant professor of sociology at Bowdoin College. She is also a research fellow in sociology at the Laboratory in Social Psychiatry, where she first learned about the analysis of interview narratives. She has published articles about women's health, medical technology, and the development of the drug DES.

Hazel Carby is Assistant Professor of English at Wesleyan University and author of *Reconstructing Womanhood: The Emergence of the Afro-American Woman Novelist,* (New York: Oxford University Press, 1987).

Susan E. Chase teaches sociology at the University of Tulsa. Her current research includes case studies of the work experiences and work context of women educational administrators, and a theoretical study of the social character of ambition.

Kathy Davis received her degree in Clinical Psychology at the Free University in Amsterdam, The Netherlands. After working as a therapist in a psychiatric outpatient clinic for several years, she helped set up the first women's studies project in Medicine at the Free University. She does research on how power works in consultations between female patients and male GPs. Research interests and publications focus on interaction between women and men in various professional service contexts and feminist methodology.

Sue Fisher is an assistant professor of sociology at Wesleyan University in Middletown, Connecticut. Her research has consistently addressed issues of gender, power and discourse. She is the author of *In the Patient's Best Interest: Women and the Politics of Medical Decisions* (Rutgers University Press) and, with Alexandra Dundas Todd, has edited the two previous volumes in this series: *The Social Organization of Doctor–Patient Communication* (1983) and *Discourse and Institutional Authority: Medicine, Education and Law* (1986). Currently she is working on a book, *Caught Between Worlds: The Case of Nurse Practitioners,* in which she analyzes the ways nurses communicate with patients against a backdrop of historical conditions which gave rise to, and now threaten, the nurse practitioner movement in the United States.

Marjorie Harness Goodwin is currently an associate professor of anthropology at the University of South Carolina. In her research she has been particularly interested in the interactive organization of language. Her monograph *Language As Social Process: Conversational Practices in a Peer Group of Urban Black Children*, to be published by Indiana University Press, is an ethnography of how children accomplish their social organization through talk during task activity, games, arguing, gossip and storytelling. Other research of hers, based on videotaped interaction, deals with how participants in talk closely monitor each other's actions (see for example "Processes of Mutual Monitoring Implicated in the Production of Description Sequences." *Sociological Inquiry,* 50 (3–4), 303–317 (1980), and "Concurrent Operations on Talk: Notes on the Interactive Organization of Assessments" (with Charles Goodwin). To appear in *IPRA Papers in Pragmatics,* International Pragmatics Association.)

Cheris Kramarae teaches sociolinguistics in the Department of Speech Communication at the University of Illinois—Urbana-Champaign. She is the author of *Women and Men Speaking;* co-editor of *Language and Power; For Alma Mater: Theory and Practice in Feminist Scholarship; Language, Gender and Society;* and *A Feminist Dictionary.* She is editor of *The Voices and Words of Women and Men,* and *Technology and Women's Voices: Keeping in Touch.*

Jo Murphy-Lawless is currently completing a history of institutionalised childbirth in Ireland at the Department of Sociology, Trinity College, Dublin. In this work she has concentrated on opening up analysis of eighteenth century obstetric discourse. Since her son was born fourteen years ago she has also been involved in counselling and support work with pregnant women in both Britain and Ireland.

Julia Penelope received her degrees from the City College of New York and the University of Texas at Austin. Her articles have appeared in Lesbian and academic journals such as *Lesbian Ethics, Linguistics, Common Lives/Lesbian Lives,* and *College English,* and she co-edited *The Coming Out Stories* (1980) with Susan Wolfe. With Morgan Grey, she is the co-author of *The Book of Found Goddesses,* and is currently working on a book about patriarchal English.

Catherine Kohler Riessman (Ph.D., Columbia University) has been an Associate Professor at Smith College since 1979 (teaching in the School for Social Work and the Sociology Department), and is currently Visiting Associate Professor of Sociology in the Department of Psychiatry at the Harvard Medical School. Her research interests and publications concern women and the health care system, gender differences in health risk associated with marital dissolution, and social class and health service use. She is completing a book on women's and men's experiences with separation and divorce in which she uses narrative analysis.

Sandra Silberstein received her Ph.D. in linguistics from the University of Michigan. Currently, she is Assistant Professor of English at the University of Washington where she teaches seminars in linguistics and literary theory, women writers, and TESOL. Author of numerous articles on reading and narrative theory, she has also authored two books in the field of TESOL. Her current research focuses on interactive theories of reading and the role of ideology in the creation of meaning.

Alexandra Dundas Todd is Associate Professor of Sociology at Suffolk University in Boston, Massachusetts. Her research interests in medical sociology and gender studies are reflected in articles on these subjects and in two edited books (with Sue Fisher) on discourse in institutions. She has just completed a book on women and health, *Intimate Adversaries: Cultural Conflict between Doctors and Women Patients.*

Susan J. Wolfe is Professor and Chair of English at the University of South Dakota, where she teaches linguistics and women's studies. Co-editor of *The Coming Out Stories,* she has also published on women and language, feminist aesthetics, and syntactic and semantic change in English.

INTRODUCTION

Theories of Gender, Theories of Discourse*

Alexandra Dundas Todd and Sue Fisher

There seems to be wide-ranging agreement that gender is an organizing principle in people's everyday experiences as well as in the theoretical work that scholars do to understand these experiences—an agreement that is reflected in the literature on gender and discourse. It is, however, an agreement fraught with disagreement. In other words while the category of gender is recognized, its construction and deconstruction are hotly contested.

In this introduction our intention is to review a range of theories providing a context for a discussion of gender and discourse. To do so we review some of the social scientific perspectives on gender and on language, suggesting the components of an ongoing process of theory construction in which to frame the articles in this book.

THEORIES OF GENDER

The Tradition

From its inception as a discipline, Sociology has had a concern with social action, an interest with ramifications for the construction of gender. Parsons, as the dominant theorist for the structural-functional position, proposed a normative theory of social action—a theory which explicitly addressed gender. On the one hand he saw society as held together by norms, values and consensus. As Safilios-

---

* We want to thank Mary Ann Clauson, Kathy Davis, Sandra Harding, Hugh Mehan and Will Wright for their helpful comments.

Rothschild (1976) pointed out there was, for him, a normative line between work and family roles. Men were instrumental; women were expressive. Men worked in the public arena; women worked in the home. Both acquired their roles through complex gender socialization. Adherence to these roles insured a noncompetitive domestic relationship. On the other hand Parsons granted a certain approval to the world he presented. The world he described was the world as it ought to be.

Symbolic Interactionists took exception to the notion that norms govern action in a direct and unproblematic way and proposed a process through which individuals acquired a sense of self. Rather than the normatively governed self of structural-functionalists, the self was acquired in interaction with others and language was the medium of acquisition. While early writers in this tradition (Cooley, 1902; Mead, 1934) were not primarily concerned with gender, their ideas provided fertile ground for feminist thinkers. If the self was acquired in interaction, the potential existed for greater flexibility. Women and men were no longer exclusively tied to expressive and instrumental roles—rather roles were acquired in interaction against the backdrop of a normative context (Bart, 1971; Safilios-Rothschild, 1971; Epstein, 1970). (We will discuss this tradition further in the next section.)

Ethnomethodologists took this normative environment as a topic of inquiry (Heritage, 1984; Mehan & Woods, 1975; Garfinkel, 1967; Cicourel, 1964). They were interested in displaying how norms were socially produced as individuals acquired both a sense of themselves and their realities. Garfinkel (1967), for example, described how "Agnes," a young person born a male, acquired the identity of a woman. According to him this transformation developed in interaction rather than as the result of either biological imperatives or normative environments. It was in and through interactions that Agnes, passing as a female, managed the presentation of herself as female. In other words she learned what other women take for granted as she accomplished the production of herself as a woman.

Most recently the interest in a gendered self has taken a psychoanalytic turn. Feminist scholars have argued that psychoanalytically the production of gendered selves and their relations to others is a process rooted in familial arrangements. This argument, like Parsons', takes structural arrangements, especially family arrangements, as its starting point. However, unlike for Parsons, domestic relations are not normatively constrained. Rather it is argued that in most cultures women, whether participating in the paid labor force or not, are primarily responsible for raising children. Both girls and boys, then, develop their sense of self and other either in relation or opposition to their mothers. In this process children simultaneously acquire an inseparable sense of themselves as social persons and as gendered persons (for examples of this work see Chodorow, 1978; Flax, 1978; Dinnerstein, 1976).

Where for Parsons there was little flexibility in the acquisition of gender, symbolic interactionist, ethnomethodologist and feminist psychoanalytic theorists see greater flexibility. This is possible since, for symbolic interactionists, gendered roles do not follow directly from societal norms; for ethnomethodologists these roles are socially accomplished; and for feminist psychoanalytic theorists changing familial arrangements changes the conditions through which gender is acquired, increasing the available options. Although these theories take different approaches—some more structural, others more process oriented—for each, communication is central to the constitution of gendered selves. While structural-functionalists rely on language as an unaddressed background resource, in each of the other perspectives we have discussed, language plays an increasingly significant part in the development of both an individual and a social identity, and in the acquisition of the social/cultural/symbolic meanings of gender.

As theory and practice go hand in hand, these theoretical gains have practical consequences: Theoretical insights have contributed to changes in personal practices and in institutional arrangements. For example women and men today have the potential to define themselves and their options in a variety of ways. These theories do not, however, simply open our eyes to the possibility of change; they also show us how difficult change is. For in their own distinct ways they illustrate how people continue to reproduce asymmetrical gender relations. The main contribution here is a deepened understanding of how gender relations are constructed and maintained. But for some this understanding is too limited. The critics claim we need a more far-reaching analysis of social institutions. It is to these critics we now turn.

The critics take the relationship between gender and the social structure as the central focus of their analysis. While Parsons assumes traditional gender roles as necessary to a functional society, the critics ask functional for whom? And while for symbolic interaction, ethnomethodology and feminist psychoanalytic theories gender is negotiated in social interaction and/or familial arrangements, critics ask what is the larger social context in which these interactions and/or domestic arrangements occur? For the critics these questions are answered differently, reflecting different theoretical positions.

The Critics

One critical perspective addresses what Harding (1986) refers to as "feminist approaches to equity issues." Women, it is argued, need the same opportunities that men enjoy: Equal educational and employment opportunities as well as more equitable domestic relations. If in all major societal institutions women have equal access to power, change will follow: New norms will emerge, social roles will be redefined, and our sense of self will be reshaped.

While promoting increased opportunity and improved institutional contexts, this argument essentially focuses on individual gain. And there can be no doubt that as women have worked to bring about change, change has occurred—legislatively, occupationally and domestically. However, unlike other more critical arguments, this perspective does not call for radical changes in the structure of society. Even so, a discussion of radical change is engendered. Some claim that the called for changes hold a radical potential. For example, Eisenstein (1981) argues that as women move toward equality, the barriers they encounter will be so firmly entrenched that they will be radicalized, forcing further, more radical changes.

Others disagree, arguing that the proposed changes do not go far enough. They claim that incremental change is always at risk of being wiped away. Citing the Reagan era as an example, they point to the rapid diminution of social gains, the increasing feminization of poverty being one example. They argue that for lasting change to occur, the nature of power needs to be understood more fully. If gender is accomplished in social interaction, family dynamics or in the search for equity—if it is relational rather than determined by nature—then we must come to understand the social relations of domination.

Marxist theories offer a more structural focus. One of the contributions of these theories is to look at the division of labor—a division in which women's place has been in the home and then the home has been devalued as the private, inconsequential sphere of social life. Further, when, in addition to domestic work, women have entered the paid work force, it has been primarily to do low-status, low-paying labor. In their often dual capacity as unpaid domestic workers and as low paid service workers, women do vital but invisible work to keep capitalism and male dominance in place—to keep in place a system in which they are largely subordinated.

While Marxist theorists critically address questions of production and the paid labor force, feminists incorporate the organization of reproduction (domestic labor) and familial arrangements into social theory to provide a fuller understanding of social life—both women's and men's. Similarly while Marxists point out that the dominant ideology provides an authoritative account of a particular reality, feminists turn our attention to how this reality is male dominated. While agreeing with the Marxist conception of class domination, these feminists point out that there is another inter-related system of oppression in operation—a patriarchal system. Patriarchal domination, they claim, is part of the conceptual scheme which structures social life for women and men alike. It plays a role in the formation of consciousness, and in the maintenance of sexist behavior as well as in such concrete institutional arrangements as the division of labor.

While both Marxist and feminist critics demystify the dominant version of reality (see Jaggar, 1983 and Smith, 1979), some feminists take the argument further. They claim that women, rather than being "subjugated knowers" (Foucault, 1980), need the power to define for themselves and to reshape the dominant ideology. For them, it follows logically that with different institutional arrangements and in a different ideological context both the creation of consciousness and the development of social relations would also be different.

Implicit in the perspectives discussed by the critics is an essentialist view of women. In feminist approaches to equity issues, the assumption is add women and stir; providing equal opportunity for *all* women will produce the necessary changes. For those offering a more structural critique, the assumption is change the system, reshape the ideology and *all* women will benefit equally. In each case women, by implication all women, are lumped together as a universal group with a specified nature. Missing in many of these critiques is an analysis of difference—difference in race, class, ethnicity, sexual identity, and individual experience. It is just this concern for difference that is addressed in the most recent trend in feminist criticism—deconstruction.

One of the best known deconstructionists, Jacques Derrida, argues that Western culture is dominated by "a series of binary oppositions which are in fact violent hierarchies" (Litvak, 1985, p. 7), for example masculine and feminine. Deconstructionists argue that these binary categories confer symmetry or declare opposition in a fictitious manner. By this we take deconstructionists to mean that while there are differences, for example between men and women or among men and women, these differences are neither enough to constitute binary oppositions—masculine versus feminine—nor unitary symmetries—man or woman.

The project for Derrida and his followers is to deconstruct these fictitious binary oppositions by revealing the discontinuities in what are typically seen as unified texts. A text can refer to a book or any work or string of words that contain internal differences. Some hold that by saying "there is nothing outside of the text," Derrida is not denying reality, material or otherwise, but rather he is claiming that we perceive reality through language. Anything said, whether written or spoken, is already "saturated with meaning" "carry[ing] the accumulated weight of history and convention" (Litvak, 1985, p. 10). For feminists this saturation is especially problematic. History and convention are patriarchal, and as such, color language, and thus women's experiences in the world as well as their experiences of themselves.

Some writers have taken deconstruction beyond the literary text to discourse, demonstrating how these oppositions perpetuate themselves as certain groups of people are stigmatized. Here we have deconstructionists talking about how language shapes our cultural realities. For example, feminists argue that women "embody the despised qualities of difference" (Litvak, 1985, p. 15). They are other and their otherness is denigrated. If our experience is, as they suggest, the experience of language, then we need to deconstruct the symmetries and oppositions of a gendered language, finding more benign differences to replace these oppositions. As such, women as a unified category and man versus woman as a binary opposition will be deconstructed.

Here we are alerted to the pitfalls of essentialism and to the importance of acknowledging similarities and differences without assuming hierarchically arranged binary oppositions. However this position, like those that preceded it, is not without problems—both politically and theoretically. Politically, as Harding (1986) points out, with the emphasis on differences among women—on their "fractured identities"—there is a potential danger with serious political ramifications. If we do not reaffirm "solidarity in our oppression," if the swing goes too far in favor of difference, the similarities which can bind women into a potent political force may be dissipated into smaller, less effective interest groups. Theoretically, this perspective is entirely ahistorical, paying little credence to institutions and to any notion of interests as operative factors structuring male-female relations. If reality is *entirely* shaped by language then we run the risk of generating theories and proposing solutions which only change language in the hopes of changing conceptual frameworks as well as history and convention. In addition, an exclusive focus on language as culture obscures the possibility of a reflexive theory—a theory in which social structure, social interaction, and the creation of consciousness are reflexively tied to language as it is used in everyday situations. In turn, language usage reflects and sustains these more structural aspects of social life.

THEORIES OF LANGUAGE

It is just this kind of reflexive relationship that has been addressed most recently by some discourse analysts whose work conceptualizes a relationship between language and context—a relationship that has heretofore been absent. The issues here are similar to problems discussed earlier and have to do in part with the direction of the analysis. For example, earlier we discussed how symbolic interaction, ethnomethodology, and feminist psychoanalytic theories focus on people's behavior. By implication, then, social change would be accomplished individual by individual, eventually building up to changes in structural arrangements. Or alternatively, how feminist approaches to equity issues as well as Marxist/Feminist theories focus on how concrete institutions and ideology influence individuals' social relationships and consciousness. In a similar way there was a dualism between the way deconstructionism located discourse as a cultural artifact and the way ethnomethodology located it as an interactional production. The language studies we are about to review share these dualities between social structure and social interaction. There is a tradition which focuses primarily on the ways institutional arrangements influence language and another where language itself is the central focus of analysis. From these dualities a synthesis is being developed. Each of these approaches implies a different relationship between language and social structure.

In the first perspective, linguistic theorists influenced by Marx offer complex views on discourse that are by no means wholly structural in nature. Volosinov (1973), for example, looks at the philosophy of signs and utterances often sounding more like a linguist than a Marxist. However, from time to time the Marxist influence is clear in passages such as the following:

> The immediate social situation and the broader social milieu wholly determine—and determine from within, so to speak—the structure of an utterance (Volosinov, 1973, p. 4).

This quote demonstrates the influence of Marx while developing the importance of language and the importance of people's mental structures. For Volosinov linguistic investigation can provide "the link between the material basis and the mental creativity of man

[sic]" (1973, p. 3), between the human psyche and the structural arrangements of society.

Coward and Ellis (1977) also seek to broaden the Marxist model. They move to incorporate some of the insights of Freudian and Lacanian theory, especially as it pertains to the "constitution of the language-using subject" (1977, p. 8). This subject is embedded in history, as well as in specific economic, political and ideological systems, and simultaneously is constructed by their place in the social structure and has the potential to reconstitute it.

> Marxism conceives at once of a subject who is produced by society, and of a subject who acts to support or to change that society. . . . [T]his human subject is constituted in ideology and by history, and at the same time acts to make history and change society, without having a full and self-sufficient knowledge of or control over the actions it undertakes (1977, p. 61).

Here the individual, seen as speaking subject and as political actor, is vital to an understanding of language and to a theory of social structure and social change. Neither the speaking subject nor the political actor can stand outside of the social system or be unaffected by it. "The subject is caught in the moment of enunciation, and is in some way constructed by it" (1977, p. 62). And while this subject participates in the production of "the social structure-in-process" (1977, p. 62), she or he is not able to manipulate or control it entirely. Both aspects of the subject—political actor and social speaker—take form in the context of ideology. What Coward and Ellis are proposing is an interrelationship between language and ideology.

> But ideology is not a slogan under which political and economic interests of a class present itself. It is the way in which the individual actively lives his or her role within the social totality; it therefore participates in the construction of that individual so that he or she can act (1977, p. 67).

Now Coward and Ellis add another level to the analysis—to political actors and social speakers they add the social construction of consciousness. The dialectic between language and ideology is crucial to the development of consciousness.

> Language and thought are inextricable: thought conceptualizes through language, and it is not a matter of one being the instrument of the other but of each engendering the other: language makes thought possible, thought makes language possible (1977, p. 79).

Language then is not merely a passive form of communication. It is an active force, inseparable from ideological, economic and political contexts, but by no means reducible to them. In fact, language is not only active, but according to Coward and Ellis, it is part of a revolutionary potential. Without an understanding of language as a symbolic system, we will lack an understanding of a revolutionary subject "constituted in history and ideological formations" (1977, p. 92). In other words we cannot understand the construction of consciousness without understanding the "dialectic between history, language, and ideology" (1977, p. 92).

The call for a multi-level analysis which takes into account the language-using subject is important. As Coward and Ellis (1977) point out, our understanding of people as active subjects and our understanding of ideology necessitate an understanding of language. People are embedded in and constructed by history and by their place in the social structure while they maintain the ability to make history and change society. Ideology is a force that contributes to: (1) the construction of the individual, (2) the development of consciousness, and (3) the ways individuals live out their roles. While in this perspective language is a central feature of the analysis, a theory of language is not well developed.

In the next perspective, speech alone becomes the topic of analysis. The focus shifts to how language is used by people who are actively participating in the production of their social reality. For example, speech act theory (Searle, 1969) is used by some to examine utterances in terms of their composition and use. The relationship between how language is used and the social action accomplished by its use is looked at in minute detail. Analyses of the simplest utterances to the most complex interactions are explored. For sociolinguists this focus leads to two bodies of research: One which demonstrates that people speak differently in different situations and another which specifies the linguistic rules associated with speech. For conversational analysts, this focus has primarily been directed toward illustrating the systematic structure of talk. While there are significant differences between sociolinguists and conversational analysts, for the purpose of our discussion they share essential points of agreement. They agree that language use is organized in patterned ways. They share the notion of communication as spoken interaction, taking linguistic performance as the topic of inquiry. For both approaches a systematic, empirical examination of speech in the social situations in which it unfolds provides the data for analysis.

Each of these theories examines the local production of talk and highlights the ways in which this talk is socially produced. While these analyses are not oriented toward either the production of consciousness or the production of revolutionary action, speech act, sociolinguistic and conversational analyses are not entirely acontextual, but context is defined very differently than it was in the Marxist-based tradition. The key issue here is the way language is used. The analytic status of context is less well developed. For example, speech act theory goes beyond the structure of the utterance to examine the ways talk "performs" various social functions. Here the words "I promise" perform the social function of promising and context is implied in this extention.

Sociolinguists and conversational analysts make the relationship between language and context somewhat more explicit. Whether demonstrating how people speak differently in different situations, specifying linguistic rules, or illustrating the systematic structure of talk, both sociolinguists and conversational analysts point to the importance of context for the study of language use. Although this tradition alerts us to the importance of studying language as a social production and provides a range of important methodological tools to do so, the status of context remains ambiguous. At best it is a background resource against which language behavior is discussed. When talk is analyzed contextually, it is analyzed in *specific* contexts: How is communication in a medical clinic or a legal office different and/or similar from naturally occurring talk? It is the talk and its social production that is of interest here. The specific relationship between context and discourse is not well articulated.

The Marxist-based and the language traditions seem to each embody a potential to enrich the other—a reflexive potential. The Marxist-based tradition has a strong theoretical perspective which includes history, economics, politics and ideology. It simultaneously calls for the inclusive use of theories of language-use and the development of consciousness. It is these called-for changes that are not well developed but needed both at the level of theory and of social action to produce what Coward and Ellis (1977) refer to as an active, revolutionary subject.

By contrast, sociolinguists and conversational analysts provide a detailed understanding of the social production of language use and concrete insight into how people interact in their everyday lives. Conversational analysis, in particular, is based on a strong theory of interaction, grounded in ethnomethodology. However, their notion of context, as we have pointed out, is invoked rather than richly developed (Mehan, 1975; Heritage, 1984). The reflexive relationship between the discourse and the larger structural considerations go unaddressed.

To our knowledge, there are no theoretical perspectives which fully incorporate all that we are calling for. There are, however, theories being developed in several disciplines—Marxist-based theories, feminist psychoanalytic and feminist theories, deconstructionism, ethnomethodology and theories of language use—which while each having their own particular focus often allude to the concerns of other theories without the detailed articulation of these concerns.

GENDER AND DISCOURSE

In the theories of gender and of language just discussed, each perspective presents itself as a relatively closed, unified theory. Whether focusing primarily on social structure or social interaction, each of these "master theories" either implicitly or explicitly ignores, competes with, or dismisses other perspectives. However, in recent work by discourse analysts the dominant perspectives in language are being drawn into a unified theory. In the first two volumes in this series, *The Social Organization of Doctor-Patient Communication* (1983) and *Discourse and Institutional Authority: Medicine, Education and Law* (1986), we joined others calling for a theory in which language bridges the gap between social interaction and social structure. To bridge this gap we looked at the micropolitics of communication. By this we meant a conception of language use which displayed the ways language both reflected and sustained institutional and cultural arrangements as it accomplishes social action.

But, how are we to incorporate the seemingly conflicting perspectives on gender?: (1) gender is socially accomplished in and through the process of talking and acting like a woman (Garfinkel, 1967); (2) gendered identities are the result of particular domestic arrangements (Chodorow, 1978); (3) discrimination on the basis of gender can be alleviated if not eliminated through legislation and affirmative action (feminist approaches to equity issues); (4) in order to change women's place in society it is important to understand and modify both capitalism and patriarchy; and, finally (5) we need to break apart the universality of gender to understand how it is constructed so it can be deconstructed in discourse—cultural discourse. How can we integrate the strengths while eliminating the weaknesses of these perspectives? How can we hope to create a unified whole?

Sandra Harding argues,

Stable and coherent theories are not always the ones to be most highly desired; there are important understandings to be gained in seeking the social origins of instabilities and incoherences in our thoughts and practices (1986, p. 243).

We find this useful for our own work. While we continue to recognize the importance of uniting social structure and social interaction, in this book we modify our call. We are not offering a unified theory. As Harding points out:

> It would be historically premature and delusionary for feminism to arrive at a master "theory," . . . with conceptual and methodological assumptions that we all think we accept (1986, p. 244).

We agree that a unified theory for gender and discourse is premature. The disciplines are too young and have been too disparate. To develop a grand, integrated theory too soon runs the risk of closing off new possibilities (even if, perhaps especially if, they are conflicting).

In an exquisitely reasoned book on science and feminism, Harding suggests instead an open-ended evolving process of theory construction. Rather than unified theories competing for master status, she argues for a more cooperative approach to theory construction—one which remains open to new theoretical developments. What is so appealing about Harding's approach is that it encourages the incorporation of exciting work being done today on the frontiers of many disciplines, even if on the surface these theories appear contradictory. Harding asks us to tolerate these contradictions, to use them productively.

Our intention in this introduction is to offer a range of theoretical views that can be drawn into an open-ended evolving process of theory construction. In this light the articles in the book are drawn from many different theoretical perspectives and offer a variety of insights on the relationship between gender and discourse. The theories in the introduction and the articles in the book work together to illuminate a reflexive relationship among social structure, social interaction, and socially constructed selves, in this case gendered selves. In this reflexive relationship, language plays a many-faceted role: It is the link between social structure and social interaction; it is the bridge between social interaction and the socially constructed self. However since neither social interaction nor gendered selves occur in a vacuum, it reflects and reinforces the social structure. In so doing, language has the potential to translate social theory into social action. This translation facilitates people's active participation in society as it gives voice to the similarities and differences in their experiences.

PLAN OF THE BOOK

In Part I, *Discourse in Interaction,* Kathy Davis and Marjorie Harness Goodwin use discourse analysis to examine transcripts of actual conversations and tie the talk to questions of power and gender. Davis enriches the literature on doctor-patient communication as she explores the subtleties of the talk between female patients and male doctors. She shows how the power of paternalism, kindly as it may be, controls the interactions and in so doing, controls women's health care.

Goodwin takes us out of the office and into the street, taping urban black girls at play in their neighborhood. She focuses on cooperation and competition in two play activities, countering some of the prevalent ideas about girls' social organization. Goodwin, in describing how girls play differently in different situations, implies a connection between gender and context. In so doing, her work undercuts an essentialist understanding of gender roles.

In Part II, *Discourse in Storytelling,* Susan Bell, Sandra Silberstein and Catherine Kohler Riessman, from different disciplines, turn to narratives as a form of discourse in understanding gender relations. Bell's article on the stories of a young woman whose mother took DES (diethylstilbestrol), takes us step by step through the events that lead to this woman's recognition of herself as a DES daughter. Bell focuses on the "core narratives" and "linked stories" to show how this DES daughter develops a new consciousness and becomes a politicized woman.

Silberstein's narratives are courtship stories. She documents the way marital partners use language in the creation of gendered selves and events and helps us understand these stories by discussing the relationship between ideology about gender roles and the courtship narratives provided by three generations of one family.

Reissman, continuing an analysis of familial arrangements, moves to the other end of the spectrum—divorce. She compares and contrasts the narrative styles of two women's divorce accounts—one woman middle class and white, the other working class and Puerto Rican. She, like others in this book, argues for a more detailed consideration of the differences in women's experiences without negating the similarities that bind women together.

In Part III, *Institutional Discourse,* Jo Murphy-Lawless and Susan Wolfe move away from discourse as the actual conversation, whether in daily life or in interview stories, to discourse in the institutional record. Murphy-Lawless focuses on the records of the first lying-in hospital in the British Isles (in Ireland) opened in 1745 to trace the male takeover of childbirth in the eighteenth century. She looks closely at the language used to legitimate a changing ideology toward reproduction, birthing women, male doctors and power.

Wolfe's discussion of current cases in the law examines the discourse of legal records with an equally critical eye. She compares the strategies of sexual politics that encourage male domination over women, with the cultural force of heterosexism to assure heterosexual domination over lesbians and gay men.

In Part IV, *Ideological Discourse,* Hazel Carby, Cheris Kramarae, Susan Chase and Julia Penelope examine how gender relations are inscribed in culture. Carby's contribution to an ideological discourse is through black women's music. She develops a framework for examining feminism, sexuality and power in black women's blues. This music expresses the contradictions faced by blacks in 1920's America—a time of much movement and change. This was a time of struggle over the different domestic and migratory interests of black women and men. In this struggle, women's voices rose up in song that continue to be heard loud and clear.

Kramarae's study of radio announcing reveals a more muted discourse. Her analysis traces programming and policy decisions from the development of radio in the 1920's to the present, showing how the voice of radio, particularly the BBC, silences women's voices, interests, and participation. She argues that the masculine organization of radio time, including programs designed for female audiences, reinforced conventional stereotypes of women. They also limited opportunities for bringing women together that might have been accomplished through innovative programming.

Penelope's interests lie in the written text and the relationship between text and reader. Is the reader complicitous or critical? Text linguists assume a complicitous relationship which, Penelope argues, is both simplistic and conservative. She uses sex-specific examples in the discourse of fiction and nonfiction to illustrate her points: First, a theory that assumes complicity underestimates the human mind, simplifying cognitive processes; second, to uncritically assume the sex-specific use of written discourse in our culture is yet another promulgation of "white, male supremacy in the guise of dispassionate inquiry."

Chase shifts the topic from ideological discourse such as music, radio, and written text to the more amorphous realm of an everyday expression—"The Woman Who Becomes a Man"—and what it signifies about gender in talk and life. Throughout her article, Chase uses this one phrase intriguingly as she moves to the heart of questions raised in feminist theory.

The articles in this volume, starting with the analysis of actual conversation in Davis' work and concluding with Chase's discussion of a single expression, make a unique move in an evolving process of theory construction. We invite you to continue this process.

REFERENCES

Bart, P. (1971, November). Sexism and social science: From the gilded cage to the iron cage, or, the perils of Pauline. *Journal of Marriage and Family, 33* (4). Nov. 1971.

Chodorow, N. (1978). *The Reproduction of Mothering: Psychoanalysis and the Sociology of Gender.* Berkeley: The University of California Press.

Cicourel, A. V. (1964). *Method and Measurement in Sociology.* New York: The Free Press.

Cooley, C. H. (1902). *Human Nature and the Social Order.* New York: C. Scribner's Sons.

Coward, R., & Ellis, J. (1977). *Language and Materialism: Developments in Semiology and the Theory of the Subject.* London: Routledge and Kegan Paul.

Dinnerstein, D. (1976). *The Mermaid and the Minotaur: Sexual Arrangements and Human Malaise.* New York: Harper.

Eisenstein, Z. (1981). *The Radical Future of Liberal Feminism.* New York: Longman.

Epstein, C. (1971). *Woman's Place.* Berkeley: University of California Press.

Fisher, S., & Todd, A. D. (1986). *Discourse and Institutional Authority: Medicine, Education and Law.* Norwood, N.J.: Ablex Publishing Corporation.

Fisher, S., & Todd, A. D. (1983). *The Social Organization of Doctor-Patient Communication.* Washington, D.C.: Center for Applied Linguistics.

Flax, J. (1978). The conflict between nurturance and autonomy in mother-daughter relationships and within feminism. *Feminist Studies, 4,* (2).

Garfinkel, H. (1967). *Studies in Ethnomethodology.* Englewood Cliffs, N.J.: Prentice Hall.

Harding, S. (1986). *The Science Question in Feminism.* Ithaca, N.Y.: Cornell University Press.

Heritage, J. (1984). *Garfinkel and Ethnomethodology.* London: Polity Press.

Litvak, J. (1985). What is deconstruction and why are they saying those terrible things about it? New Brunswick, ME: Unpublished paper, Bowdoin College.

Mead, G. H. (1934). *Mind, Self and Society.* Chicago: University of Chicago Press.

Mehan, H., & Wood, H. (1975). *The Reality of Ethnomethodology.* New York: John Wiley.

Safilius-Rothschild, C. (1971). A cross-cultural examination of women's marital, educational and occupational options. *ACTA Sociologica, 14,* 96–113.

Safilius-Rothschild, C. (1976). Dual linkages between the occupational and family systems: A macrosociological analysis. In M. Blaxall & B. Reagan (eds.) *Women and the Workplace: The Implications of Occupational Segregation*. Chicago: University of Chicago Press.

Searle, J. (1969). *Speech Acts*. Cambridge: Cambridge University Press.

Volosinov, U. N. (1973). *Marxism and the Philosophy of Language*. New York: Seminar Press.

PART I

Discourse in Interaction

CHAPTER 1

Paternalism Under the Microscope[1]

Kathy Davis

Faculty of Medicine
Vrije Universiteit Amsterdam
The Netherlands

INTRODUCTION

Interaction between men and women inevitably involves asymmetrical relations of power. If this is taken as a "social fact"[2]—which is what I propose we do—then any face-to-face encounter between the sexes should serve as a good starting place for investigating power and gender. In this paper, I shall be taking a closer look at one such encounter: the general practice consultation where the patient is a woman and the physician a man. If my contention is true

---

[1] The present research is part of a research project being conducted at the Faculty of Medicine of the Vrije Universiteit in Amsterdam. For their critical remarks and helpful suggestions on an earlier draft of this paper, I would especially like to thank Willem de Haan, Greta Noordenbos, Nelly Steffens, Brian Torode, Petra Mangold, and Tony Hak. My thanks also go to those people who read it and "just" liked it.

[2] My use of quotation marks here does not mean that I doubt that sexism is a social fact. Even a small sample from the abundant feminist literature and research which has accumulated over the past decade provides sufficient empirical verification. Moreover, the present inquiry was conducted under the auspices of a women's studies project. This was helpful as it enabled me to skip over the issue of having to prove *that* unequal relations of power exist between the sexes, and get right down to the business of showing *what* they look like in a specific setting.

On the contrary, I am following a practice found among the more qualitatively-minded social scientists who maintain that social facts are not only "out there" in the Durkheimian sense of recognizable, external forces which we can all agree upon, but are continually and reciprocally constructed by individuals in various social settings. It is this construction process which I wish to delineate.

that sexism does not grind to a halt before the doctor's office, but rears its (ugly) head there as well, it should be viewable within the actual consultation.

My focus will be on how a woman patient's initial presentation of complaints are diagnosed and treated in the course of the consultation. I suspect that this process does not occur strictly on the basis of medical or scientific criteria, but may be tied up with the construction of asymmetrical gender relations as well. The relevant question, then, is how can power be exercised within the specific context of the general practice consultation? Are women subject to particular forms of domination and subordination within this setting? A related, and in my view, even more important issue is what women themselves are doing. Are they the passive victims of the medical professional or do they engage in covert and overt forms of resistance?

Thus, this paper will be dealing with some of the "hows" of power and gender relations at the micro-level of medical talk. As luck would have it, this proved by no means an easy subject to investigate. For this reason, I shall begin by tackling the thorny issue of how I was able to move from a structural (and feminist) critique of the health care system, which was my starting point, to what I actually saw happening in my data; i.e. transcriptions of consultations between male General Practitioners (GPs) and female patients. I shall show how my research process reflected the very problem I was attempting to come to grips with. This will be followed by a theoretical discussion of one specific way power may be exercised; namely, paternalism or the "for-her-own-good" approach. Using one of my consultations, I shall demonstrate how paternalism works within medical talk. Finally, an attempt will be made to link these (micro-) findings to some of the larger issues of social control and the relations of power between female patients and male physicians.

FROM FEMINIST CRITIQUE TO DATA

My first step was to familiarize myself with the available literature on women and health care. Since the advent of the feminist movement in the late '60s, considerable attention has been paid to this subject and, as Elizabeth Fee (1983) has noted, if feminists have had a great deal to say about health care, it has, by and large, been critical. Women's bodies and reproductive functions are subject to rampant medicalization. Normal functions like menstruation, pregnancy, menopause, etc. have been transformed into matters requiring constant medical surveillance. From the moment she enters puberty, a woman becomes, by virtue of her female-ness, "sick." (Ehrenreich & English, 1979; Oakley, 1979; Roberts, 1981; Laws, 1983.)

Physicians don't treat women's complaints seriously; problems are frequently regarded as psychological in origin. Dysmenorrhea or pain in labor may be attributed to a "faulty outlook" or infantile colic to the mother's insecurity or anxiety (Lennane & Lennane, 1973). Accompanying the notion that it's "all in her head," is the negative stereotype of the female patient as someone who takes up the busy doctor's time with a host of vague symptoms and endless complaining (Scully & Bart, 1973; Lorbeer, 1976; Fidell, 1980; Lipset, 1982).

The medical profession is—and has been historically—a primary agent in the social control of women. Doctors have frequently and with considerable success managed to channel women's dissatisfaction away from active or collective protest to the safer paths of endurance and acceptance (Ehrenreich & English, 1979; Cloward & Piven, 1979; Donzelot, 1979). By means of benevolent medical advice, they have been helped to view their difficulties as instances of personal pathology, essentially internal to the individual woman. Thus, boredom or anxiety may be smoothed away with a chat, a prescription for Valium, or the promise of another appointment (Barrett & Roberts, 1978; Cooperstock, 1978; Standing, 1980).

This critique informed my general perspective on women and health care and was meant to provide a backdrop for my investigation of actual general practice consultations. Armed with Glaser and Strauss (1967) notions concerning "theoretical sampling," I had every intention of using this critique as a kind of "sensitizing concept," useful for coming to terms with the "problem area," but to be laid aside when no longer useful. Thus, whereas I did expect to learn something about power relations between women and men in medical interaction, I did not expect the above-mentioned phenomena to emerge neatly from my data. I was going to remain open to the possibilities my material had to offer.

What my material had to offer proved—to say the least—surprising. As I began listening to the taped general practice consultations at my disposal,[3] my initial reaction was, first and foremost, this: the GPs seemed unabashedly and unswervingly *nice!* They were friendly, interested, empathetic, and obviously bent on providing their pa-

---

[3] The tapes are part of the TRIPT-collection of 400 audiotapes of general practice consultations held in 50 practices in five urban settings in The Netherlands. The GPs were fairly young, having taken their medical exams after 1969. All had received vocational training (Thomassen, 1982).

tients with quality care. I could easily detect traces of training in good listening skills as well as familiarity with the tenets of progressive or holistic medical approaches. Many were noticeably reticent about prescribing psychotropic drugs.

My response was mixed. At first, I was inclined to reject these tapes as exceptional. They did not correspond with what I had been reading about women's experiences with physicians so they must be in some way unusual. Upon returning to the larger collection of tapes and listening to them, however, I discovered that, by and large, they all shared this same quality of intimacy and niceness.

At this point, I might simply have concluded that the problem of medical sexism no longer exists. Perhaps the treatment of women patients in The Netherlands is exceptional. General practice training programs may indeed have succeeded in instilling nonsexist attitudes in their trainees.[4] I am a sceptic, however. I decided to have another look. After re-examining my tapes at length, I discovered that they were, in fact, full of instances of the kinds of phenomena the feminist critique of the health care system had brought to light: GPs making moral judgments about women's roles as wives and mothers, psychologizing women's problems, not taking their complaints seriously, massive prescription of tranquilizers, usurpation of women's control over their reproduction—in short, it was all there, just waiting to be investigated.

Considering the by-now extensive body of literature on the subject, this is not surprising. What *is* surprising, however, is that these instances, while available in my material, were not immediately so. In fact, they nearly escaped my attention altogether. It was precisely the intimate, pleasant quality of the medical encounter itself that made issues like power and control continually seem like something else. For example, was the GP telling a joke in order to put the patient at ease or was he interrupting her troubles talk, conveying that what she had to say was irrelevant to the business at hand?

It was, ultimately, this experience of sensing that "something" was wrong without being able to put my finger on the source of that feeling which caused me to stop dead in my tracks. A kind of conversational *dé jà vu*. I was reminded of the countless, everyday experiences of being ignored, not being taken seriously, the minor daily insults and jokes which are part of women's conversational lot in life.

---

[4] Vocational training has only been compulsory since 1973. In the attempt to promote General Practice to a medical specialism, considerable attention has been paid in training programs to developing therapy skills as well as presenting more sophisticated approaches to etiology and treatment than the strict medical model had to offer.

And, of course, I recognized the all-too-familiar occurence of emerging from conversations feeling vaguely dissatisfied or even humiliated, *without being able to say why*. It is this last element which particularly interests me here.

The micro-insults, which are part of the fabric of talk between men and women, are bad enough in and of themselves. When they are also unidentifiable as such, however, the problem becomes infinitely more serious. Should one venture a protest, the other party may immediately retreat behind the other, also-present face of the interaction ("Only joking, lady!"), leaving one unconvinced, but without a leg to stand on (just another humorless female).

My initial confrontation with my data convinced me that this Janus quality which permeated the general consultations of my data played an important if not essential role in the construction of relations of dominance and subordination between the GP and the patient. It therefore became my task to analyze *how* it works.

FROM DATA TO THEORY. 'PATERNALISM' AS THEORETICAL CONSTRUCT

In order to describe the subtle, but effective ways power is being exercised in my data, I needed a concept of power which combines the element of benevolence with the elements of dominance and subordination.[5] Fortunately, there is such a concept. Moreover, it has even been implicated as a feature of doctor–patient relationships. This concept is *paternalism*. There are several reasons for selecting paternalism as a useful theoretical construct for organizing my data.

To begin with, it entails, by definition, limiting the freedom of another person by means of well-meant regulations. In this way, benevolent intentions are combined with relations of power. The person in authority may restrict and coerce, but only for the good of the other (Sorenson & Bergman, 1984).

Paternalism—again, by definition—implies a relationship of asymmetry. The original model for a paternalistic relationship is that of parent and child (Sorenson & Bergman, 1984).[6] It is not limited,

---

[5] For a sophisticated theoretical treatment of power and domination in interaction, as well as critical discussion of how power has been dealt with in mainstream sociology, the reader is referred to Giddens (1976, 1979).

[6] Interestingly, Sorenson and Bergman (1984) use the word "parent" for describing the paternalistic relationship, although the root of the word "paternal" refers to fathers. In fact, the aspect of exercising control, beneficent or otherwise, is absent from the equivalent word for motherly behavior, namely, maternal. Male scientists, particu-

however, to this particular constellation, but might be applied to other relationships where a similar inequality in responsibility and/or need exists. There is nothing new about referring to doctor–patient relationships as paternalistic. In fact, in a recent issue of *Theoretical Medicine* (5, 1984) devoted entirely to the problem of paternalism and autonomy, it was at no point questioned that paternalism was anything but a necessary and integral part of any medical encounter. In fact, it is, by definition, that kind of encounter. The issue, then, was rather how to avoid the pitfalls of too much paternalism for the patient's autonomy; i.e. a problem of degree.

Women have, historically, been the objects of medical paternalism (Ehrenreich & English, 1979). Not only have various experts had plenty of advice to give women about how they might best view themselves as well as how their lives might best be managed, but this advice has been manifestly presented as "for her own good." Thus, if paternalism is a routine feature of medical encounters generally, it should be particularly familiar to women as patients.

These considerations, along with my initial confrontation with my data, make paternalism a useful starting point for organizing and, ultimately, delineating the elusive and complicated phenomena described above. I shall now return to my data. Using a general practice consultation, an attempt will be made to show how paternalism works at the micro-level of the medical consultation. In particular, I shall be interested in its role in the construction of power relations between a male physician and a female patient.

BACK TO THE DATA: AN ANALYSIS OF THE INTERACTION BETWEEN A GP AND AN OLD WOMAN

I shall now take a look at one of the consultations from my data. The GP is in his early thirties and has a practice in a working-class neighborhood in an urban center in The Netherlands. The patient, an elderly woman, has clearly been to see him regularly as there is talk throughout the consultation about various well-known complaints: her arthritis, stiffness in her knees, water retention.

This time, however, she comes with another problem. Her oldest daughter has just discovered that she has a double uterus. The pa-

larly those connected with the helping professions, have been particularly eager to pinpoint the effects of bad parenting to mothers (maternal deprivation, schizophrenogenic mothers, etc.). It would seem that they are strangely reticent to have the potentially thorny issue of paternalism linked to fathers; i.e. males.

tient is worried that this means her daughter won't be able to have children.

The entire consultation takes 8 1/2 minutes and may be divided into three segments.

In the first, the patient introduces the double uterus as a topic and engages in what Jefferson (1980) has called "troubles talk".[7] This segment is interrupted after about two minutes when the GP asks a medical question ("But about those heart palpitations . . ."). What follows is a medical dialogue (West, 1984) with the GP inquiring about various symptoms, checking into the patient's present medication and taking her blood pressure. The patient provides the information requested without embarking on any more troubles telling. This segment takes up about half of the consultation. The third segment begins during the last two minutes of the consultation, when the patient returns to her initial trouble, her daughter's double uterus. The rest of the consultation is devoted to talk around that topic. Thus, the consultation has an overall structure something like Troubles Talk → Medical Talk → Troubles Talk.

Excerpts have been selected, chronologically, from each of these segments. Each example will be examined in detail in terms of how it constructs paternalism as routine feature of the medical encounter. In particular, I shall demonstrate how each instance displays the GP as well as the encounter as being *benevolent* while, at the same time, the patient's activity is being *curtailed or limited*.

EXCERPT 1[8]

P: My oldest daughter - she's been married for six years and she
      would love to have a baby now, after all, huh?   but
                                                  ⌊Mmhmm
      now: there's been an
15   examination and well: she's - she seems to have a double *uterus*.

---

[7] Jefferson has done considerable work on troubles talk (1980, 1984; Jefferson & Lee, 1981), which she describes as a "robust phenomenon" having its own characteristics, sequential organization, and membership categories. One feature of troubles talk, however, is that it is subject to constant disordering within a conversation. This may be due to improper alignment by reference to the membership categories (troubles teller–troubles recipient) or activity contamination, as, for example, when a troubles recipient suddenly engages in advice giving as opposed to providing appropriate affiliative responses to the trouble being told. The disruption of the patient's troubles-telling may also be observed in the present interview, where it must suddenly give way to medical Q–A sequences or problem solving activities.

[8] The original transcripts were in Dutch. I have translated them for the purpose of this paper. An attempt was made to preserve something of the idiomatic quality of the

D: *Oh!* ((surprised))
P: Have you ever heard of that?
D: It happens sometimes yeah. Sure enough.
P: And well: - yeah -   and then you
20   (All rabbits have them, I believe, but-

     work (
            Mm
     yourself up there again (about it, huh?
                                (Yes

This segment contains the patient's initial presentation of her
trouble. She is upset (lines 19–21) and the reason for this is that her
daughter, who wants to have children, has just discovered that she
has a double uterus. Not only does she provide the GP with the
"facts," but she also supplies information which, although extraneous to the trouble at hand, can help him appreciate its seriousness.
She indicates that her daughter is married, has been married for six
years, and does not have children yet. Moreover, her daughter doesn't
just want to have a child now; she would *love* to have one. All of this
information, presented economically in the first utterance, helps to
establish the double uterus as a problem of some urgency.

Whether the GP 'hears' the matter as urgent will depend, in part,
on whether he shares certain background assumptions[9] with the pa-

---

talk, while preserving the actual word order as much as possible. The entire transcript
of the consultation is numbered from lines 1–176 and the excerpts used in this paper
are taken from this transcript. 'P' refers to the patient and 'D' to the doctor.

Transcription symbols include:

(indicates simultaneous utterances as in
       there again (about it
                   (Yes
((   ))indicates the occurrence of the phenomenon described within the double brack-
       ets as in ((coughs))
((2.0))indicates a pause of two seconds
,   indicates a pausing fall in tone
.   indicates a stopping fall in tone
-     indicates a halting, stammering cut off tone when at the end of a sound or a
      connecting flow from the last sound when at the start of a sound
:   indicates an extension of the sound it follows
?   indicates a rising inflection
!   indicates an animated tone

emphasis is indicated by italics, capitalization, or both, depending on the relative
volume.

[9] See Polanyi (1979) for a discussion of how members engaged in storytelling go to
great lengths to ensure that recipients will "get the point." They must be able to
understand what makes a story worth telling in the first place and this recognition is
constrained by what makes any set of events story-worthy within a particular culture.

tient. For example, he will, at the very least, need to sympathize with what it might be like for a woman who wants to get pregnant not to be able to. Moreover, if he believes that marriage makes having children compulsory, then six years of childnessness will account for the present situation being a matter of considerable concern. We do not know whether the GP uses such knowledge as a resource for understanding the present trouble. What is apparent, however, is that such information is provided by the patient as a *possible* resource. The GP is being helped to understand the present situation as something definitely worth worrying about. In this way, his cooperation is being enlisted in producing troubles telling as mutual endeavor as well as laying the groundwork for an affiliative "troubles-receptive" hearing (Jefferson, 1980).

In addition to aligning the GP as troubles recipient, the patient appeals to him in his position as medical authority. She does not merely engage in troubles talk for its own sake, but requests information from the GP, based on an assessment of his probable expertise.[10] The patient organizes her troubles-telling in such a way that the GP may appreciate the seriousness of her trouble and provide appropriate commiseration. Should that fail, however, he has the option of falling back on his position as medical expert and supplying the information requested. Let us take a look at what he does.

To begin with, he establishes himself as someone who has indeed "heard" of the problem before (line 18). He then proceeds to elaborate on this by providing an additional piece of information; namely, that rabbits have them (double uteri) too.

I shall now examine this remark as a possible candidate for medical paternalism. The first thing to be said about the GP's utterance is that it constitutes an *interruption*. The patient has the floor and seems about to continue her troubles-telling ("and well . . .") when he, rather abruptly, takes it away from her. This might be viewed as a violation of the "only-one-party-may-speak-at-a-time" rule (Sacks et al., 1974). Unlawful attempts to gain conversational control can be symptomatic of asymmetrical interactional power (West, 1984).

Unfortunately, interruptions are not that simple. Neither do they automatically signify that a power imbalance exists between the con-

---

In the above example, the event of the 'double uterus' would be less story-worthy in a culture where it is not considered problematic if women can't have children.

[10] This request is not made directly—"Tell me what you know about a double uterus"—but rather indirectly. See Labov and Fanshel (1977) for a discussion of how members may produce and hear requests that some activity be performed as well as the lengths they will go to make such requests indirectly or in a mitigated fashion.

versational partners. An interruption can also mean that the GP has made a mistake in transition timing; i.e. he thought that the patient was 'finished' with her turn or was hesitating because she didn't know how to continue, allowing him, therefore, to take over.

In addition to marking an error, an interruption can display a listener's competence. In other words, the GP may have been following the patient's talk so closely that he is able to anticipate what she will say next and says it for her. This display of independently achieved knowledge displays alignment.

Thus, even if we conclude that the GP has interrupted that patient, we cannot be sure whether he is doing so in order to regain control over the conversation (*bad* news for the troubles teller) or because he wants to demonstrate that he's listening to her and sympathizes with her trouble (*good* news). Depending on how we interpret the interruption, it becomes obstructive or supportive to the patient's troubles-telling. The issue becomes even more complicated if we take a look at what this particular interruption is about.

At first glance, the GP's observation concerning rabbits and their reproductive organs appears to be a *joke*.[11] As such, the GP is inviting the patient to laugh along with him. This is the appropriate and conventional response to a joke. By introducing a joke, the GP has, in a sense, not only taken over the floor, but he has started a story of his own, thereby placing the patient in the position of recipient. In other words, not only is she prevented from continuing her own troubles-telling, but she must now respond with laughter to his "story."

This particular joke, however, follows the patient's talk about a trouble. As such, it could also be viewed as an attempt to *reassure* the patient. Taken in this way, the joke becomes a perfectly appropriate and, in fact, affiliative response to a trouble-telling.

A "hearing" of the GP's rabbit-observation as reassuring hinges on the patient being able to perform one or both of the following steps. She must be able to view the *fact* that the GP would make a

---

[11] I am using the term "joke" rather loosely here. Scherzer (1985) maintains that there is a distinct difference between "joking" (nonserious communicative behavior) and a "joke" (full-fledged discourse form, complete with a setup and punch line). If we accept the above remark as an attempt at humor on the part of the GP, then it takes on an in-between status. The patient's description of the double uterus provides the setup for the GP's unexpected punch line.

Whereas other interpretations of the utterance are possible (and will be suggested further on in the text), this one is a particularly benevolent one as far as the GP's intentions go. Others, which have been suggested to me by less kindly readers, are: he didn't know what else to say, maybe that's what they learn in medical school, or it was the first thing that came to mind when he heard the complaint 'double uterus'. My own inclination here was to give the GP the benefit of the doubt.

joke in the midst of a troubles-telling as an indicator that her present difficulty can't be all that serious. This means that she believes that jokes do not belong in the same category as serious problems. Or, she might find the content of the joke as such reassuring. Everyone knows how prolific rabbits are, so if they are able to reproduce in such awesome numbers despite having a double uterus, there may be hope for the patient's daughter. Of course, in order for this to work as a reassurance, the patient must be able to make the link between rabbits and her own daughter. We have, unfortunately, no way of knowing whether or not she manages to do this. In other words, we do not know whether the comment worked as a reassurance. At this point, we can only say that the GP's remark *might* have been produced and/or heard as a well-intentioned attempt at reassurance.

If it is *not* heard as a reassurance, however, what then? The patient might find herself confused that the GP should suddenly begin to talk about rabbits, out of the blue as it were. Or, she might take offense at the fact that her daughter is being compared to a rabbit at all. More importantly, however, she might view the remark as a *trivialization* of her daughter's present distress as well as an indicator that he does not take what she (the patient) is saying, seriously.

It is precisely this ambiguity which makes the rabbit remark not only difficult to respond to, but more devastating to the ongoing troubles-telling than a mere interruption could ever be. If the patient laughs, she acknowledges that a joke has been told and that she has been competent in "getting the joke," thereby establishing their interaction as a harmonious, even friendly, endeavor. Simultaneously, however, she relinguishes her position as troubles-teller and (implicitly) lends credence to the notion that her "troubles" were in actual fact "a laughing matter." Her reasons for coming to the doctor don't have to be taken seriously.

If, on the other hand, she treats the GP's remark as a rude interruption or as an insult ("Listen, are you calling my daughter a rabbit, or what?"), he may legitimately retreat behind the other (janus) face of his joke; namely, that he was (a) only trying to reassure her, or (b) just making a little joke. She will then have to account for why she is so upset about something so patently well-intentioned.

How does the patient deal with this highly complicated obstacle to her troubles-telling? To begin with, she does not laugh. Instead, she pauses midstream, allowing the GP to bring his utterance to completion. In this way, minimal acknowledgement is provided for the interruption. She then 'proceeds where she left off', i.e. she repeats her initial starter and introduces the utterance as a next step in the ongoing troubles-telling ("and then . . ."). There is, of course, no way of knowing whether this is what she would have said, had she not been interrupted.

Upon closer inspection, her utterance appears to be a recapitulation of the "point" of her talk. "You get worked up" is not only a description of how *she* feels, but, by means of the general "you," how anyone under normal circumstances would feel, as well. In this way, she attempts to establish the grounds for her present trouble, which she has, perhaps, come to feel might be unclear to the GP.

Thus, she can be viewed as re-embarking on the business of alignment. By repeating her "point," the GP—despite his previous blunder—may yet be brought to recognize what the problem is.

EXCERPT 2

D: Do you still have muscular pain?

P: *Often. Very often.*(When I, well, for example, have been
                  Hmm

walking for a long time, when I, well, like go down-downtown,
you know(and then at a *certain moment*
       Mm

95   *WELL:* ((complaining)) then uhh—I can't *stand* it any
more— then do I ever get a pain in those *muscles* of
(Mmhmm

mine- especially in my *thighs*—

D: Do you also take them every day then, those(little yellow
                                     No:

pills(or
     No

100   just every once in awhile.

P: Just once in awhile.

D: Yeah(hh). Then you get a handful from me.
((4.0))

P: Oh and-

D: I *would* say go downtown *more often.* Then you'll get more used
105   to it.

P: *NOW* you just might(be right(an ointment. Yes.
                     Yeah   And an ointment

Please.

((5.0))

D: Now I am *more* in favor of you — after you've been downtown,
110   rubbing your muscles with that ointment(than
                                        Yeah-

that you immediately take some *pill,* right.

P: Yeah.

> D: O.K.?
> P: Yes.
> 115 D: Otherwise your life will start to be one continuous string of
> *pills*- ((loudly)) No, no thank you. Because uhh— ((laughs))
> I'd rather not.
> ((3.0))
> D: I'll just help you into your coat, just like at the hairdresser's.

This segment comes somewhat later on in the consultation, following a lengthy stretch of medical talk, in which the GP checks up on
various medications the patient has been taking for minor ailments (a
sore toe, water retention, muscular pain). The consultation is coming
to an end. In this fragment, the talk moves from a trouble (muscular
pains) to some advice for treating it (more little yellow pills, frequent
walks, ointment) to a closing segment ("I'll just help you into your
coat . . .").

Whereas the previous segment was organized as a troubles-telling,
this stretch of talk has a question–answer format. It is the GP who is
asking the questions and formulating relevant dimensions of the
problem or treatment. The patient is predominantly engaged in
providing the information requested or confirming the GP's formulations. In terms of control over the production of the ongoing interaction, the GP appears to have the reins firmly in hand. The only independent starter produced by the patient is found after a lengthy
pause (line 102) and is immediately interrupted.

Question–answer sequences are an interactionally sound way of
maintaining control over a conversation, the question constraining
the next speaker to provide an answer, thereby allowing the first
speaker to ask another question (Schegloff & Sacks, 1974).[12] Not
only does the present structure of the talk put the GP in a position of
control, but the activity in which he engages does so as well. In this
segment, the topic is not so much the patient's painful experience,
but rather what she might do to alleviate it. The general context, in
fact, is one of checking up on the various remedies she is currently
taking.

In this segment, the GP gives advice. The patient, as advice-recip-
ient, has the interactional choice of accepting or rejecting it. As
Jefferson and Lee (1981) have pointed out, members exhibit a prefer-

---

[12] That the issue of Q–A sequences is a tricky one, not easy to establish when a
question is a "question," has been discussed thoughtfully by West (1984). She also
investigates the role question strategies play in medical interaction and how they
construct unequal power relations.

ence for accepting advice, suggestions, or recommendations (whether or not they actually follow them up in daily life). This is an interactional issue, due to the extra 'work' rejections entail.

Thus, the present example displays the GP in a position of control in terms of the topics being discussed as well as the conversational form the talk will take. His activity sets limits on the activity which may be (appropriately) produced by the patient.

Whereas there seems little reason here to doubt that an asymmetry in interactional power is being displayed at this particular juncture of the consultation, there are different ways of evaluating it. This is, by no means, a matter of consensus among medical sociologists. Hughes (1982) views interactional control within the medical interview as essential for the production of orderly and coherent talk in a situation where members have unequal competence. The practice of engaging in highly directive question and answer sequences is beneficial not only for the GP, but also for the patient who must, after all, learn the ropes of the medical encounter. According to Hughes, then, the above fragment would be an example of medical interaction in the patient's best interests.

Aside from the relative merits of Hughes' point of view, I would contend that it rests on certain assumptions which the outside observer must be prepared to accept. The first is that physicians possess an interpretative scheme which enables them to control medical talk in a way which can be beneficial, i.e. that they know what they are doing. The second assumption is that patients do not possess such a scheme; i.e. do not know what they are doing. Although accepting the validity of such assumptions provides for the intrinsic benevolence of medical Q–A sequences, it is not the only way benevolence may be discovered. A fragment may also be investigated in terms of how it is constructed to *appear* benevolent.

We can now take a closer look at the second part of Excerpt 2 (lines 102–118). This is where the GP provides the patient with advice for her problem of muscular pains. His advice consists of the following: she gets another handful of pills from him (line 102), she is told to take walks downtown more often (line 104–105), and she receives an ointment (lines 108–111). Each bit of advice is constructed in a characteristic and, I would suggest, paternalistic way.

Let us begin with the "little yellow pills." It is the GP who introduces this particular topic in the ongoing interview. He wants to know if the patient is still taking them. Her response is that she is, but "only once in awhile." Despite her dramatic recount of how painful her muscles have been (lines 95–97), she displays a marked reticence about taking pills. The GP's reaction is to give her another handful. She did not ask for them directly and he clearly frames this offer as his own initiative (line 102). Based, perhaps, on her exemplary behavior of not taking too many pills ("then"), he gives her some more.

In the course of describing the pain, the patient provides an example of a situation in which it is particularly bad; i.e. after long walks downtown. Based on this account, the GP suggests that she should go downtown "more often." Then she'd "get used to it." The implication is twofold. To begin with, the patient is presented as someone who does not take walks often enough. And, more important, her current muscular pain becomes viewable as a result of this faulty behavior.

Based on the information provided, there is no way of knowing whether this is true. Another reading, namely, that the patient does take walks, even long ones, would certainly be just as plausible, especially if we stick to what she actually has said. In terms of giving advice, however, it does come in handy to display the patient as doing something which is not good for her. This enables the GP to come to the fore as someone who has a better suggestion.

His final piece of advice is offered in a similar way. He suggests that she might try an ointment. This elicits an enthusiastic response from the patient (lines 106–108), which is followed by a remark that *he* would *rather* she used the ointment after taking a walk instead of a pill.

This utterance is constructed in such a way that the GP is displayed as the person who wants the patient to take the ointment whereas she, when left to her own devices, might be just as likely to take pills. Although there is no basis for such pill-happy behavior on the part of the patient (on the contrary), nor for the GP's reticence in prescribing them (also on the contrary), this remark does work to set his advice off from the patient's own inclinations. In other words, she does not display the proper behavior and he is placed in the position of having to remind her to mend her ways, "for her own good."

This stance receives the final flourish (line 115), as the GP remarks that "otherwise" (i.e. if she doesn't do what he says), her "life will start to be one continuous string of pills".

The issue here is not whether or not the GP's advice is sound. It may well be. The advice is not being justified, however, on the grounds of its correctness. On the contrary, the patient herself must supply the rationale for it. By appearing, first, as *not* behaving in her best interests, his advice may subsequently be displayed as warranted. This pattern is repeated, as we have seen, in each of the instances above. Not only is the patient being advised, but she is being advised "for her own good."

Let us turn to the patient now. What options does she have when confronted with such manifestly well-intentioned advice? As advice recipient, the easiest course to take, interactionally speaking, is to accept suggestions (Jefferson & Lee, 1981). This will presumably not be too difficult since the advice itself seems to be in accordance with what she already does or what she would probably want to do. What grounds could she have for rejecting the GP's advice? Unfortunately, by accepting the advice, she also, implicitly, confirms the definition of herself as someone who is not doing the "right" things and of the GP as someone who knows better than she does what is "right" for her. The patient may not find this problematic, of course. However, if she does, she has very little choice, in terms of the interaction, but to accept it. It would take considerable conversational expertise to reject this relationship definition. She would need to engage in meta-talk and formulate their relationship as a topic in its own right ("Are you saying I don't take enough walks?"). Whereas professional helpers are adept at this conversational maneuver (Schwartz, 1979; Davis, 1986), it is not a readily available option for clients and patients. Moreover, even if the patient did engage in "meta-linguistic listening," it is unlikely that she would do so at this juncture in the consultation. She is already being helped into her coat. The consultation is coming to a close.

The interactional control exercised in this fragment begins with sequential ordering. The patient is subject to the constraint imposed by elicitation practices. Moreover, as recipient of advice, she will be likely to accept it due to the interactional consequences a rejection would entail. The greatest restriction to her activity, however, is not provided by membership categories. It is the fact that the activities are so manifestly being performed "for her own good." How, then, can she possibly refuse without questioning the relationship itself or disrupting the quality of the interaction?

EXCERPT 3

```
     D:   I can imagine that that- that fear of whether or not you'll be able
135        to have children(        that that can make you really very
           tense(              (Yes
              (Yeah
           on the other hand, I tend to say, yeah(hh): ((rapid)) you're
           better off with a double uterus than with just one arm, but, yeah-(
140  P:              ((snorts)) YEAH:
           yes but, you can go without children, too, of course, but,(
                                                                      (Yes
```

that IS NOT the way it's supposed to be, of course, right?

D: That's - it's annoying-   that
the ones who

145   *do* want to have them-   they can't   have them the
             Yeah, they-   Yeah-
uh- the ones who don't want to have them they   get
                                    Yeah

them anyway.

Yeah but   let's look a little more at the

150 P: And what can I do now-

D: sunny side for the time being-

P: in your opinion about my nervousness?

D: Uhh- uh I would like to do *nothing* about it for the time being.

155   Look, I can give you a pill   because uh- but that nerv-
                      Yeah:
ousness, you *do* use that to *work through* the problem with your
daughter.

P: Yeah(hh).

D: Yeah: all that worrying, you'll *keep* doing that of course   and
                                         Yes

160   well I could sweep that under the table with a pill   but I
                                        No:
think we'd just get a kind of unnatural situation
                                      Yeah: of course
that you uhh- now if it gets too *out of hand* - then yes-

165   Yeah: well
we could   uh- have another   talk- but then I'd rather
yeah   talk   another   time
talk about *problems* than about pills.

P: Yeah(hh).

This excerpt is taken from the final stages of the consultation. The patient has recycled her initial trouble—her daughter's double uterus. The GP provides a medical-type explanation of the "anomaly" in which he describes it as a normal stage in every woman's physiological development; the patient's daughter just got "stuck." It doesn't necessarily mean that she won't be able to have children.[13] The pa-

---

[13] The present paper is not about how GPs dispense or withhold medical information. See Fisher (1983) and Fisher and Todd (1986) for a good example of how that is done in a doctor–patient interview. It is interesting, however, to note that, whereas the GP's information is correct, it is also somewhat incomplete. Uterine malformations can (and often do) cause a host of clinical problems, for example: dysmenorrhea, renal troubles, infertility, repeated miscarriage, premature labor, uterine rupture, transverse or breech births, retained placenta, prenatal and postpartum blood loss (Stolk, 1975). Thus, whereas a double uterus does not necessarily mean that a woman can't get

tient responds to this emotionally; she finds it "sad," "terrible" for her daughter. I shall now examine how this "trouble" is dealt with and, ultimately, the advice the patient receives for it. Like the excerpts before it, this occurs in a specific, i.e. paternalistic, way. It does *not*, however, occur without a struggle.

If we view the segment in terms of the GP's activities, it may be divided roughly into a joke (lines 137–139), a platitude (lines 144–151) and advice (lines 154–168). Each activity will be examined in terms of how it limits the patient's activity as well as how benevolence is being constructed. In each case, the patient's contribution to this production process will be examined.

The Joke

Unlike the first example, where the GP launched a joke concerning the patient's troubles mid-sentence, this joke is embedded in a rather lengthy utterance. It begins with an affiliative remark (lines 134–136). Not only does he provide an assessment of her difficulty as something which would cause anxiety and "a whole lot of tension," but he indicates that he can understand that it would do that.

As response to the patient's troubles-telling, such a response is more than adequate. It displays considerable affiliation with her present dilemma.[14]

What follows (lines 137–139), I have chosen to regard as a "joke." This joke may belong to the initial affiliative response (Jefferson, 1984). Before considering this possibility, however, I would like to describe how I (or anyone else) might come to see this particular utterance as belonging to the general category of speech events called "jokes."

What would happen, for example, if we regarded it as a simple assertion of something this particular GP "tends to" say. You're better off with a double uterus than with one arm. Applied to some "generalized other" (you = anyone/everyone), or some general bodily state (having one or two arms, one or two uteri), we are faced with the unproblematic task of agreeing or disagreeing with the statement. Problems arise, however, when prior talk is considered. The assertion needs to be linked to the ongoing talk which was, as the reader will

woman can't get pregnant or have a normal birth, it would be going a little too far to say she has 'nothing to worry about'.

[14] For a troubles-telling to proceed, the troubles recipient needs to be properly aligned. This alignment, which entails a display of emotional reciprocity or commiseration with the person in trouble, will need to be ongoingly displayed if the troubles-telling is to proceed.

recall, not about general states or affairs, but particular individuals; namely, the patient and her daughter. Fortunately, the preceding talk did contain a topic which returns in this utterance; namely, the double uterus. The patient's daughter has one. Perhaps the "you," then, is not so general after all, but is being directed at the daughter as someone who happens to possess a double uterus. She could then compare herself or her present predicament with that of someone with "only one arm." Unfortunately, this is where we run into difficulties again. Who is this (concrete) one-armed person with whom the patient's daughter might compare herself?

The suspicion begins to arise that the remark is, perhaps, not linked to the prior talk at all, but rather has nothing much to do with anything. Before I come to such a conclusion, I would like to consider some other possibilities. After all, one of the basis tenets of conversation analysis (Schegloff & Sacks, 1974) is that talk is an orderly affair and that members go to great lengths to display that orderliness as well as their appreciation of it. Before we accuse the GP of such an interactional breach of conduct, let us consider how this remark might possibly be connected to prior talk after all.

One possibility is that the remark might be viewed as a joke, or, more appropriately, something of a pun. Puns are plays on words, often embedded in a proverb or commonplace statement (Scherzer, 1985). Thus, the GP might be making a word play on the number of bodily parts in the context of a commonplace "things could be worse."[15] Attached to the preceding affiliative assessment of the problem, it might be viewed as a qualifier of the patient's anxiety. Her trouble is bad, but not *that* bad. Qualifiers of this type might well be viewed as a further display of alignment to the troubles-telling. As Jefferson and Lee (1981) have pointed out, in everday troubles talk recipients go to great lengths to ensure that the person with the trouble remain "one among others." She may have problems, but she is still expected to participate in the ongoing activities of the community (pp. 416—417). In this way, such a joking commonplace might work to bring the patient (and her daughter) "back into the fold." Her difficulty becomes a part of the human dilemma; something we can all identify with.

Aside from providing a troubles-responsive display of affiliation, the utterance might also allow participants a chance to "laugh together." Laughter as time-out from troubles talk (Jefferson, 1984) can provide welcome relief from the more serious activities involved in a medical encounter. Moreover, laughing is something friends do

---

[15] A similar (both in form and content) English proverbial equivalent is: "Better a bird in the hand, than two in the bush."

together. In an institutional setting, it can lend the intimate touch of a chat between friends.

Joking is frequently done in institutional settings, particularly in medical ones. As Gordon (1983) has pointed out, it is an important way of establishing rapport among the medical staff without things getting too personal or intimate. It is a way of letting off steam.

Unfortunately, jokes as a device for establishing rapport are a bit tricky when the object of the humor is the one with whom rapport is being established. Humor occurs in situations where participants are relatively uninvolved in the object of their mirth (Korsmeyer, 1978). If we can laugh at the slapstick slipping-on-a-banana-peel routine, it is because this misfortune belongs to another person. Thus, if laughter unites those laughing together, it distances them from those they are laughing at. Finding the joke "funny" and, consequently, being able to join in a companionable "laughing together" with the GP rests on the patient's being able to distance herself from her daughter. Moreover, she must also be able to distance herself from herself, as someone who has, up until now, regarded her daughter's predicament as anything but a laughing matter.

The reassurance noted by Jefferson and Lee (1981) has as its focus the person with the trouble rather than the trouble itself. Thus, if she is admonished not to take things so seriously, it is not because her trouble is not considered worth talking about. On the contrary, reassurance displays intimacy with the person; you're one of us *in spite of* your trouble. This runs counter to the distancing which a joke requires. In view of the above and the rather contradictory demands it makes on the patient as conversational partner, it is not surprising perhaps that the utterance "flops" as joke. The patient interrupts the GP with a snort. In her next turn (lines 140–142), she reformulates her trouble as a serious one. Not only is having children a good thing, but it is described as the way things are supposed to be. The use of a "generalized other" (you) as well as words like "of course," appeal to the GP as member, someone who will know how "things should be."

At this point, a rather ticklish situation has emerged. The joke hasn't provided an opportunity for a laugh; nor has it worked as a display of sympathetic alignment to the ongoing troubles-telling. The patient has formulated her problem as a serious one. The question now arises: will the GP confirm this—finally—as an accurate reading of what their talk has been about?

A Platitude

This segment (lines 144–151) is located between a joke (which flopped) and an extended stretch of advice-giving. It contains elements of both and serves to link the definition of the trouble, which is now under negotiation, to a closing segment in which advice can be given and the patient may, having already been helped into her coat minutes ago, finally leave the office.

The GP produces an utterance, a candidate reading of the trouble, which has a similar format to the previous joke. He displays alignment with the trouble itself (it's a nuisance) and a commonplace concerning people who want to have children and can't, whereas those who don't want them, get them anyway. Unlike the prior joking platitude, this utterance is more carefully constructed. It is linked to what the trouble itself is about.

The GP displays awareness that the problem is being able to have children or not, rather than the presence of one or two body parts. He also makes use, much as the patient did in *her* formulation, of possible shared background assumptions. The platitude is, for example, based on shared knowledge that: (a) some women want children and some women don't (b) some women can have children and some women can't (c) these categories can appear in various combinations with the result that (d) a woman can find herself wanting something which she can't have and (e) when faced with this dilemma one possible action to take is to look at the sunny side. Whereas this remark also has the message not to take things so seriously, the patient is not being invited to laugh at the problem but to consider it as part of the "human dilemma."

The GP thus does finally exhibit an awareness of the interactional difficulties that treating troubles as joking matters can entail. He does not, however, confirm the patient's prior reading of her problem as a serious one. Despite the fact that her problem has yet to be considered seriously, this does not prevent him from dispensing some helpful advice. Unfortunately, the patient seems not to have developed the appropriate philosophical outlook. She interrupts the GP[16] (line 150) and asks him, directly, what he thinks she should do about her nervousness. Whatever else this utterance is, it does not constitute an acceptance of advice-just-offered. In fact, it is not even a rejection of advice. By requesting advice herself, the patient demonstrates that—up until now—no advice has been given. In view of the fact that the GP has just provided advice ("look at the sunny side"), the patient's utterance might be heard as an indirect challenge to him in his position as medical authority.[17] After all, physicians are sup-

---

[16] In order to appreciate how unusual this is, the reader is referred to West (1984). Interruptions are, by far, according to her study, the prerogative of the physician.

[17] See Labov and Fanshel (1977) for a discussion of how such indirect requests can serve as a criticism. When a person makes a request in a situation where she shouldn't

posed to give advice. The patient's remark also cuts off any further talk about this particular trouble.

Some Advice

What follows this patient-initiated request for advice is a lengthy stretch of advice-giving on the part of the GP (line 154–168). The advice is to do *nothing*. Whereas this rather bald suggestion is softened slightly by "for the time being" (line 154), it is not very consoling. Fortunately, it does not remain in this unadulterated form, but is subject to some accounting.

To begin with, the GP explains that he could give her a pill for her nervousness, but this would only serve to obfuscate the problem (line 160), creating an "unnatural" situation (line 161) and, ultimately, getting rid of the very nervousness which she needs to work through the difficulties with her daughter (lines 155–157). In addition to being a commendable display of some of the more progressive trends in medicine today,[18] the implication is that the patient has asked for tranquilizers and the GP, once again, is warning her against them. If this excerpt is strangely reminiscent of an earlier one, it is so in more ways than one. Once again, the patient has not actually requested tranquilizers. Perhaps she would like them, but it is, in fact, the GP who brings them up here. Employing what she has said before as a resource for understanding her request (lines 150–153), we might even assume that her general reluctance to take pills could mean that pills are not what she wants to have done about her nervousness. Still, this remains speculation. What we *do* know is that she has requested help; a possible indication that help has—as of yet—not been forthcoming.

We have seen that the GP's account serves, once again, to display the patient as engaging in an activity which is not in her best interests (asking for tranquilizers) and himself, on the other hand, as a champion of exactly those interests ("I would like to do nothing;" i.e. not have you take tranquillizers). In this way, an account is constructed of his advice as "for her own good." Aside from being benevolent, this account has an additional feature. It creates a lopsided

---

have to make the request, it can be heard by the other person as a challenge to his or her performance in a particular role (p. 94).

[18] His advice shows remarkable similarity to some of the tenets held dear by holistic medicine with its emphasis on nontechnological solutions to health problems and individual responsibility (Berliner & Salmon, 1980) or the newer, comprehensive approaches to disease which extend beyond the somatic to include psychological and even social dimensions (Mechanic, 1979; Conrad & Kern, 1981, for example).

picture of both what the patient is doing as well as what the GP is not doing.

Let us assume, for example, that the GP would not only like to do nothing about the present problem, but is, in fact, *unable* to do anything. In that case, the account works to cover up this unfortunate state of affairs. Her (and our) attention are directed away from his regrettable inability to help and focused instead on the possibility that at some later date ("when things get out of hand"), he *could* do something about it (tranquilizers being a kind of help, albeit a problematic kind). The fact that nothing is being done *now* has nothing to do with his *powers*, but rather his *preferences* as medical expert.

The GP does not leave the patient with empty hands. In his summary statement (lines 165–168), he displays an optimistic orientation to her problem and future treatment; namely, she can always return for a chat. *He,* personally, would rather talk about problems.

This may come as somewhat of a surprise to the reader—and possibly to the patient as well. The question might arise why he didn't engage in a bit more of this therapeutic activity in the present consultation. On the other hand, if he presents it as something he not only prefers to do, but suggests doing in the future should she run into difficulties, she may begin to wonder whether he did talk about her problems and she just missed it. Unfortunately, we have no way of knowing whether the patient had trouble coming to terms with this discrepancy in the GP's professed intentions and his actual conversational behavior. Following a brief exchange of pleasantries, the consultation is brought to a close.

DELINEATING PATERNALISM

Having examined some excerpts from a consultation between a male GP and a female patient in detail, I shall now return to my original research problem; namely, how power is exercised at the level of medical interaction and, more specifically, how benevolent control or paternalism might work to construct asymmetrical relations of power between the participants. Taking a step backwards from my actual data, I shall now discuss what it has revealed about paternalism in medical talk.

The first question is, of course, how the two dimensions inherent in the concept itself—control and benevolence—can be constructed simultaneously within a consultation. This will be followed by a discussion of how the fact that these dimensions occur *simultaneously* can produce a new, and, ultimately, more intensive and effective form of control. And, finally, I shall be turning to the current critique of medicine as an instance of social control, particularly over women (Ehrenreich, 1978; Ehrenreich & English, 1979). What do the present findings concerning how paternalism works at the micro-level of a general practice consultation have to say of relevance concerning these broader issues?

Paternalism: Benevolence and Control

In its most general sense, power is connected to human agency (Giddens, 1976). What this means is that everyone has, at least to some degree, the capacity to "intervene in a series of events so as to alter their course" (p. 111). Nevertheless, few will deny that members have asymmetrical access to resources and skills for achieving outcomes. Thus, some members may exercise power "over" other members. This is where power is linked to domination or control.

In the present interview, the GP was able to exercise considerable control over how the ongoing topic talk was structured. This was done in accordance with his professional system of relevance, i.e. diagnosis and treatment. Inevitably, it entailed limiting the patient's troubles talk. For example, we saw that he was able to "interrupt" her initial presentation of her problem. He could engage in extended medical question–answer sequences, give advice, and provide candidate formulations of her difficulties. Ultimately, her initial complaint could be labelled as "nothing to worry about."

Each of these activities might be viewed as an instance of the interactional exercise of power. Moreover, there is clearly a somewhat unequal distribution of resources available to the participants in this particular encounter. The patient generally allowed herself to be interrupted, provided "responses" to the GP's "questions," and presented her own initiatives in a mitigated fashion, demonstrating considerable deference to his position as medical expert. At no point did she directly confront his reading of the problem, although there are indications that she was not necessarily in agreement with it.

All of this is fairly straightforward and, as Hughes (1982) has pointed out, potentially of mutual advantage to both parties. After all, the patient will presumably expect to have her difficulties "assessed" and hope that some form of help be forthcoming. Moreover, she will have some general background assumptions concerning how a physician "should" behave as well as "what usually happens when you see a doctor" (Stimson & Webb, 1975), enabling her to view this as a routine instance of a general practice consultation.

In addition to producing orderly medical talk, the GP also devotes considerable interactional effort towards displaying the encounter as a benevolent one. This begins with attentiveness to ritual conventions like greetings, helping the patient into her coat, reminding her not to forget her bag when she leaves, etc. He also provides affiliative responses throughout the patient's troubles-telling in the form of "listening noises" (hmm's and ja's) as well as occasionally underlining how bothersome the difficulties must be for her. This kind of interactional work belongs to the conversational behavior routinely exhibited by members in order to support or affirm their social relationships (Goffman, 1971). It is in everyone's interest that the encounter be "pulled off" as pleasantly as possible, with a minimum of (interactional) muss and fuss. Such considerations obviously do not apply to everyday, face-to-face encounters alone, but make themselves felt in institutional ones as well.

In the present interview, the GP did more than pay attention to minimum politeness conventions, however. He engaged in considerable joke-telling. Platitudes were produced to remind the patient that her difficulties are not all *that* terrible, but rather just part of the human condition. Such activities could easily be found in a situation where participants are friends or acquaintances. In fact, it is precisely this sort of activity which constructs an encounter as a friendly one. Thus, by joking and talking about the commonplace, the GP provides the institutional encounter with a friendly, even intimate touch.

In addition to constructing the consultation as a pleasant, friendly affair, the GP executes his professional duties (diagnosis and suggestions for treatment) in such a way that his good intentions are displayed. As we have seen, he does more than commiserate with her difficulties. He attempts to reassure her. His advice is not simply a detached suggestion of what she could do, but presented as in her best interests. In short, it is clear that control and benevolence are by no means mutually exclusive phenomena. They can (and do) coexist harmoniously within a consultation. In other words, a GP may exercise control over the consultation, thus limiting the patient's activity and her power to define the situation. At the same time, he may produce displays of his good intentions as well as engage in the production of friendly social talk. The question now becomes whether this activity, which West (1984) has aptly called the "social cement" of the medical encounter, can be regarded as a separate dimension of the consultation, running parallel to the actual business of doing medical talk and of little consequence to it. What would happen if these "inconsequential niceties" were directly implicated in the very exercise of control? It is to this possibility I shall now turn.

Paternalism: Control Through Benevolence

Paternalism pervades the consultation as a whole. It is not simply involved in producing orderly topic talk or in giving the interaction a pleasant, intimate quality. It also determines how the patient's problem may ultimately be defined, the kind of advice she receives, the possibilities she has for influencing the course of the unfolding consultation, as well as how the social relationship between the participants is being constructed. I shall deal with each of these issues briefly in order to show how benevolence may work to produce a new, and, in fact, far more effective form of control over the medical encounter.

Let us return to the patient's initial presentation of her problem. She has gone to the GP because she is worried about her daughter. She can't sleep; thinks about it all the time. The question she asks the physician in his capacity as medical expert is whether a double uterus can, in fact, impair her daughter's ability to have children. She may, of course, also wish to elaborate what this particular event means for her; her concern for her daughter; her own desire to have grandchildren, etc. Her experience will be—at least, for her—a part of the problem as well.

What sort of answer does the patient receive? Not only is she instructed that the presence of a double uterus is of little consequence, medically speaking—a point which might be worthy of debate—but she is consistently constrained to treat it as something which is not worth worrying about to begin with.

However pleasant jokes and platitudes may be in ordinary social encounters, when they are produced in response to a trouble, the effect is automatically to *trivialize* it. The patient may enjoy being able to laugh during a consultation, but here she will have to do so at the expense of taking herself and her daughter seriously. It can, of course, be reassuring to compare one's experience with that of another person. In this way, a sense of community is established; we're all in this together. In this case, a respect for the individual's suffering is combined with the attempt to help her cope with and, ultimately, get along with living her life. In the present interview, reassurance was also constructed by means of comparing the patient's plight to that of others (rabbits, one-armed individuals, people who do and don't want children). It was done, however, in the context of a devaluation of her experience. In other words, the price tag of being reassured was to regard her troubles as a laughing matter, scarcely meriting serious attention.

Considering that the patient's present difficulty was consistently treated as something of little consequence, we might expect that she be sent home empty-handed. After all, in the absence of a problem, the rationale for medical (or other) intervention would seem to be lacking. This did not, however, prove to be the case in the present consultation. On the contrary, the patient received numerous helpful suggestions, not only for the complaints she came with, but various other ones as well.

This advice was offered in a specific and systematic fashion. To begin with, the patient was displayed as someone behaving in ways detrimental to her own well-being (not taking walks, preferring pills to the less medical–technical solutions, etc.). This was followed by some advice from the GP which was presented as running counter to the unfortunate behavior previously established. In this way, the GP emerges as someone with the patient's best interests at heart. His benevolence, however, is constructed by virtue of *her* inability to take good care of herself when left to her own devices.

The issue is not simply that the patient is placed in the position of getting advice she didn't ask for. There is no reason why spontaneously offered advice should not be good advice as well. Accepting advice offered in the manner just described, however, entails an implicit confirmation of her own irresponsibility in terms of her health and well-being. She may be "helped," but only at the expense of her position as autonomous agent.

At this point, the conclusion might seem warranted that the patient's initial complaint had been reduced to a triviality and that she herself has emerged from the consultation, albeit on somewhat dubious grounds, as someone in need of professional guidance in matters concerning her general health and well-being. The patient, of course, may agree with this outcome of the consultation and leave the doctor's office feeling reassured, convinced that she, indeed, has nothing to worry about. On the other hand, she might not agree with this definition of her problem (and herself).

It is unlikely that, in that case, she would openly and in so many words express disagreement with the GP's assessment, but she might well express a lack of compliance covertly. "Yes, but . . ." followed up by a counter-example is a useful interactional strategy for "resistant" patients in conversations with professional helpers (Davis, 1986). This presupposes, however, that the patient have a clear picture concerning what is happening in the consultation. In other words, she must be able to see *that* her complaint is being trivialized and that she is being treated as an incompetent person in terms of managing her own health.

Unfortunately, a clear view is precisely what the patient in this interview could *not* have. The consultation continually appears as something it is not; i.e. a friendly chat between friends. This constrains the kinds of activities in which she may appropriately engage. It is never easy, interactionally speaking, to reject advice, particularly when it is well-intentioned. Refusing to laugh at a joke will, at the very least, require a bit of accounting, if the conversation is to proceed without a snag. The patient, like the GP, will have a vested interest in constructing the medical encounter as a pleasant and harmonious affair. In the present interview, however, the patient is not only constrained by routine social conventions. She is also being confronted with two separate and, in some senses, mutually exclusive definitions of the situation as well as the social relationship between the participants. Not being able to act "appropriately" can easily lead to not being able to "act" at all, a conversational double bind.

In view of the above, it is not surprising that the patient would find it difficult to exercise control over how her problem was defined. What *is* surprising, is that she managed to resist at all.

Up until now, paternalism has been discussed in terms of what it might mean for the patient's experience as well as her ability to determine what happens within the consultation. I shall now turn to a final feature of paternalism; namely, how it may construct a social relationship in which the GP's position as medical authority may be established. Let us consider the dilemma which the patient's complaint presents for the GP. It is clearly a complaint which he can do little about. The patient's daughter isn't his patient. Aside from providing some general information about the double uterus as medical anomaly, he is, in fact, powerless to help her. He is more or less relegated to lending a sympathetic ear to her troubles. This presupposes, of course, that he was indeed able to sympathize with them. Judging from his responses throughout the consultation, there is reason to believe that this was not the case. Given the situation that he has been presented with a complaint he cannot empathize with and which he is unable to alleviate, he has two options. He may do nothing at all; i.e. explain to the patient that he can't help her. A bitter pill to swallow, perhaps, but truthful. On the other hand, he may *pretend* to do something about the complaint.

Tranquilizers are one way of dealing with this dilemma. Prescribing tranquilizers, however, particularly for difficulties like the patient's, is no longer as acceptable as it once was. It will, at the very least, require some accounting, a fact of which this GP seems only too well aware.[19] Thus, he finds himself in the unfortunate position of *having* to provide help as medical expert and not having anything but inferior help to provide.

This is where paternalism makes it fortuitous entrance. Instead of having to admit that he could do nothing for the patient, the GP was able to equivocate. He could cover up two separate but related facts; namely, that (a) he couldn't do anything about the patient's current distress and that (b) he, in fact, did not do anything about it. He was able by the end of the consultation to appear as someone who had not only provided sympathy, but advice as well. And the patient could return home with the illusion that she had been helped.

It is my contention that control and benevolence are not simply separate dimensions of the medical encounter. On the contrary, I would like to suggest that benevolence itself may be employed as a *resource* for control. Ultimately, this control is far more effective, potentially, than control exercised by means of organizing topicality within the consultation or engaging in straightforward advice giving. It is precisely the conflation of control and benevolence that serves to construct asymmetrical power relations between the participants which are effective because they are unidentifiable as such. Paternalism worked as a medium for controlling how the patient's experience, the medical encounter, and the social relationship between the participants could be defined. Moreover, its Janus face limited the patient's opportunities for exercising control, overtly or covertly, over the situation more completely than would have been possible by more obviously authoritarian or repressive means. In this way, undisputed medical authority could be established over an area which might not otherwise have fallen unproblematically under the GP's jurisdiction. Unfortunately, the effects of paternalism cannot be limited to the general practice consultation. It is to its potential effects *outside* the doctor's office, particularly for women, that I shall now direct my attention.

PATERNALISM, SOCIAL CONTROL AND THE INSTITUTION OF MEDICINE

It is by no means a new idea that the medical system serves important social control functions (Illich, 1976; Ehrenreich, 1978; Conrad &

---

[19] For a sensitive discussion of how physicians can be both concerned about preventing their patients from becoming dependent on medical solutions to their problems while, at the same time, prescribing tranquilizers en masse, the reader is referred to Gabe and Lipshitz-Phillips (1984).

Schneider, 1980). In their critique of modern medicine, Ehrenreich and Ehrenreich (1978) maintain that the institution of medicine "promotes acquiesence to a social system built on class- and sex-based inequalities in power" (p. 61). They then proceed to sort out the different types of social control which are exercised.

The first, disciplinary control, is basically geared towards keeping people out of the system and on the job. Such control is characterized by difficulties in obtaining medical services and discourteous treatment for those who receive them. This control is applied most readily to the poor and ethnic minorities.

The other type of control is cooptative or expansionary. I shall be focusing on it, partly because it is, according to Ehrenreich, on the rise, and partly because it resembles the phenomena I observed in my consultations between GPs and women patients. This second form of control features low barriers to entry into the medical system. People are actually encouraged to seek the services of medical professionals, even in situations where they are not sick (contraception, advice for marital problems, etc.). Those who enter the system are treated sympathetically. In this way, large numbers of people can be brought under medical surveillance and "into the fold of professional management of various aspects of their lives" (Ehrenreich & Ehrenreich, 1978: p. 49).

The content of the control is primarily ideological. Messages are transmitted about the way people should be, thus influencing how they will behave. The doctor–patient relationship proves an ideal medium for the transmission of such messages with its features of intimacy combined with authoritarianism. Not only is the physician in a unique position of being able to convey just about any message he would like to convey,[20] but:

> Given the intimacy and authoritarianism built into the relationship, and the prestige and presumed expertise of the doctor, the patient is likely to take such messages much more seriously than he or she would from other people. (p. 64)

Not only is this form of social control particularly effective, but it is selectively applied to social groups. In particular, women as patients are subject to this kind of control.

---

[20] I have used "he" because this is the routine situation. In The Netherlands, 94% of GPs are male (whereas two thirds of the patients are female). Particularly, when it comes to the transmission of ideological messages we might expect them to reflect the social group to which doctors generally belong: white, upper-class males.

In their classic study, Ehrenreich and English (1979) describe how women have, historically, been subject to well-intentioned control on the part of various experts. After usurping their age-old skills and authority in the field of health and reproduction, men set themselves up as the undisputed authority of nearly every aspect of women's lives. Not only were their bodies and reproductive functions subject to constant medical surveillance and intervention, women's minds became the objects of male attention as well. They delved into her "psychology," discussed how she should raise her children, and even had suggestions to make about how she should clean her house. Whereas the content of the advice changes over the years, two features remained consistent.

To begin with, women's experience was defined by men rather than by women themselves. These definitions were frequently derogatory, moralistic, or just plain inaccurate. Even when the judgements were not harmful, the message was consistently that women did not have anything of consequence to say about their lives and experiences.

The second feature of the advice was that it was inevitably presented as being "for her own good." This proved necessary, as medical advice has historically been quite dangerous to women's health and well-being. The crux of social control over women by medical and other helping professions may be located in the privatization of their experiences (Smith & David, 1975; Smart & Smart, 1978; Barrett & Roberts, 1978; Cloward & Piven, 1979; Hearn, 1982). Women are required to view their difficulties and discontent as a matter of individual inadequacy. It is not surprising that they seek medical solutions for them.

Another related aspect is that women learn to look to men to tell them what's wrong with them. Their own versions lack authority, requiring confirmation by a male (professional). As Bleier suggests (1984), male power over women is based on

the soft, subtle, intellectual control, which through the hysterization and medicalization of women's bodies and psychiatrization of their minds taught women their *need* to be subservient to men, though it speaks the language of love . . . (p. 182)

Thus, cooptative forms of social control in medicine not only serve to define women's difficulties in a particular direction; i.e. as evidence of her personal inadequacy or as inconsequential in terms of her life and situation, but it also defines her relationship to men in a particular way. The relationship is one of subordination and dependency.

In the present interview, the patient's experience was consistently negated. Little more than lip service was paid to the very real effects the presence of a double uterus can have on a woman's ability to have children or to have them without serious complications. The patient's and her daughter's very valid worries were thus discounted or treated as "nothing to worry about." Even if the grounds for her fears had been less solid than they, in fact, were, it can hardly be denied that the patient's distress *was* very real. She "thought about" it all the time, had difficulties sleeping and, ultimately, even went to the doctor about it. Throughout the consultation, she was instructed to view her experience as well as her feelings about it as a trivial and even slightly ridiculous matter. None of this is new, of course. Women are frequently referred to humourously. In fact, as Korsmeyer (1978) points out, talk about women is almost automatically accompanied by a less-than-serious atmosphere. Humor is one of the prime weapons in the battle against women's equality.

Not only does the patient discover in her talk with the GP that her experience isn't important and that her own worries are invalid, but she also learns that she does need his services, perhaps even more than she thought she did when she sought them in the first place. Her own reckless or unfortunate behavior in matters concerning her health make it advisable that she look to him, the medical expert, for guidance. Thus, not only is her experience discounted and trivialized, but her need for medical surveillance is confirmed.

CONCLUSION

In the present inquiry, I have attempted to show how power relations between the sexes might be constructed at the level of face-to-face interaction. I began with the assumption that power is not simply a relevant feature of political organizations or social groups, but integral to social life, even, and perhaps especially, at the micro-level of everyday encounters. Analogously, gender relations are not only structural to patriarchal society, but are ongoingly constructed and reproduced by individual men and women. Whereas these issues are often dealt with as theoretical concerns or transformed into generalizations suitable for empirical verification, I have taken a routine situation—a general practice consultation between a male physician and a female patient—as starting point for my investigation. By placing it under the microscope, as it were, I hoped to uncover what Henley (1977) calls the "micro-political structure of daily life." It is a modest step towards the development of grounded theories about the relations of domination and subordination between men and women.

Whereas I believe this to be an essential undertaking,[21] it is, by no means, an easy one. Knowing that power is implicated in the production of social interaction does not mean that it is always possible to "find" it.

Using my own experiences as researcher as well as my initial confrontations with my data, I began to unravel some of the difficulties inherent in identifying how power can be exercised in the context of a medical consultation. My own difficulties mirrored the difficulties a patient might also have in coming to terms with the Janus face of paternalism. There is, conversationally speaking, no "appropriate" response to it. Accepting the benevolence with appreciation means allowing your experience and your definition of self to be treated as inconsequential. Resisting this kind of control would mean disrupting the pleasant character of the encounter which is in the interest of both participants. More important, however, such a disruption would be problematic to justify. The GP could with perfect equanimity retreat behind the other, ever-present dimension of the encounter. Thus, it is hardly surprising that it may pass by unnoticed, or, at least, unmentioned.

It is my contention that paternalism is what makes general practice an extremely effective location for exercising control over how women see themselves and their difficulties. It has real and obvious advantages for greasing the wheels of medical interaction.

Unfortunately, paternalism cannot be limited to general practice. It plays a major role in the everyday experience of being female. It is my hope that by uncovering its subtle maneuverings in one specific instance, a medical consultation, we may all be helped in identifying (and ultimately) combatting Janus when and where he rears his head.

REFERENCES

Barrett, M., & Roberts, H. (1978). Doctors and their patients. The social control of women in general practice. In C. Smart & B. Smart (Eds.), *Women, Sexuality, and Social Control*. London: Routledge and Kegan Paul.

---

[21] I am not alone in this conviction. For a discussion of the importance of linking micro- and macro-levels of analysis when attempting to come to terms with social phenomena, the reader is referred to Knorr-Cetina and Cicourel (1982). In terms of medical talk, this issue has been specifically addressed by Fisher and Todd (1985). A feminist rendition of the same idea; i.e. the necessity of attaching our theoretical and structural accounts of women's oppression to everyday contexts can be found in Stanley and Wise (1983).

Berliner, H. S., & Salmon, V. W. (1980). The holistic alternative to scientific medicine: History and analysis. *International Journal of Health Services, 10* (1), 133–147.

Bleier, R. (1984). *Science and Gender. A Critique of Biology and its Theories on Women.* New York: Pergamon Press.

Cloward, R. A., & Piven, F. F. (1979). Hidden protest: The chanelling of female innovation and resistance. *Signs, 4,* 651–669.

Conrad, P., & Schneider, J. W. (1980). *Deviance and Medicalization. From Badness to Sickness.* St. Louis: The C. V. Mosby Co.

Conrad, P., & Kern, R. (Eds.). (1981). *The Sociology of Health and Illness: Critical Perspectives.* New York: St. Martin's Press.

Cooperstock, R. (1978). Sex differences in psychotropic drug use. *Social Science and Medicine, 12B,* 179–186.

Davis, K. (1986). The process of problem (re)formulation in psychotherapy. *Sociology of Health and Illness, 8*(1).

Donzelot, J. (1979). *The Policing of Families.* New York: Pantheon Books.

Ehrenreich, B., & English, D. (1979). *For Her Own Good.* London: Pluto Press.

Ehrenreich, B., & Ehrenreich, J. (1978). Medicine and social control. In J. Ehrenreich (Ed.), *The Cultural Crisis of Modern Medicine.* New York: Monthly Review Press.

Ehrenreich, J. (Ed.). (1978). *The Cultural Crisis of Modern Medicine.* New York: Monthly Review Press.

Fee, E. (1983). Women and health care: A comparison of theories. In E. Fee (Ed.), *Women and Health: The Politics of Sex in Medicine.* Farmingdale, N.Y.: Baywood Publishing Co.

Fidell, L. S. (1980). Sex role stereotypes and the American physician. *Psychology of Women Quarterly, 4*(3), 313–330.

Fisher, S. (1983). Doctor talk/patient talk: How treatment decisions are negotiated in doctor–patient communication. In S. Fisher & A. D. Todd (Eds.), *The Social Organization of Doctor–Patient Communication.* Washington, D.C.: Center for Applied Linguistics.

Fisher, S., & Todd, A. D. (Eds.). (1985). *The Social Organization of Doctor–Patient Communication.* Washington, D.C.: The Center for Applied Linguistics.

Fisher, S., & Todd, A. D. (1986). Friendly persuasion: The negotiation of decisions to use oral contraceptives. In S. Fisher & A. D. Todd (Eds.), *Discourse and Institutional Authority: Medicine, Education, and Law.* Norwood, N.J.: Ablex Publishing Co.

Gabe, J., & Lipshitz-Phillips, S. (1984). Tranquillizers as social control? *The Sociological Review, 32*(3), 524–546.

Giddens, A. (1976). *New Rules of Sociological Method: A Positive Critique of Interpretative Sociologies.* London: Hutchinson.

Giddens, A. (1979). *Central Problems in Social Theory.* London: The Mac-Millan Press, Ltd.

Glaser, B. G., & Strauss, A. L. (1967). *The Discovery of Grounded Theory: Strategies for Qualitative Research.* New York: Aldine Publishing Co.

Goffman, E. (1971). *Relations in Public*. Middlesex: Penguin.

Gordon, D. P. (1983). Hospital slang for patients: Crocks, gomers, gorks and others. *Language in Society, 12*(2), 173–185.

Hearn, J. (1982). Notes on patriarchy, professionalization and the semi-professions. *Sociology, 16*(2), 184–202.

Henley, N. M. (1977). *Body Politics, Power, Sex, and Non-verbal Communication*. Englewood Cliffs, N.J.: Prentice-Hall.

Hughes, D. (1982). Control in the medical consultation: Organizing talk in a situation where co-participants have differential competence. *Sociology, 16*(3), 359–376.

Illich, I. (1976). *Limits to Medicine*. London: Marion Boyars.

Jefferson, G. (1980). On 'trouble-premonitory' response to inquiry. *Sociological Inquiry, 50*(3/4), 153–185.

Jefferson, G., & Lee, J. R. E. (1981). The rejection of advice: Managing the problematic convergence of a 'troubles-telling' and a 'service encounter'. *Journal of Pragmatics, 5*, 399–422.

Jefferson, G. (1984). On the organization of laughter in talk about troubles. In J. M. Atkinson & J. Heritage (Eds.), *Structures of Social Action. Studies in Conversation Analysis*. Cambridge: Cambridge University Press.

Knorr-Cetina, K., & Cicourel, A. (Eds.). (1982). *Advances in Social Theory and Methodology. Towards an Integration of Micro- and Macro-Sociologies*. Boston: Routledge and Kegan Paul.

Korsmeyer, C. (1978). The hidden joke: Generic uses of masculine terminology. In M. Vetterling-Braggin, F. A. Elliston, & J. English (Eds.), Totowa, N.J.: Littlefield, Adams and Co.

Labov, W., & Fanshel, D. (1977). *Therapeutic Discourse. Psychotherapy as Conversation*. New York: Academic Press.

Laws, S. (1983). The sexual politics of premenstrual tension. *Women's Studies International Forum, 6*(1), 19–31.

Lennane, K. J., & Lennane, J. R. (1973). Alleged psychogenic disorders in women—a possible manifestation of sexual prejudice. *New England Journal of Medicine, 288*(6), 288–292.

Lipset, D. R. (1982). The painful women: Complaints, symptoms, and illness. In M. T. Norman & C. C. Nadelson (Eds.), *The Woman Patient* (Vol. 3). New York: Plenum Press.

Lorbeer, J. (1976). Women and medical sociology: Invisible professional and ubiquitous patients. In M. Millman & R. Moss Kanter (Eds.), *Another Voice. Feminist Perspectives on Social Life and Social Science*. New York: Octagon Books.

Mechanic, D. (1979). *Future Issues in Health Care*. New York: The Free Press.

Oakley, A. (1979). A case of maternity: Paradigms of women as maternity case. *Signs, 4*(4), 607–631.

Polanyi, L. (1979). So what's the point? *Semiotica, 25*(3/4), 207–241.

Roberts, H. (Ed.). (1981). *Women, Health and Reproduction*. London: Routledge and Kegan Paul.

Sacks, H., Schegloff, E., & Jefferson, G. (1974). A simplest systematics for the analysis of turn-taking in conversations. *Language, 50,* 696–735.

Schegloff, E., & Sacks, H. (1974). Opening up closings. In R. Turner (Ed.), *Ethnomethodology.* Middlesex: Penguin Books.

Scherzer, J. (1985). Puns and jokes. In *Handbook of Discourse Analysis.* London: Academic Press.

Schwartz, H. (1979). On recognizing mistakes: A case of practical reasoning in psychotherapy. In H. Schwartz & J. Jacobs (Eds.), *Qualitative Sociology. A Method to the Madness.* New York: The Free Press.

Scully, D., & Bart, P. (1973). A funny thing happened on the way to the orifice: Women in gynaecological textbooks. *American Journal of Sociology, 78,* 1045–1050.

Smart, C., & Smart, B. (Eds.). (1978). *Women, Sexuality, and Social Control.* London: Routledge and Kegan Paul.

Smith, D., & David, S. (Eds.). (1975). *Women Look at Psychiatry.* Vancouver: Press Gang Publishers.

Sorenson, J. H., & Bergman, G. E. (1984). Delineating paternalism in pediatric care. *Theoretical Medicine, 5*(1), 93–104.

Standing, H. (1980). Sickness is a woman's business? Reflections on the attribution of illness. In The Brighton Women and Science Group (Eds.), *Alice Through the Microscope. The Power of Science over Women's Lives.* London: Virago.

Stanley, L., & Wise, S. (1983). *Breaking Out: Feminist Consciousness and Feminist Research.* London: Routledge and Kegan Paul.

Stimson, G. V., & Webb, B. (1975). *Going to See the Doctor: The Consultation Process in General Practice.* London: Routledge and Kegan Paul.

Stolk, J. G. (1975). Clinical implications of congenital uterine malformations. In T. Eskes et al, (Eds.), *Aspects of Obstetrics Today.* Amsterdam: Exerpta Medica.

Thomasma, D. C. (Ed.). (1984). Autonomy and the doctor–patient relationship. *Theoretical Medicine, 5*(1).

Thomassen, J., et al. (1982). Het TRIPT-project: Een data-collectie uit zeventig huisartspraktijken. *Huisarts en Wetenschap, 25.*

West, C. (1984). *Routine Complications: Troubles with Talk Between Doctors and Patients.* Bloomington: Indiana University Press.

CHAPTER 2

Cooperation and Competition Across Girls' Play Activities*

Marjorie Harness Goodwin

Department of Anthropology
University of South Carolina

In an attempt to characterize women as speaking "in a different voice," recent research on female interaction patterns has tended to examine those features of female communication which are clearly different from those of males to the exclusion of those which females and males share in common. For example, cooperative aspects of female language usage have been examined (e.g., Brown, 1980; Maltz & Borker, 1982), while ways in which disagreement may be expressed have been largely ignored. Investigations of girls' play have also neglected to analyze the full range of female interactional competencies. According to Piaget (1965: p. 77), Lever (1976: p. 482), and Gilligan (1982: pp. 9–20) the lack of complex rule structure and forms of direct competitiveness in girls' games [as for example are found in marbles (Piaget, 1965) or team sports (Lever, 1976)] limits their opportunities for practicing negotiational skills. Lever, making use of interview rather than ethnographic data, argues that, while playing games, girls are incapable of handling conflict without disruption of the ongoing activity (1976: p. 482).

Detailed ethnographic study of girls in play situations (Goodwin, 1985; Hughes, in press) presents a different view of girls' competen-

---

* An earlier version of this paper was presented at the American Folklore Society 1986 Annual Meeting and at the Indiana University Sociolinguistics Seminar. I am indebted to Charles Goodwin, Barrie Thorne and Linda Hughes for helpful and insightful comments on an earlier version of this analysis.

55

cies. In my studies of urban black girls I found that, with respect to boys, while some of girls' activities are conducted with what appears to be minimal disagreement or competition (Goodwin, 1980b), others provide for extensive negotiation (Goodwin, 1980a; Goodwin, 1985; Goodwin & Goodwin, 1987). The forms of social organization which girls select to carry out their play vary across different types of play activities. In order to investigate such variation, this paper focuses on a single type of speech sequence, yet the primary one through which children achieve organization in domains of play: sequences of "directives" or speech actions that try to get another to do something (Austin, 1962), and their responses. Directives will be examined within two play contexts—activities in which children are accomplishing a task and pretend play—as well as within cross-sex and caretaking situations. In this way it will be possible to examine how girls' directives and social organization take different forms across various activities.

For comparative purposes I will first summarize findings regarding how boys conduct themselves in a specific task activity, making slingshots and organizing a slingshot fight.[1] The types of hierarchical differences they establish between participants while performing a task permeate all aspects of their peer activities (comparing one another, arguing, storytelling, etc.). Next I will analyze how girls interact as they undertake a comparable task activity—making rings from the rims of glass bottles. In contrast to the boys, when girls organize tasks they select a more egalitarian form of social structure, avoiding the creation of distinctions between participants. Such a form of organization is consistent with the way in which they normally conduct their daily interactions with one another. When the full repertoire of female interaction patterns is investigated it can be seen that girls exhibit ways of formulating and sequencing their talk which display both cooperative and competitive forms. For example, in the activities of repairing utterances or disagreeing with one another girls use argumentative speech forms shared by the boys (Goodwin, 1983; M. H. Goodwin & C. Goodwin, 1987). Girls do not, however, customarily use bald commands, insults and threats—actions which are commonplace among the boys. Such actions are reserved for situations in which girls sanction the behavior of one of their members. Nonetheless the forms of accounts girls use in directive sequences express concerns that are distinctive from those used by the boys. Across different domains, girls exhibit a range of ways of

---

[1] For more detailed analysis of how the boys organized their slingshot fight see Goodwin (1980b) and Goodwin and Goodwin (in press).

executing decisions about courses of action and evolve distinctive forms of social organization.

FIELDWORK AND BACKGROUND FOR THE STUDY

The present study is based on fieldwork among a group of children in a black working class neighborhood of West Philadelphia whom I encountered during a walk around my neighborhood. I observed them for a year and a half as they played on the street, focussing on how the children used language within interaction to organize their everyday activities. The children (whom I will call the Maple Street group) ranged in age from four through 14 and spent much of the time in four same age/sex groups (older and younger girls and older and younger boys). Here I will be concerned principally with children in the older age group, from 10–13. As they played on the street after school, on weekends and during the summer months I audiotaped their conversation. In gathering data I did not focus on particular types of events that I had previously decided were theoretically important (for example stories or rhymes) but instead tried to observe and record as much of what the children did as possible, no matter how mundane it might seem. Moreover I tried to avoid influencing what the children were doing. The methods I used to gather data about the children were thus quite different from those characteristically used in psychological and sociological studies of children's behavior; in such studies efforts are typically made to systematically collect particular types of information deemed to be theoretically important in a carefully controlled fashion. Rather than being based on a laboratory model, the methodology I used was ethnographic, and designed to capture as accurately as possible the structure of events in the children's world as they unfolded in the ordinary settings where they habitually occurred. Therefore I did not have to rely on what subjects or interviewees might tell a researcher and could observe the conduct of children in a range of situations.

ALTERNATIVE FORMS OF DIRECTIVES

The ways in which speakers format their directives and sequence turns to them provide for a range of possible types of social arrangements between participants. Some directive/response sequences display an orientation towards a differentiation between participants, and result in asymmetrical forms of relationships. Others, by way of contrast, display an orientation towards seeking to minimize distinctions between participants and result in more egalitarian or symmetrical arrangements of social relationships. Within different clusters there may also be a division of labor with respect to the delivery of certain types of moves. This has consequences for the type of social organization a group evolves.

Directives have been discussed as forms of "social control acts" ["moves in which there is a clear intention to influence the activities of the partner" (Ervin-Tripp, 1982: p. 29)] and "persuasive talk" (Cook-Gumperz, 1981). One way in which directives may be formatted is in a very straightforward or "aggravated" (Labov & Fanshel, 1977: pp. 84–86) way, as imperatives (i.e., "Do X!"). Alternatively, directives may take more softened or "mitigated" (Labov & Fanshel 1977: pp. 84–86) forms, as requests ("Could you please do X?"). Aggravated forms of directives have been analyzed by a number of researchers of children's interaction as displaying control vis-à-vis the recipient (Mitchell-Kernan & Kernan, 1977; Cook-Gumperz & Corsaro, 1979; Andersen, 1978; Becker, 1982, 1984; Cazden, Cox, Dickerson, Steinberg, & Stone, 1979; Wood & Gardner, 1980; Cook-Gumperz & Corsaro, 1979; Garvey, 1975; Ervin-Tripp, 1982). Indeed Mitchell-Kernan and Kernan (1977), Ervin-Tripp (1982), and Becker (1982, 1984) argue that children use imperatives not to effect actual behavior change but rather to test and make assertions about relative positions among participants. Imperatives thus constitute the currency with which speakers may attempt to define a position of relative superiority over recipients. In addition to the selection of the verb in the directive, Ervin-Tripp (1982: pp. 29–30) notes that the *head act* (the principal verb) may be accompanied by "supporting explanations, attention getters, vocatives, and polite markers." She further states that social information about role, rank, distance, etc. can be manifested "through nuancing by markers, such as saying *please,* using slang, address forms, minimizers, conditionals, or past tense" (Ervin-Tripp 1982:33).

THE ORGANIZATION OF A TASK AMONG BOYS

Making slingshots from wire coat hangers is a pastime which could be organized in a variety of different ways. The slingshot is an individual instrument, and, in theory, play with it could be construed as an individual activity in which all participants fend for themselves, the only preparation being that each have a slingshot and an adequate supply of "slings." Among the boys of Maple Street, however, the activity of making and using slingshots became organized into a competition between two separate "sides" or teams (not unlike those in football or basketball) with a hierarchical organization of participants on each team.[2] The slingshot fight itself was preceded by an extended preparation period during which, not only were weapons and slings made, but the organization of the group was also negotiated. All of the elements in this process, such as the allocation of necessary tools, the spatial organization of participants, where the preparation would occur, who would provide materials, who had rights to resources, when the activity was to move from stage to stage, what battle strategy would consist of, etc., became the focus for status negotiations between participants.

The Formatting of Leaders' Directives and Accounts in a Boys' Task Activity

One key resource that was used in negotiation among the boys about their relative status was alternative formats for asking or ordering someone else to do something. A typical way that one party attempted to display or establish his position with respect to another party was by making directives in the form of explicit commands to that party rather than as hints, suggestions, or indirect requests. In organizing the sling shot session the team leaders, Michael and Huey, constructed their directives using the imperative form ("Do X!"). In the terminology developed by Labov and Fanshel (1977: pp. 84–86) they thus choose relatively "aggravated" or explicit directive forms. The following data are transcribed according to the system developed by Jefferson and described in Sacks, Schegloff, and Jefferson (1974: pp. 731–733). A simplified version of this transcription system appears in the Appendix. The citation after each example gives the date of the conversation and the transcript page from which the example is taken.

(1)   10/19/70/20

Michael: *All* right. Gimme some rubber bands.
Chopper: ((*Giving rubber bands to Michael*)) Oh.

---

[2] The organization of boys' activities into "teams" has been extensively commented upon by a number of researchers, most notably Lever (1974, 1976). Among the Maple Street boys, even the making of go carts evolved into play divided into two highly competitive "pit crews," each with its own professional secrets regarding the manufacture of the carts.

(2)   10/19/70/107

> Huey: Go downstairs. I don't care *what* you say you aren't—
>   you ain't no good so go down*stairs.*
> Bruce: ((*Moves down the steps*))

(3)   10/19/70/136

> ((*Regarding coat hanger wire*))
> Michael: Give it to me man. Where's yours at. Throw that piece of
>   shit out.
> Chopper: ((*Gives Michael his cut-off piece of hanger*))

The turn containing the imperative arguing for the speaker's relative control vis-à-vis the recipient may be accompanied by various types of "semantic aggravators" (Becker, 1982: p. 8) i.e., threats, phrases demanding immediate action, etc., which display the speaker's view of the recipient's subordinate status. As is shown in examples 2 and 3, negative descriptions of the other (e.g., "you ain't no good") or of his objects (e.g., referring to one of Chopper's slings as "shit") may accompany the imperative to further denigrate the recipient's character. In response to these sequences, recipients comply with the requests. Of course other types of next responses, such as counters, are possible next moves, as in lines 2, 4, and 7 of the following:

(4)   10/19/70/16

		((*Michael asks for pliers*))
1	Michael:	Gimme the thing.
2	Poochie: →	Wait a minute. I gotta chop it.
3	Michael:	Come on.
4	Poochie: →	I gotta chop it.
5	Michael:	Come on Poochie. You gonna be with
6		them? Give it to me. I'll show you.
7	Poochie: →	I already had it before you.
8	Michael:	So? I brought them out here. They
9		mine. So I use em when I feel like it.

In this sequence Michael responds to counters with actions which argue for his ultimate control of the situation. For example in line 5 through his question "You gonna be with them?" Michael counters Poochie by threatening to make Poochie be on another team. In lines 8–9 Michael refutes the relevance of Poochie's counter by arguing that he has ultimate jurisdiction concerning the allocation of resources. In other instances when players counter Michael or Huey's imperatives, the leaders display their authority by reminding subordinates that they can also make them leave their property (i.e., "Get off my steps." or "I'll tell you to get out of *here* if I *want* you to.")

The imperative forms of the leaders' actions differ from the ways in which other players formulate actions to Michael and Huey. Requests for information such as "Can I have some hangers?" or "Can me and Robert play if Robert be on Huey's team?" are used in actions to team leaders. In contrast to the actions which Michael and Huey use towards their teammates requests for information display deference towards the addressee and permit options in the way in which recipient should respond. When answering such mitigated types of directives, those assuming leadership positions do not comply with the proposed actions, as in examples 1–3, but instead provide arbitrary definitions of the situation (example 5), return imperatives (example 6), and flat refusals (example 7):

(5)   10/19/70/71

   Bruce: Can me and Robert play if Robert be on Huey's team?
   Michael: IT'S ALREADY TOO MANY OF US.

(6)   10/19/70/57

   ((*Tokay takes a hanger*))
   Tokay: Can I have some hangers?
   Michael: Put that thing back!

(7)   10/19/70/152

   Robby: Michael could I be on your side?
   Michael: *Heck* no!

A form of asymmetry is established through the alternative ways in which directives and their responses are formated. While Michael delivers aggravated actions getting compliance in return, his teammates issue mitigated directives receiving counters as next moves.

Michael's actions are not only direct and aggravated but also arbitrary. To see the import of this it is important to note that not all direct imperatives constitute degrading actions to a recipient. Thus in many cases the situation of the moment itself warrants the use of directive formats that in other circumstances would be seen as aggravated. For example in the midst of a game of jump rope girls yell "Watch out!" as a car comes, or "Go ahead Nettie!" to urge a player to take her turn. Similarly, imperatives may be appropriate in work settings where differences in rank call for the subordination of one party to the other (Ervin-Tripp, 1976: p. 29). However, the directives Michael issues display no obvious reason why certain tasks need to be performed "right now" except for his own whims. The use of "need statements" (Ervin-Tripp, 1976: p. 29), "desire statements" (Ervin-Tripp, 1982: P. 30) or "explicit statements" Ervin-Tripp,

1982: p. 35) has been argued (Garvey, 1975: pp. 52, 60; Ervin-Tripp, 1976: p. 29) to constitute among the most aggravated ways of formulating a directive. For example:

(8)   10/19/70/38

Michael: PL:IERS. I WANT THE PLIERS! Man y'all gonna have to get y'all *own* wire cutters if *this* the way y'all gonna be.
Nate: Okay. Okay.

(9)   10/19/70/54

→   Michael: Everybody. Now I don't need all y'all down here in this little space. Get back *up* there. Get *up* there. Now! Get back up there please.

In brief, through the way in which Michael constructs his directives he proposes his superior status with respect to others, and others' inferior positioning vis-à-vis him. He uses actions which imply that he independently can define for others how the task should proceed and how their actions can be interpreted. In response others assuming an inferior position with respect to him often provide compliance through either a nonvocal carrying out of the requested action (as occurred in examples 1–3) and/or signals of vocal agreement (as in examples 1 and 8.)

Instructing Others

There is one aspect of Michael's performance as team leader—instructing his subordinates—in which the use of aggravated social control acts appears less arbitrary. The job of teaching teammates how to make slings makes use of a participation framework common to other teaching situations. Instructing implies an asymmetrical relationship of participants, with the teacher providing actions such as getting the attention of the subordinates, giving them information, and criticizing them (Cazden, et al., 1979: p. 210). Assertions, such as "See this how we gonna do ours." in example 10 below may stand for speech acts with directive force. Frequently, as in the next two examples, an account for why the stated course of action should be pursued is provided: either that leader's way is a superior way of executing the task, as in example 10, or simply that the leader has a particular plan for how the activity should take place (example 12):

(10)   10/19/70/58

Michael: See this how we gonna do ours. It's a lot better and faster. Bend that side and then we bend this side too.

(11)   10/19/70/106

    Michael: Look I wanna show you how to do it so when you get the things you gonna know how to do it.

(12)   10/19/70/99

    Michael: I know what we gonna do. Poochie, a- after I cut these up all y'all- all y'all gonna cut these things off and Poochie gonna bend them and I cut em. And I just chop em. And then y'all pick em up. And they be ours.

Michael, as leader of his group, not only prescribes the working procedures and division of labor for sling making; in addition he dictates team strategy:

(13)   10/19/70/156

1	Michael:	Now. Re*mem*ber what I sai:d. And
2		don't try to shoot till
3	Tokay:	Like- like they in sight?
4	Michael:	That's *r*ight.
5	Tokay:	What if they ain't.
6	Michael:	But if they- if they hidin in some
7		bushes, don't you shoot.=You let them
8		waste theirs. Count for the man how
9		many he waste. Then after he waste as
10		many as you got you let him shoot his.
11		But then you let him waste some more.

As is clearly illustrated by this example, Michael's role as leader of the peer group is ratified through the types of actions, such as Tokay's requests for information (lines 3 and 5), which are initiated towards him. Because Michael is felt to be in control of knowledge regarding the craft, his opinion and assistance is summoned repetitively:

(14)   10/19/70/107

               ((*Michael illustrates bending and cutting coat hangers*))
    Michael: You bend it over like that and when- when you finish I'll show you how to just do these.
→   Tokay: After it break, stomp down?
    Michael: Just clap em.

(15)   10/19/70/99

    Michael: After I cut these up
→   Poochie: Who turn is it.

> Chopper: Mine. Mine. *Uh* uh. Ain't it my turn Michael,
> Michael: ((*nods yes*))
> Chopper: See?

In the next example not only is Michael's expertise requested by Chopper (lines 1, 5–6, 11, 13); but also Poochie (line 9) explicitly states that the boys treat Michael as the person in command:

(16)   10/19/70/21

1	Chopper: →	I want- Member it was a lot more- Kay I
2		want some more like you- like the one
3		you had for me before.
4	Michael:	It's small. / / It's all right.
5	Chopper:	But you had fixed it before. It was
6		good and small.
7	Michael:	I will. I will. And boy you keep
8		lettin me / / see your head.
9	Poochie: →	They- they don't know how to / / do it.
10		That's why they ask Michael so much.
11	Chopper:	My boy Michael'll do it.
12	Michael:	Yeah yeah yeah yeah.
13	Chopper:	Michael can you-
14	Michael:	Man I'm doin it already.

Vaughn and Waters (1980: p. 361) [discussing research by Chance and Jolly (1970)] have argued that "the *structure of attention* within a group, rather than aggressive or agonistic interactions, priority access to food, objects, mates, and so forth" should be "used to draw the outlines of social organization." Although *visual* attention was the form of attention investigated in the ethological studies reviewed in Vaughn and Waters (1980: pp. 361–362), as can be seen in these data, his peers give to Michael their primary attention in the form of requests towards Michael regarding various aspects of the play activity in progress.

Although Michael is frequently in control of instructing, other participants may attempt to occupy a similar position; for example in the following, Poochie attempts to teach Nate the proper way of holding a slingshot:

(17)   10/19/70/158

> Poochie: How you shoot them. You supposed to hold the whole
> thing.
> Nate: I am!
> Poochie: Talkin about holdin the whole- You holdin one *part* of it.
> Nate: I am not.

Poochie: I don't know what then.
Nate: Dag. Stop boy. Should be mindin your business.
           ((*Talk switches to debate between Raymond and
           Chopper*))

Note that in response to Poochie's instructions Nate counters and
eventually provides the last argumentative utterance of the instruction exchange. By way of contrast, argumentative sequences which
develop in response to Michael's instructions frequently end with
Michael having the last word. For example in the following, throughout several turns Chopper objects to Michael's giving him instructions (lines 7, 10) until Poochie (line 15) aligns himself with Michael's
position. In line 16 Chopper accepts Michael's delineation of the task
activity.

(18)   10/19/70/99

```
1    Michael:    I know what we gonna do. Poochie, a-
2                after I cut these up all y'all- all y'all
3                gonna cut these things off and Poochie
4                gonna bend them and I cut em. And I
5                just chop em. And then y'all pick em
6                up. And they be ours.
7    Chopper:    Heck no.
8    Michael:    What you talkin
9                about.
10   Chopper:    And then we try to grab for
11               them?
12   Michael:    No. Poochie bend your
13               hanger. And then I smash
14                  ⸢smash and then chop it.
15   Poochie:   ⸤You go get em.
16   Chopper:    Oh all right.
```

In attempting to enforce his definition of the situation following
objections Michael can provide an account which alludes to his ultimate control of the play situation. For example in the following he
argues that the spatial arrangement for manufacturing slings is overly crowded:

(19)   10/19/70/14

```
1    Michael:    Wait wait wait. Now what do you wanna
2                make first. You wanna sling
3                shot.=Right?
4    Raymond:    Yeah.
5    Michael:    What do you want.
```

	6	Raymond:	I know how to make one.
	7	Poochie:	I know how to make both of em.
	8	Michael:	Man I told you it's gettin a little crowded up here.

As proprietors of the house where play occurs both Michael and Huey can exert considerable leverage in getting boys to do what they want them to do, in that they can threaten them with having to leave the premises:

(20)   10/19/70/35

((*Michael asks for rubber bands, from Huey who is making a slingshot board with rubber bands and pliers*))

	1	Huey:	I'm not finish. I got two more hangers
	2		to go.
	3	Chopper:	Dag he always usin them. See I swear.
	4		I was usin em before Huey and he gonna
	5		come up and take em.
	6	Huey:	Oh you shut up. / / You didn't do
	7		nothin with yours.
	8	Chopper:	Why don't you make me faggot.
→	9	Huey:	Get off my *steps*.
	10	Chopper:	No. You get on my steps. I get on
	11		yours.
	12	Huey:	I haven't been on your steps.

(21)   10/19/70/122

((*Michael moves into Poochie's space*))

	Poochie:	Get outa here.
→	Michael:	Hell it's my house.
	Poochie:	You always gettin in the way. You talkin about we can't even come up there.
	Huey:	That's *right*. It's mine *too*.
	Poochie:	So.
→	Michael:	I'll tell you to get out of *here* if I *want* you do.
	Huey:	Yep.

Thus, despite the fact that participants other than those acting as team leaders may initiate instruction sequences or counter the instructions from them, there is an asymmetry with respect to whose instructions are treated as binding. Considerable power resides in the party who sponsors a task activity at his home, and this may account for the differential success with which his proposals are eventually heeded.

Summary of Observations on How Boys Construct Task Activities

Within the boys' group a pattern of asymmetry in the formatting and usage of directives and their responses develops in the interaction between players, creating the positions of leaders and followers. Michael and Huey, who assume the position of leaders for this activity, issue bald imperatives to others and characteristically get compliance. These commands concern every aspect of the slingshot making, including access to resources, site for play, procedure for manufacturing "slings", future battle strategy, etc. Many of their imperatives contain insult terms or implicit comparisons which place the recipient in a degraded position with respect to the speaker; accounts that accompany Michael and Huey's directives propose that the activity should be performed because of their personal definition of the situation or needs of the moment, rather than any requirements of the current activity. Michael assumes the position of instructor vis-à-vis the others, and the other boys ratify this claim. A division of labor develops with respect to the distribution of various types of actions. Boys other than Michael and Huey do not initiate new phases of the activity through giving bald imperatives; instead they use more mitigated forms, requests for information. Michael's position in the group is displayed and validated in a number of different ways: through issuing direct commands while receiving indirect requests and through contradicting proposals and requests of others, while expecting and getting compliance to his own.

THE ORGANIZATION OF GIRLS' TASK ACTIVITY

In this section I will analyze how girls go about organizing a task activity which is comparable to that of the boys, making rings from glass bottle rims. In making the rings, girls carefully scrape bottle rims over metal manhole covers or other rough surfaces so that the rims break evenly, leaving as few jagged edges as possible. The jobs faced by girls in making their objects do not substantially differ from those faced by boys; they involve procuring and allocating resources and establishing techniques for the objects' manufacture. Thus, in making rings the girls must decide where they will get the bottles necessary to make the rings, how many bottles are needed, who should break the bottles, how precisely the rims of bottles should be broken over metal manhole covers, how used bottles should be disposed of, and how the rings should be decorated.

The Formatting of Directives and Accounts in Girls' Task Activity

With the exception of the domain of pretend plan, hierarchical forms of organization are uncommon in girls' play. In accomplishing a task activity girls participate jointly in decision-making with minimal negotiation of status. This process is both reflected in and achieved through the selection of syntactic formats for the production of directives as well as forms of accounts which are quite different from those selected by the boys. The following provide examples of the types of directives typically found among the girls:

(22)   9/28/70/72

((*Girls are searching for bottles from which to make rings.*))

Terri: Well let's go- let's go around the corner- Let's let's go around the corner where whatchacallem.

(23)   9/28/70/79

((*Girls are looking for bottles.*))

Terri: Let's go. There may be some more on Sixty Ninth Street.
Sharon: Come on. Let's turn back y'all so we can safe keep em. Come on. Let's go get some.

(24)   9/28/70/79

((*Girls are looking for bottles.*))

Sharon: Let's go around Subs and Suds.
Pam: Let's ask her "Do you have any bottles."

Whereas boys' directives typically constitute commands that an action should be undertaken at the time the imperative is issued, girls' directives are constructed as suggestions for action in the future. Syntactically the forms utilized by the boys generally differentiate speaker and hearer. One party is either ordering another to do something, or alternatively, requesting action from some other party. By way of contrast the verb used by the girls, *'let's'* (generally used only by the boys when shifting a major phase of the activity underway)[3] includes both speaker and hearer as potential agents of the

---

[3] Among the boys, 'let's' is used when a boy proposes to move to a new stage of an activity in utterances such as "Let's play some football Poochie. Two against two." or "Michael! Let's get a game." 'Lets' was used two times during the boys' slingshot making session reported on here. Michael requested (a) that boys move around to the back of the house to make slings ("Let's go around back and make some slings") and (b) that boys move from a stairwell to a cement backyard area ("All right. It's too crowded in here. Let's go somewhere.")

action to be performed,[4] thus mitigating the appearance of control. *Let's* signals a proposal rather than either a command or a request and as such shows neither special deference towards the other party (as a request does) nor claims about special rights of control over the other, (as a command does). Thus, through the way in which they format their directives, the girls make visible an undifferentiated, 'egalitarian' relationship between speaker and addressee(s), that differs quite markedly from the asymmetrical, hierarchical relationship displayed in boys' directives.

The structure of directives used to organize making rings is not different from the types of actions which are used to direct other girls' activities which involve a joint task, as can be seen in the examples below in which participants undertake playing jacks (example 25), jumping rope to a particular rhyme called "one two three footsies" (example 26) and hunting for turtles (example 27).

(25)   10/19/70/14
       Darlene: Let's play some more jacks.

(26)   10/20/70/61
       Pam: Let's play "one two three footsies." First!

(27)   8/2/71/12
       ((*searching for turtles*))
       Pam: Let's look around. See what we can find.

In alternation to the use of *'let's'* the auxiliary verbs *'gonna'* with a plural subject and the modal verbs *'can'* or *'could'* can also be used to format an action as a mitigated directive form (Blum-Kulka & Olshtain 1984: p. 203), proposing a suggestion or a joint plan as in the following which occur in the midst of making glass rings:

(28)   9/28/70/78
       Sharon: We gonna paint em and stuff.

(29)   9/28/70/84
       Pam: We could go around lookin for more bottles.

(30)   9/28/70/80
       ((*Discussing keeping the ring making secret from boys.*))
       Terri: We can *l*imp back so nobody know where we *g*ettin them from.

---

[4] According to Blum-Kulka and Olshtain (1984: p. 203), such a "point of view" provides a more mitigated form of directive.

In some cases the overt tentativeness of the modal is further intensified through the use of terms such as *maybe:*

(31) 9/28/70/77

Terri: Maybe we can slice *them* like that.

Directives which include verbs such as *gotta* (which place more demands on recipient than modal verbs) may also contain an account providing explicit reasons for why an action should be undertaken. Characteristically, such accounts consider the benefits which would accrue to all members of the group:

(32) 9/28/70/73

Sharon: Pam you know what we could do, (0.5) We gotta *clean* em first, We gotta *clean* em.
Pam: Huh,
Sharon: We gotta *clean* em first, / / You know,
Pam: I know.
→   ₍₍Cuz they got germs.
Sharon: [[Wash em and stuff cuz just in case they
→   got germs on em.
          ₍₍And then you clean em,
Pam: [[I got some paints.
          (3.5)
Sharon: Clean em, and then we *clean* em and we gotta be careful with em before we get the glass cutters. You know we gotta
→   be careful with em cuz it cuts easy.

In circumstances of urgency, e.g., when the safety of a group member is at stake[5], imperatives constitute the appropriate and even expected form (Brown & Levinson, 1978: pp. 100–101). Characteristically, when imperatives are used by girls they are accompanied by accounts which take into consideration the situation of the addressee, such as her safety:

(33) 9/28/70/41

          ((*Regarding Pam's finger cut while making glass rings*))
          Sharon: Pam don't you lick your own blood.

---

[5] Grant (1984: p. 108) in her study of peer interaction in a desegregated school found that "black girls were above the mean in care-giving in four classrooms."

→   That way it gonna go right back there
through your body.

(34)   9/28/70/46

((*Terri and Sharon attempt to put mercurochrome on
Pam's cut finger.*))
Terri: Take it out now Pam.
Pam: No I'm not.
Terri: Get- it ain't gonna hurt you girl. You
→   got- and you want to get your hand
infected and they take- they take the hand taken off?

Thus despite the relative infrequency of imperatives used in organizing girls' task activities, there are nevertheless circumstances which
occur when imperatives constitute the most appropriate form of directive. The type of account which girls offer to support their imperatives during task activities contrast markedly with the accounts
accompanying boys' commands. Rather than arguing that an action
should be performed because of one party's personal desires, girls'
imperatives deal with the requirements of the current activity.

Instructing Others

When girls use imperatives during instruction they may qualify their
talk in ways which are sensitive to both the form of their social
organization and other aspects of context. In the next example girls
actively negotiate who has the right to address others with imperatives while demonstrating how to break the glass rim of the bottles;
it is not assumed that any one party has exclusive rights to instruct
another. When Pam takes over the job of teaching in lines 11–18 she
uses a range of paralinguistic cues to frame her talk (Goffman, 1974),
or contextualize it in a particular way (Gumperz, 1982). Thus she
speaks with singsong intonation, caricaturing a teacher (lines 14–18)
and colors her talk with laughter.

(35)   9/28/70/10

1 Pam: Get that one. Here! Yeah give it to
2   her.
3   (2.0)
4 Sharon: This won't know the difference.
5 Pam: Get outa the street.
6   (0.8)
7   See you gotta do it real hard.
8 Sharon: Gimme this. I wanna do it. You're

```
 9                cracked. I wanna show you how to do
10                it. I know how to do it Pam!
11   Pam:         I know. I ju- So you won't have to
12                break it. Like y'know. Do it like ((as she demon-
                  strates scraping it against a metal manhole cover the
                  correct angle for getting a smooth bottle rim))
13   Sharon:      Yeah.
14   Pam:      ⌐((singsong instructing voice)) But when
15             │ you get at the end you do it hard so.
16             │ the thing would break off right, eh heh
17             │ heh! ((laughing at style of teaching))
18             └ Harder!
19   Sharon:      Do it harder.
20   Pam:         Eh heh heh! // Oh:.
```

The negotiation which takes place here has features of what developmental psychologists Stone and Selman (1982: pp. 169–179) describe as a considerably advanced form of "social negotiation strategy." They note that in the "collaboration" stage of negotiation children make use of various paralinguistic expressions to "communicate multiple, often ironic, meanings" (Stone & Selman, 1982: p. 175), employing "a contrast between the form they use and the form generally used in peer interaction." Here, while instructing others, Pam gives them orders in lines 1–2, 5, and 7; Sharon in lines 8–10 counters that she wants to do it herself and does not need any instruction from Pam. Such active objection to letting another issue orders is congruent with the ways that the girls in other contexts actively monitor each other for actions that could be seen as claiming that one girl is setting herself above the others. When Pam takes up the instructor role again in lines 14–18 she modifies the intonation of her voice; by adopting a singsong lilt she mocks the way she is delivering her instructions to the group. Through this caricaturing of the talk of an instructor Pam distances (Goffman, 1961: pp. 120–132) herself from the teaching role she is currently enacting, thereby making herself a more equal partner in the play.

This sequence of instructing thus differs from comparable ones among the boys (examples 10–13). Michael took his instructor role quite seriously, with little deviation from a strict interpretation of his notion of himself as someone superior to the others present. Interaction from other parties supported the image of Michael as more knowledgeable than others (see examples 13 and 16) and portrayed their current social relationships as asymmetrical. By way of contrast, Sharon's objections to Pam's teaching challenge the position of superordination Pam has adopted. Pam begins modifying her role as instructor when Sharon objects, and eventually even laughs at her own speaking style. The negotiation in this sequence thus resembles the symmetrical features of roles observable in other phases of task activities, with girls extending to one another equivalent types of actions and avoiding the appearance of hierarchy.

Achieving Symmetry in Interaction within Girls' Directive Sequences

It was noted earlier that asymmetry among the boys was displayed not only in the formatting of particular directives, but also in the differential usage of both directives and responses to them. In the boys' group generally only the party acting as leader issued the directives prescribing actions for others, and he responded to others' directives with refutations. In the girls' group, however, proposals for certain courses of action can be made by many different participants, and the girls generally agree to the suggestions of others. For example:

(36)   9/28/70/73

　　　　Sharon: You can get people to cut this though,
　　　　Pam: Yep.

(37)   9/28/70/80

　　　　Terri: Hey y'all. Let's use these first and then come back and get the rest cuz it's too *m*any of em.
　　　　Sharon: That *right.*
　　　　Terri: We can *l*imp back so nobody knows where we *g*ettin them from.
　　　　　　　　　　(0.8)
　　　　Sharon: That's right.
　　　　Terri: And w- and wash our hands. And wash your hands when you get *f*inish now.
　　　　Sharon: If the boys try to follow us we don't know. Okay?
　　　　Terri: Yep.

Thus in terms of both how directives are constructed, and the way in which others respond to them, the girls' system of directive use displays similarity and equality rather than differentiation among group members.

Other task activities that the girls engaged in, such as searching for turtles, are organized in comparable ways. It has been seen that when initiating a new activity, rather than signaling new phases of the activity with a command, girls issue proposals about future courses of action. An even less coercive way of moving into a new phase can be accomplished through simply making a statement about one's own future plans, and waiting to see what others' reactions to one's assertion consist of. For example in the next fragment, in which the girls plan a turtle hunting expedition, Nettie (in line 1) states what she is going to do. Others subsequently offer their reactions to the idea. Pam (line 3) is in agreement while Delin (line 9) (who is too young to go off the street anyway) and Sister (line 12) reject the invitation.

(38) 8/2/71/14

```
 1  Nettie:  I'm gonna catch me a turtle at Cobbs
 2           Creek.
 3  Pam:     Me too. I'm gonna catch / / me a
 4           turtle.
 5  Nettie:  You goin over there with me?
 6  Pam:     Yeah. Wanna go now?
 7  Net:     Yeah.
 8           (1.8)
 9  Delin:   I don't wanna.
10  Pam:     Wanna go?
11           (1.0)
12  Sister:  I done caught one.
13           (2.0)
14  Nettie:  Well we done it- we didn't caught one
15           yet. You goin?
16  Pam:     Wanna go with us?
17  Candy:   Mm yeah!
18  Pam:     I'm gonna catch me a turtle. Well
19           were we gonna put him at. Could-
20           could- could- could- could we find a
21           thing?
22           (1.6)
23  Nettie:  I get me a little plastic bag from somewhere.
```

In this sequence we find that both Nettie and Pam have equivalent say in setting up the expedition. Though Nettie first suggested the activity, Pam rather than Nettie explicitly asks first Sister (line 10) and then the ethnographer (line 16) whether or not they wish to go. In line 6 when Pam proposes the time for undertaking the activity, it is agreed to by Nettie. Potential participants in the activity are free to choose whether or not they want to participate. In responding to actions as well as in initiating courses of action, girls avoid establishing a differentiation of power between one another. When Pam (lines 19–21) brings up a potential problem, how the girls are going to carry their turtles home, Nettie mentions what *for her* constitutes a possible solution, without obliging Pam to do the same.

Throughout the turtle hunting expedition plans are discussed in terms of what individual girls wish to do, without any forcible defining for others what their course of action need entail. The activity is interpreted as one in which parallel courses of action may take place rather than as one requiring a central authority to coordinate disparate aspects of it. Girls do not dictate courses of action for others and accept a range of possible ways of executing the activity. For example in the following Pam disagrees with Nettie about the type of rocks she wants for her turtle. However Pam produces her disagreement in a mitigated way, by contrasting the type of rocks she would like to have with the type proposed by Nettie:

(39) 8/2/71/9

> Nettie: I want me the kind of rocks like in the front of my garden?
> Pam: I'm a get *me* some *li*ttle rocks hon, little rocks.

In the organization of this activity, all are invited to participate, and there is little differentiation into specialized roles. Girls can, however, distinguish themselves through variations in statements concerning how they choose to carry out similar activities, as is evident in example 39 above. Yet participants do not enforce their versions of what the activity should be, but instead provide *descriptions* of their own courses of action to be reacted to by others. Such a situation is consistent with the less coercive nature of the girls' directives as well as the relative infrequency with which the girls use the imperative form during constructive play.

Although girls do not characteristically respond to directives in ways which show one party superior to another, they do counter one another's proposals for action. Argumentation is as common an activity in the girls' group as it is among boys or in mixed-sex groups (Goodwin & Goodwin, 1987). The following is an example of a directive/counter sequence in the midst of a task activity:

(40) 8/2/71/8

		((*On reaching a city creek while turtle hunting*))
1	Pam:	Y'all gonna walk in it?
2	Nettie:	*Walk* in it, You know where that
3		water come from? The toilet.
4	Pam:	So, I'm a walk in it in my dirty feet.
5		I'm a walk in it and I don't care if it
6		do come.=You would / / easy wash your
7		feet.
8	Nettie:	((*to ethnographer*)) Gonna walk us
9		across? Yeah I'll show y'all where you
10		can come.

In this example negotiations occur with regard to directives. The directive initially posed by Pam in line 1 ("Y'all gonna walk in it?") is countered by Nettie (line 2). Pam then opposes Nettie's counter to her (line 4). Subsequently, in the midst of Pam's turn (line 6) Nettie interrupts to reinstate Pam's initial request and issue a second directive regarding where to step in the creek. Upon completion of this fragment, each of the major parties to the conversation has both given a directive and countered the other's action. The form of the argumentation, however, has not attempted to affirm the relative superiority of one party with respect to the other. The directives in lines 1 and 8 are requests for information and in line 6 the directive is framed as a proposal using a modal verb. Moreover the counters do not flatly refuse prior actions; instead they provide first (lines 2–3) an argument against the appropriateness of the suggested action and second (line 4) an argument against the consequentiality of the suggested action. The directive/counter sequences promote a symmetrical rather than an asymmetrical social situation in that counters to proposals are themselves considered counterable, and a proposal initiated by one party may be reinstated subsequently by another.

Summary of Findings about Differences in the Organization of Task Activities among Girls and Boys

Though boys and girls make use of a common system of directives for the coordination of behavior in task activities, they construct these actions in quite different ways. By selecting alternative directive forms and responses and by creating differing divisions of labor with respect to who can issue particular forms, they build different forms of social organization. Boys' directives are formatted as imperatives from superordinate to subordinate, or requests, generally upward in rank. The usage of alternative asymmetrical forms for the directive, such as the request and the command, is differentially distributed among members of the boys' group; however, among the girls all have access to similar types of actions. Girls characteristically phrase their directives as proposals for future activity and frequently mitigate even these proposals with a term such as *maybe*. They tend to leave the time at which the action being proposed should be performed somewhat open, while a boy in a position of leadership states that he wants an action completed *right now*. Syntactically the directives of the boys differentiate speaker from hearer. Among the girls, however, the party issuing the directive is usually included as one of the agents in the action to be performed. From the point of view of cognitive psychologists who study "social perspective taking" ["an individual's capacity to coordinate psychological perspectives of self and other" (Stone & Selman, 1982: p. 164)] and "social negotiation strategies" (Stone & Selman, 1982) it can be argued that girls' directives *display* taking into consideration the other's point of view to a far greater extent than boys' directives do.[6] Thus the details of how participants select to build a turn either requesting another to do something or responding to talk make relevant two contrasting modes of interaction; hierarchical or more egalitarian social organization may be proposed through the syntactic structures which are chosen. Though within task activities a symmetrical form of social organization is established by the girls in their same-sex group in other circumstances, girls can select more aggravated forms and construct quite different forms of social organization.

DIRECTIVE USE IN PLAYING HOUSE

Girls on Maple street distinguish between various types of directives and degrees of mitigation, as is apparent from the ways in which they talk about alternative polite and impolite forms:

(41)   4-7-71-24

        ((*Concerning a 4-year old girl, Delin*))
    Nettie: Delin wanted to come in the house. I said "You say 'ex*cuse* me.'=*N*ot '*mo*:ve.'"

(42)   10/20/70/48?

        ((*Pam describing how she confronted another girl*))
    Pam: I s'd *I* said "You c'd *roll* your eyes all you *want* to. Cuz I'm *tellin* you. (0.5) *T*ellin- I'm not *ask*in you." And I ain't say no plea:se *ei*ther.

A major circumstance in which girls make use of aggravated directives is when taking care of younger children and enacting such roles in their favorite pastime, playing house. For example when girls give directives to younger children in their charge, they frequently use aggravated forms or imperatives which resemble those their mothers use in disciplining them.[7] Directives may be accompanied by ac-

---

[6] This is not meant to imply that boys are *in fact* less able to deal with the perspective of the other than girls are.

[7] Studies comparing child-rearing practices of black parents with those of Euro-American (Bartz & Levin, 1978 ; Baumrind, 1972) and Chicano parents (Bartz & Levin, 1978) report "a pattern of increased strictness, high control, and high support (nur-

counts which can explicitly describe a benefit (such as safety) for the recipient of the imperative as in example 44:

(43)   9/28/70/11

Sharon: Stay out of the street now man. Come on punk. Hurry up Glen.

(44)   9/28/70/8

((*Sharon cautions Delin to stand away from girls making glass rings*))

Sharon: Delin you get back cuz I don't want nothin fallin in your eyes or in your face. Get back. Get back.

(45)   9/14/70/8

((*Delin puts down the hood of her jacket on a windy day*))

Terri: *Don't* put that down. Put that back *up*! It's sup*posed* to be that way.

Such types of actions constitute the models for communication which takes place when older children play house with younger children.

Here a specific episode of playing house will be investigated. In order to provide a point of reference for observations made about interaction occurring within this session of pretend play, a diagram of dramatized kinship relationships will be provided. Deniece and Sharon, who enact "sisters" who are "mothers," establish two separate households at the onset of this session.[8] As this diagram shows, Aisha (age 10) is a childless sister of Deniece (10) and Sharon (12). At the onset of play Pam (12), Brenda (8), and Terri (age 12, who frequently acts as parental child[9] taking care of younger sibling Brenda) are the children of Deniece. However during the session Terri negoti-

---

turance) among African-American parents" (McLoyd, Ray, & Etter-Lewis, 1985: p. 40). The white middle class mothers studied by Bellinger and Gleason (1982) deliver directives which appear far more mitigated than those I found in black mother–child interaction.

[8] The importance of female sibling ties among black families has been discussed by Aschenbrenner (1975); Ladner (1971); McAdoo (1983), and Stack (1974). McLoyd, Ray and Etter-Lewis (1985: p. 41) and Pitcher and Schultz (1983) report that among preschool children there is little development of the father/husband role during pretend play.

[9] Commenting upon the role of parental child within black families, McLoyd, Ray, and Etter-Lewis (1985: p. 40) state "Older children often assume caretaking responsibilities for younger children (Aschenbrenner, 1975; Lewis, 1975; Young, 1970) and, as a consequence, may acquire advanced role-taking skills."

ates a position as sister of Deniece, Sharon and Aisha. Priscilla (7) and Shahida (5) are Sharon's children.

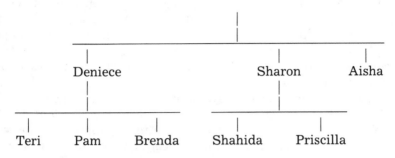

The Structure of Directives and Accounts in House

When playing house girls enacting the role of mother address their "children" with directives that are very similar in structure to those that mothers or caretakers use. Such patterning is consistent with other research on role playing among children's groups (Andersen, 1978: p. 89; Corsaro, 1985: p. 82; Ervin-Tripp, 1982: p. 36; Garvey, 1974, 1977; Mitchell-Kernan & Kernan, 1977: pp. 201–207; Sachs, in press) which has demonstrated that directives constitute the principal means through which children realize positions of dominance and submission between characters such as those in the mother/child relationship. "Mothers" typically deliver imperatives to their "children":

(46) 10/24/70/13

   Deniece: Hurry up and go to bed!

(47) 10/24/70/4

   Sharon: BRING THOSE CARDS BACK, BRING THAT BOOK IN THE HOUSE AND C:OME HOME! Don't *climb* over that way. You climb over the *right* way.

(48) 10/24/70/52

   Sharon: PRISCILLA, BRENDA, SHAHIDA, GET IN THE CAR! Get in the car. Sheila and Brenda, and all y'all get in the car.=Where Priscilla at. GET IN THE CAR. YOU GOIN OVER *MY* HOUSE. GO ON OVER AND GET- UH- WHERE'S PRISCILLA AT.

In addition to the job of enacting the roles of characters relative to one another, a principal task for participants is determining what scene is being enacted and making visible that scene. Directives not only constitute the principal ways in which roles in house are dramatized; they also provide the means through which the stage is set and the plot line is developed, as scene-changing guides are embedded in them and reference is made to nonpresent objects and spaces as well as future undertakings.

Accounts which accompany mothers' directives (such as "IT'S TIME TO GO *IN.*=YOU GOTTA GO TO *SCHOOL* TOMORROW!") supply warrants for the imperatives, culturally appropriate reasons for why activities should be done in specific ways. They thus provide the primary ways that participants playing house develop domestic roles and introduce new information into the ongoing action. Consequently the accounts within 'house' may be more elaborated than those that occur in actual interaction between caretakers and their charges:

(49)   10/24/70/21

> Deniece: Well if you don't want to go to sleep, don't go. But don't disturb your sisters. Just because *you* don't wanna go. (2.8) Maybe *they* wanna go to sleep. You don't know:: that. (3.6) That goes for *all* a you. Whether you not my-children or not. You *too.* (2.2) *Don't* let this happen again.

In providing accounts girls playing mother talk about measures that must be heeded for the safety and well-being of members of a group. Thus they express concerns which are similar to those in accounts during girls' task activities.

The positions of those in control in house (as with the boys' slingshot episode) are maintained not simply through the issuing of directives which maintain a particular format. They are also manifested through the *receipt* of various forms of action from others. The actions enacted by smaller children are largely requests for permission, actions which imply an asymmetry of role relationships:[10]

---

[10] Corsaro (1985: p. 83) also found that requests for permission were most frequently used by children playing younger children to "mothers" and constituted a way of displaying subordination. McLoyd, Ray, and Etter-Lewis (1985: p. 37) found that 'children' used more direct forms with each other than with their 'mothers'. Gordon and Tripp (1984: p. 308) argue that "true permission requests imply that the addressee has control over the speaker and that the speaker's wishes are subject to the hearer's approval."

(50)   10/24/70/1

Brenda: Mommy can um Aisha play with our baby brother?

(51)   10/24/70/2

Shahida: Can I hold your book?

(52)   10/24/70/48

Brenda: Mommy may *we* go out and play,

When speaking outside an enacted role concerning details of the drama, requests for information are also used to address girls who manage the activity:

(53)   10/24/70/3

Pam: How old am *I,*

With respect to the roles of mother and children there is thus a form of asymmetry built into the structure of behavior which closely models that in caretaker/child interaction as well as that in leader/follower interaction among the boys during task activities.

Although Maple Street girls playing the roles of subordinates in 'house' display deference through their requests for information they do not always display deference through their *responses* to imperatives, as has been reported for other groups (i.e., Corsaro, 1985: p. 83). Excuses rather than agreements are provided in the examples that follow in line 4 of example 54 and in lines 2, 6 and 8 of example 55; a counter accusation occurs in line 7 of example 54.

(54)   10/24/70/13

```
1  Brenda:    Maanaa. I want some peanuts.
2  Terri:     Well you ain't gettin none.
3  Deniece:   Hurry up and go to bed!
4  Brenda:  → ((whining)) I was just eating a peanut.
5  Deniece:   GO TO BED! YOU SUPPOSED- YOU SUPPOSED
6             TO GET YOURS IN THE MORNINGTIME.
7  Brenda:  → ((whining)) Well You eating them all
8             u:p.
9  Deniece:   Do you want me to tell her to go- uhm
10            make you go to bed?
```

(55)   10/24/70/4

```
1  Sharon:    COME ON PRISCILLA.
2  Pris:    → We playin cards.
```

3	Sharon:	I DON'T CARE *WHAT* YOU PLAYIN.=COME
4		ON.=IT'S TIME TO GO *IN*.=YOU GOTTA GO TO
5		*SCHOOL* TOMORROW!
6	Pris:	→ SHAHIDA TOOK THE CARDS,
7	Sharon:	SHAHIDA!
8	Pris:	→ Shahida took / / some a the cards.
9	Sharon:	BRING THOSE CARDS BACK, BRING THAT
10		BOOK IN THE HOUSE AND C:OME *HOME!* Don't
11		*climb* over that way. You climb over the *right* way.
12		

In examples 54 and 55 mothers Deniece and Sharon persist over several turns in their strategies to attempt to get their children Brenda and Priscilla to comply with directives. Mothers' imperatives are repetitively answered by children's counters as children negotiate their roles with respect to their caretakers.

Girls playing sisters also negotiate aspects of play through directives and accounts appropriate to their roles. For example consider the following dispute between older siblings Pam and Terri and younger sibling Brenda.

		((*Pam and Terri are arguing over who gets to play with the doll.*))
1	Pam:	The baby's hair. Stop.= I had it first.
2		I had the baby before you.
3	Brenda:	You're waking up the te(hh)dy bear.
4	Terri:	I want the baby in the bed.
5	Brenda:	You're waking up the teddy bear.
6	Pam:	*I* had it before *y*:ou.
7	Brenda:	You're waking up my *teddy* bear.
8	Pam:	Well I don't have to *p*lay with you
9		no more.
10	Sharon:	Okay I'm comin over.
11	Brenda:	Waking up the *teddy* bear.
12	Pam:	See I had it before *her*.=And she just
13		wanna / / fix her *hair*.
14	Sharon:	I know!

In this example there is a kind of symmetry with respect to the types of actions which girls of an equivalent position (children) but of different ages enact. While arguing among themselves, Pam (a sister younger than Terri) and Terri (a girl playing older sister and parental child) provide actions appropriate to their roles. Pam (lines 1–2, 6, 12) claims that she had the doll first while Terri provides a statement of her personal wants: "I want the baby in the bed." As the sequence progresses, Pam (lines 8–9) steps outside of the realm of play with a warning: "Well I don't have to play with you no more." Assuming the role of commentator on the argument between her older sisters, Brenda issues complaints (lines 3, 5, 7, 11) fitting her position as younger child within the house frame: "You're waking up my teddy bear."

By framing directives as requests for information, girls playing younger children display their subordination vis-à-vis girls playing mother. However as examples 54–56 show, girls playing children do not assume passive roles in 'house.' Instead considerable negotiation occurs among girls playing subordinate roles, in both their responses to girls playing roles of mother and among themselves.

Asymmetry in Roles in Playing House

Symmetrical types of exchanges take place within house in interactions in which siblings exchange equivalent argumentative forms (as in example 56) and "mothers" exchange stories about their "children." By comparison with task activities, however, there is a minimum of egalitarianism in decision making. In so far as those acting as children play subordinate roles there is asymmetry built into the activity itself. In addition girls who play the role of mother act in the capacity of stage manager. As overseers of the unfolding drama, both Deniece and Sharon monitor the actions of participants, commenting on them in utterances such as "Hey Brenda you supposed to be sleep." or "Priscilla you can't hear them." For example, in the following Deniece and Sharon, as commenters on Brenda's actions, describe for her appropriate behavior as a child (line 1) and warn her of her precarious tenure in the play through a negative categorization of her behavior ("not even *playing* right") (lines 4–5), commands (lines 6 and 8) and an account "THAT'S WHY NOBODY WANT YOU FOR A CHILD." (lines 6–7):

(57) 10/24/70/13

```
1  Deniece:  HEY BRENDA YOU OUGHTTA / / be sleep!
2  Terri:    I can't even get her in the bed.
3  Deniece:  I know.
4  Deniece:  SHE'S NOT / / EVEN PLAYIN RIGHT. SHE
5            NOT EVEN PLAYIN RIGHT.
6  Sharon:   BRENDA PLAY RIGHT. THAT'S WHY NOBODY
7            WANT YOU FOR A CHILD.
8  Deniece:  GET IN THERE AND GO TO SLEEP!
```

Girls in the position of "mother" can thus dictate for others dimensions of play *outside* the frame of play as well as within it. They not only can control who has rights to play what roles but also who can be members of the group. In example 57, important with respect to issues of social organization is the fact that while Deniece's actions towards Brenda are produced as complaints using third-person references, Sharon (line 6) delivers an imperative directly to Brenda. As the party who takes control of duties of principal stage manager, Sharon assumes the right to issue commands to players, even those not her own children.

Asymmetry is extended to other aspects of the activity as well. For example, while one might expect a certain equality among two girls who play mother, only one of them characteristically makes decisions for the group. In the present case Sharon assumes the right to change frame through "pretend" directives and in general it is she who plays the role of stage manager:

(58)   10/24/70/28

Sharon:	Hey y'all.=Pretend it's a- like- it's about twelve o'clock. =okay?
Deniece:	It's twelve o'clock in the afternoon so y'all should settle down.
Sharon:	Don't be too late.
Terri:	I'll fix their lunch!

(59)   10/24/70/15

Sharon:	Come on.=Pretend it's two o'clock in the morning.
Deniece:	OH: I'm goin to bed.

(60)   10/24/70/2

Sharon:	Pretend it's gettin night time.=
Terri:	Good night children!

Responses to pretend directives are not randomly distributed among participants. While many girls are present, generally the person responding to a request to pretend is another girl situated in an equivalent role. In these examples Deniece, a household head, and Terri, an older child performing caretaking responsibilities, are the ones who reply to Sharon's overt proposals for shifts in activity. Their talk elaborates the relevance of the directives for current and future activities. While not all initiations of frame shifts are begun by girls in the "mother" role, those who pass final judgment on proferred frame switches do overwhelmingly occupy that position. Thus asymmetrical role relationships are played out during 'house'.

Positions of subordination and superordination between Deniece and Sharon are further evident in forms of interactions between them. Deniece repetitively displays deference to Sharon. In the following, for example, Deniece relays a request made by someone in her household to Sharon rather than responding to it herself:

(61)   10/24/70/22

> Terri: Okay. Pretend it's just about seven o'clock in the morning.
> Deniece:→ What time is it Sharon, (1.8) What time is it Sharon. (0.6) *Sh*aron what time is it.
> Sharon: Seven o *clock.*
> Deniece: In the morning.

Meanwhile Sharon asserts her position as above that of Deniece in a variety of ways, for example by issuing imperatives to her:

(62)   10/24/70/5

> Sharon: Where Deniece go. You better get your children in the *house.*

(63)   10/24/70/7

> Sharon: Hey- you should beat your children cuz- You let her do her hair when she supposed to be in bed.

Repetitively Sharon's definition of the situation is asserted above Deniece's. In the following, after Sharon states that she has to fix dinner (lines 1–2), Deniece (line 3) offers an alternative plan of action using a modal verb: "*They* could eat dinner with *us,*". This suggestion is flatly opposed in a next turn by Sharon (lines 4–5), and subsequently the group follows up on Sharon's plan.

(64)   10/24/70/3

> 1 Sharon: Don't sit over here or stand over here
> 2   cuz I gotta fix dinner.
> 3 Deniece: *They* could eat dinner with *us,*
> 4 Sharon: No *uh* uh I'm fixin- I brought all this
> 5   food out here and they gonna eat over here.

Not only do girls establish hierarchical arrangements among members of their groups. In addition they form coalitions against particular girls. Among the Maple Street girls, as occurs among other girls' groups (i.e., Eder & Hallinan, 1978; Lever, 1976; Thorne & Luria, 1986), negotiating who is to be included within the most valued roles is an important feature of social organization. Within task activities girls were positioned in equivalent identities. Greater social differentiation is possible while playing house as the division into families and households provides for the playing of alternative roles. The position of sibling to the party playing principal decision maker is the most coveted position. In the particular session of playing house being examined, Sharon's best friend Aisha had no difficulty acquiring the identity of sibling sister. However considerable negotiation took place regarding Terri's identity in a similar slot. In the following the girls conspire to exclude Terri from the position of sister to Sharon:

(65)   10/24/70/12

```
 1   Terri:     I'm not your daughter.=all right? Um,
 2              I'm- I'm her sister.
 3   Deniece:   N:OO! / / You-
 4   Sharon:    YOU CAN'T BE STAYIN WITH ME!
 5   Terri:     I know.=I'm staying with her! But I
 6                 [[can-
 7   Deniece:   [[YOU- Uh uh! You- you my daughter.
 8   Terri:     Mm mm.
 9   Deniece:   Uh huh, / / Until Pam get back.
10   Terri:     Pam your daughter.
11   Deniece:   [[I know.=I-
12   Sharon:    [[WELL HOW CAN YOU BE HER SISTER,
13   Deniece:   UH HUH BECAUSE WE S:/ /ISTERS, HOW CAN
14              YOU BE HER SISTER.
15   Sharon:    NOW HOW CAN YOU BE MY SISTER,
16   Deniece:   How can you be my / / sister.
17   Aisha:     That's r- that's right.
18                 (0.8)
19   Aisha:     We all three sisters.
20   Sharon:    I know.
21   Aisha:     Well how come you don't wanna be
22                 [[her daughter.
23   Brenda:    [[THERE SHARON, AISHA / / AND
24   Terri:     I'm another sister.
25   Brenda:    [[There Sharon and Aisha is her-
26   Sharon:    [[N:O.
27   Brenda:    Is your- and / / she-
28   Sharon:    WELL YOU STAY HERE WITH HER.
```

The dispute about Terri's position in playing house begins in lines 1–2, where Terri proposes that she enact the role of Deniece's sister rather than her daughter. This proposal is first objected to by Deniece (line 3) with "N:00!" and then by Sharon (line 4): "YOU CAN'T

BE STAYIN WITH ME!" Deniece counters Terri again in line 7, arguing that Terri is her "daughter," rather than sister. The dispute becomes more intense when Sharon (lines 12, 15, 20), Deniece (line 9, 13–14, 16), and Aisha (lines 17, 19) argue that they are the only ones who can be sisters in playing house. The argument nears closure when Terri (line 24) states "I'm another sister." Subsequently Sharon (line 28) concedes that she can be a sister under the condition that she live with Deniece. In this way Sharon terminates the dispute while distancing herself from Terri. Thus in the midst of dramatic play, as in other of their interactions (Goodwin, 1982), girls take considerable care to delineate their friendship alliances. Though an issue which is highly charged is debated, the girls continue playing together for nearly an hour after this dispute.

CONCLUSION

Various researchers (Lever, 1976; Gilligan, 1982: p. 242) have proposed that the structure of games itself influences the form of social organization that children evolve. As the argument goes, because girls do not participate in complex games (team sports having a large number of players, high degrees of interdependence of players, role differentiation, rule specificity, and competitiveness), with respect to males females are considered less able to develop the negotiational skills which prepare one for "successful performance in a wide range of work settings in large, formal organizations" (Lever, 1974: pp. 240–241).

As can be seen from the data on playing house within a fairly unstructured form of play (that is, a form of play with relatively few explicit rules), an incipient hierarchy emerges. As within any focused gathering or activity requiring the close coordination of participants in differentiated roles, decisions regarding how the play is to proceed must be made from moment to moment; this allows for the emergence of the role of manager of the activity. Though both girls playing mother as well as the girl who is "parental child" may give directives to children in the play frame, one girl in particular controls the staging of the activity. She makes frequent use of imperatives in her talk, and in general uses explicit speech forms to oversee aspects of the activity. Concurrently those in positions subordinate to principal character (as both characters in the drama and actors in the dramatic play) display their positions of subordination vis-à-vis those in a position of authority, thereby constructing a complimentarity of roles. Within dramatic play girls further create a differentiation of participants through the ways in which they criticize certain girls or exclude them from valued positions. Alliances of girls against particular individuals are played out in a fashion which resembles alliance formation in a gossip event called "he-said-she-said" (Goodwin, 1980a). Supportive evidence for girls' competence in developing elaborated forms of social organization while playing games comes from Hughes' (1983, in press) studies of white middle class girls; within a nonteam game such as "foursquare", girls evolve quite sophisticated forms of social organization which entail contests between incipient teams.

The form of social organization which evolves in the midst of pretend play differs from that which characterizes girls' task activities. Girls, in contrast to boys, interpret task activities as needing relatively little control. In coordinating the actions of participants, events are treated as involving parallel rather than tightly interdigitated events, which are typical of a game such as jump rope or house. Girls make use of actions which include the speaker as well as others within the scope of the action and suggest rather than demand courses of next action. In addition, making decisions regarding what happens next is rotated among group members. When imperatives are used in this frame they are in some way modified from the bald forms which occur among the boys, either through accounts which specify safety of the individual involved, or benefits for the entire group. During the giving of instructions, imperatives are further modified through the shading of laughter and mimicry which surrounds them.

Thus girls exhibit a range of different types of social organization in the organization of their activities. Many studies of gender differences tend, as Thorne (1986: p. 168) argues, to promote the notion of "separate worlds" of males and females—"to abstract gender from social context, to assume males and females are qualitatively and permanently different." Here I have attempted to show that some features of girls' activities resemble the ways in which boys hierarchically structure their play. However, while girls in a stage manager position direct play in ways similar to the ways that boys in a leadership position make decisions for the group, the accounts they provide to support their imperatives speak to female rather than male concerns.

The findings reported here would thus seem to counter many of the prevalent notions about girls' social organization. Typically girls are seen as avoiding direct competition and spending little time on "negotiational involvements" (Lever, 1976; Sutton-Smith, 1979; Gilligan, 1982); such a view supports the view of females as powerless speakers. As I have argued here, within the 'house' frame, girls devote considerable attention to negotiating features of their play, making use of language which expresses disagreement in an aggravated fashion. Moreover, such negotiation takes place without the disruption of the ongoing activity or a breach in social relationships, as is frequently argued to occur among girls (Lever, 1976: p. 482; Gilligan, 1982: pp. 9–10). The form of differentiated social organization within a comparatively large cluster that girls evolve within playing house defies the often cited typifications of girls as interacting within small groups or friendship pairs (Waldrop & Halverson, 1975; Eder & Hallinan, 1978; Maltz & Borker, 1982). The fact that girls' social organization varies substantially across different domains makes it imperative that studies of girls' play or interaction be grounded in detailed analysis of specific contexts of use.

APPENDIX

TRANSCRIPTION

Data are transcribed according to the system developed by Jefferson and described in Sacks, Schegloff, and Jefferson (1974: pp. 731–733). The following example has been constructed to contain a variety of relevant transcription devices in a brief example. It is not an accurate record of an actual exchange. Features most relevant to the analysis in this paper are identified below:

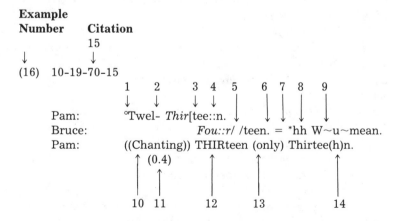

1. *Low Volume:* A degree sign indicates that talk it precedes is low in volume.

2. *Cut-Off:* A dash marks a sudden cut-off of the current sound. Here, instead of bringing the word "twelve" to completion, Pam interrupts it in mid course. *Italics:* Italics indicate some form of emphasis, which may be signaled by changes in pitch and/or amplitude.

3. *Overlap Bracket:* A left bracket marks the point at which the current talk is overlapped by other talk. Thus Bruce's *"Thirteen"* begins during the last syllable of Pam's *"Fourteen."* Two speakers beginning to speak simultaneously are shown by two left brackets at the beginning of a line.

4. *Lengthening:* Colons indicate that the sound just before the colon has been noticeably lengthened.

5. *Overlap Slashes:* Double slashes provide an alternative method of marking overlap. When they are used the overlapping talk is not indented to the point of overlap. Here Pam's last line begins just after the *"Four"* in Bruce's *"Four*teen."

6. *Intonation:* Punctuation symbols are used to mark intonation changes rather than as grammatical symbols:
    - A period indicates a falling contour.
    - A question mark indicates a raising contour.
    - A comma indicates a falling-raising contour.

7. *Latching:* The equal signs indicate "latching"; there is no interval between the end of a prior turn and start of a next piece of talk.

8. *Inbreath:* A series of 'h''s preceded by a dot marks an inbreath. Without the dot the 'h''s mark an outbreath.

9. *Rapid Speech:* Tildas indicate that speech is slurred together because it is spoken rapidly.

10. *Comments:* Double parentheses enclose material that is not part of the talk being transcribed, for example a comment by the transcriber if the talk was spoken in some special way.

11. *Silence:* Numbers in parentheses mark silences in seconds and tenths of seconds.

12. *Increased Volume:* Capitals indicate increased volume.

13. *Problematic Hearing:* Material in parentheses indicates a hearing that the transcriber was uncertain about.

14. *Breathiness, Laughter:* An 'h' in parentheses indicates plosive aspiration, which could result from events such as breathiness, laughter or crying.

15. *Citation:* Each example is preceded by a citation that locates the tape and transcript where the original data can be found. *Example Number.*

REFERENCES

Andersen, E. S. (1978). Learning to speak with style: A study of the sociolinguistic skills of children, Unpublished Ph.D. Dissertation, Department of Linguistics, Stanford University.

Aschenbrenner, J. (1975). *Lifelines: Black Families in Chicago*. New York: Holt, Rinehart and Winston.

Austin, J. L. (1962). *How to Do Things with Words*. Oxford: Oxford University Press.

Bartz, K. W., & Levin, E. S. (1978). Childrearing by black parents: A description and comparison to anglo and chicano parents. *Journal of Marriage and the Family, 40*, 709–719.

Baumrind, D. (1972). An exploratory study of socialization effects on black children: Some black–white comparisons. *Child Development, 43*, 261–267.

Becker, J. (1982). Children's strategic use of requests to mark and manipulate social status. In S. Kuczaj II (Ed.), *Language Development v. 2: Language, Thought and Culture* (pp. 1–35). Hillsdale, N.J.: Lawrence Erlbaum Associates.

Becker, J. A. (1984). Implications of ethology for the study of pragmatic development. In S. Kuczaj II (Ed.), *Discourse Development: Progress in Cognitive Development Research*, (pp. 1–17), New York: Springer-Verlag.

Bellinger, D. C., & Gleason, J. B. (1982). Sex differences in parental directives to young children, *Sex Roles, 8*, 1123–1139.

Blum-Kulka, S., & Olshtain, E. (1984). Requests and apologies: A cross-cultural study of speech act realization patterns (CCSARP). *Applied Linguistics, 5*, 196–213.

Brown, P. (1980). How and why are women more polite: Some evidence from a mayan community. In S. McConnell-Ginet, R. Borker, & N. Furman (Eds.), *Women and Language in Literature and Society* (pp. 111–149). New York: Praeger.

Brown, P., & Levinson, S. C. (1978). Universals of language usage: Politeness phenomena. In E. N. Goody (Ed.), *Questions and Politeness Strategies in Social Interaction* (pp. 56–311). Cambridge: Cambridge University Press.

Cazden, C., Cox, M., Dickerson, D., Steinberg, Z., & Stone, C. (1979). 'You all gonna hafta listen': Peer teaching in a primary classroom. In W. Collins (Ed.), *Minnesota Symposia on Child Psychology* (Vol. 12, pp. 183–231). Hillsdale, NJ: Lawrence Erlbaum Associates.

Chance, M. R. A., & Jolly, C. J. (1970). *Social Groups of Monkeys, Apes and Men*. London: Jonathan Cape.

Cook-Gumperz, J. (1981). Persuasive talk—the social organization of children's talk. In J. L. Green & C. Wallat (Eds.), *Ethnography and Language in Educational Settings* (pp. 25–50). Norwood, N.J.: Ablex.

Cook-Gumperz, J., & Corsaro, W. (1979). Social–ecological constraints on children's communicative strategies. *Sociology, 11,* 411–434.

Corsaro, W. A. (1985). *Friendship and Peer Culture in the Early Years.* Norwood, N.J.: Ablex.

Eder, D., & Hallinan, M. T. (1978). Sex differences in children's friendships. *American Sociological Review, 43* 237–250.

Ervin-Tripp, S. (1976). 'Is Sybil there?': The structure of some American English directives. *Language in Society, 5,* 1–289.

Ervin-Tripp, S. (1982). Structures of control. In L. C. Wilkinson (Ed.), *Communicating in the Classroom* (pp. 27–47). New York: Academic Press.

Garvey, C. (1974). Some properties of social play. *Merrill-Palmer Quarterly, 20,* 163–180.

Garvey, C. (1975). Requests and responses in children's speech. *Journal of Child Language, 2,* pp. 41–63.

Garvey, C. (1977). *Play.* Cambridge, MA: Harvard University Press.

Gilligan, C. (1982). *In a Different Voice: Psychological Theory and Women's Development.* Cambridge, MA: Harvard University Press.

Goffman, E. (1961). *Encounters: Two Studies in the Sociology of Interaction.* Indianapolis: Bobbs-Merrill.

Goffman, E. (1974). *Frame Analysis: An Essay on the Organization of Experience.* New York: Harper and Row.

Goodwin, M. H. (1980a). 'He-Said-She-Said': Formal cultural procedures for the construction of a gossip dispute activity. *American Ethnologist, 7,* 674–695.

Goodwin, M. H. (1980b). Directive/response speech sequences in girls' and boys' task activities. In S. McConnell-Ginet, R. Borker, & N. Furman (Eds.), *Women and Language in Literature and Society* (pp. 157–173). New York: Praeger.

Goodwin, M. H. (1982). 'Instigating': Storytelling as social process. *American Ethnologist, 9,* 799–819.

Goodwin, M. H. (1983). Aggravated correction and disagreement in children's conversations. Journal of Pragmatics, 7, 657–677.

Goodwin, M. H. (1985). The serious side of jump rope: Conversational practices and social organization in the frame of play. *Journal of American Folklore, 98,* 315–330.

Goodwin, M. H., & Goodwin, C. (1987). Children's arguing. In S. Philips, S. Steele, & C. Tanz (Eds.), *Language, Gender, and Sex in Comparative Perspective.* (pp. 200–248). Cambridge: Cambridge University Press.

Goodwin, C., & Goodwin, M. H. (In press). Interstitial argument. In A. Grimshaw (Ed.), *Conflict Talk.* Cambridge: Cambridge University Press.

Gordon, D., & Ervin-Tripp, S. (1984). The structure of children's requests. In R. L. Schiefelbusch & J. Pickar (Eds.), *The Acquisition of Communicative Competence* (pp. 295–321). Baltimore: University Park Press.

Grant, L. (1984). Black females' 'place' in desegrated classrooms. *Sociology of Education, 57,* 98–111.

Gumperz, J. J. (1982). *Discourse Strategies*. New York: Cambridge University Press.

Hughes, L. A. (1983). Beyond the rules of the game: Girls' gaming at a friends' school. Unpublished Ph.D. dissertation, University of Pennsylvania, Graduate School of Education.

Hughes, L. A. (in press). The study of children's gaming. In B. Sutton-Smith, J. Mechling & T. Johnson (Eds.), *A Handbook of Children's Folklore*. Washington, DC: Smithsonian Institution Press.

Labov, W., & Fanshel, D. (1977). *Therapeutic Discourse: Psychotherapy as Conversation*. New York: Academic Press.

Ladner, J. A. (1971). *Tommorrow's Tommorrow: The Black Woman*. New York: Anchor Books.

Lever, J. R. (1974). Games children play: Sex differences and the development of role skills. Unpublished Ph.D. Dissertation, Department of Sociology, Yale University.

Lever, J. (1976). Sex differences in the games children play. *Social Problems, 23*, 478–487.

Lewis, D. (1975). The black family: socialization and sex roles. *Phylon, 36*, 221–237.

Maltz, D. N., & Borker, R. A. (1982). A cultural approach to male–female miscommunication. In J. Gumperz (Ed.), *Communication, Language and Social Identity* (pp. 196–216). Cambridge University Press.

McAdoo, H. P. (1983). *Extended Family Support of Single Black Mothers*. Columbia, MD: Columbia Research Systems.

McLoyd, V. C., Ray, S. A., & Etter-Lewis, G. (1985). Being and becoming: The interface of language and family role knowledge in the pretend play of young African American girls. In L. Galda & A. D. Pellegrini, (Eds.), *Play, Language, and Stories: The Development of Children's Literate Behavior* (pp. 29–43). Norwood, NJ: Ablex.

Mitchell-Kernan, C., & Kernan, K. T. (1977). Pragmatics of directive choice among children. In S. Ervin-Tripp & C. Mitchell-Kernan (Eds.), *Child Discourse* (pp. 189–208). New York: Academic Press.

Piaget, J. (1965). *The Moral Judgment of the Child* (1932). New York: Free Press.

Pitcher, E., & Schultz, L. (1983). *Boys and Girls at Play: The Development of Sex Roles*. New York: Praeger.

Sachs, J. (in press). Preschool boys' and girls' language use in pretend play. In S. Philips, S. Steele, & C. Tanz (Eds.), *Language, Gender and Sex in Comparative Perspective*. Cambridge: MA: Cambridge University Press.

Sacks, H., Schegloff, E. A., & Jefferson, G. (1974). A simplest systematics for the organization of turn-taking for conversation. *Language, 50*, 696–735.

Stack, C. (1974). *All Our Kin: Strategies for Survival in a Black Community*. New York: Harper and Row.

Stone, C. R., & Selman, R. L. (1982). A structural approach to research on the

development of interpersonal behavior among grade school children. In
K. H. Rubin & H. S. Ross (Eds.), *Peer Relationships and Social Skills in
Childhood,* (pp. 163–183). New York: Springer-Verlag.

Sutton-Smith, B. (1979). *Play and Learning.* New York: Gardner Press.

Thorne, B. (1986). Girls and boys together—but mostly apart: Gender arrangements in elementary school. In W. W. Hartup & Z. Rubin (Eds.),
Relationships and Development (pp. 167–184). Hillsdale, N.J.: Erlbaum.

Thorne, B., & Luria, Z. (1986). Sexuality and gender in children's daily
worlds. *Social Problems, 33,* pp. 176–190.

Vaughn, B. E., & Waters, E. (1980). Social organization among preschool
peers. In D. R. Omark, F. F. Strayer, & D. G. Freedman (Eds.), *Dominance Relations: An Ethological View of Human Conflict and Social
Interaction* (pp. 359–379). New York: Garland STPM Press.

Waldrop, M. F., & Halverson, C. F. (1975). Intensive and extensive peer
behavior: Longitudinal and cross-sectional analyses. *Child Development, 46,* 19–26.

Wood, B., & Gardner, R. (1980). How children 'get their way': Directives in
communication. *Communication Education, 29,* 264–272.

Young, V. H. (1970). Family and childhood in a southern Negro community.
American Anthropologist, 72, 269–288.

PART II

Discourse in Storytelling

CHAPTER 3

Becoming a Political Woman: The Reconstruction and Interpretation of Experience Through Stories*

Susan E. Bell

Bowdoin College
Brunswick, Maine
and
Laboratory in Social Psychiatry
Harvard Medical School
Boston, Massachusetts

Narrative reconstruction is an attempt to reconstitute and repair ruptures between body, self, and world by linking up and interpreting different aspects of biography in order to realign present and past and self with society (Williams, 1984, p. 197).

INTRODUCTION

From 1940 to 1971, DES (diethylstilbestrol) was prescribed to pregnant American women to prevent miscarriage. Between 500,000 and three million U.S. women (DES daughters) were exposed to DES prenatally when their mothers took it. As a result of their exposure to this drug, DES daughters are vulnerable to reproductive tract prob-

* A version of this paper was presented at the XI World Congress of Sociology, New Delhi, India, August 1986. Research funds were provided by a postdoctoral fellowship from NIMH (5 T32 MH 1426-08) and by a grant from the faculty research fund, Bowdoin College. Thanks are due to Elliot Mishler, Catherine Kohler Riessman, Sue Fisher, and Alexandra Todd for their comments.

lems, including miscarriages, infertility, and vaginal and cervical cancer (Apfel & Fisher, 1984). This paper is an analysis of how one DES daughter has understood and responded to these risks at different stages in her life. To interpret this woman's experience, I begin by discussing some of the effects of DES exposure. I then analyze three stories that she told during an interview. The stories are linked together, and explain the role of her exposure to DES in the process of becoming a politically active woman.

The risk of problems related to DES exposure is both known and unknown. For example, up to 90% of DES daughters have adenosis, a condition in which cells that are normally found in the cervix are found on the walls and surfaces of the vagina, posing as yet unknown health risks. Just over 500 DES daughters have been diagnosed with clear cell adenocarcinoma (vaginal cancer). The risk of DES daughters developing clear cell adenocarcinoma is estimated to be 1/1000 through the age of 24. In contrast, the total death rate from all causes for women between the ages of 20 and 25 is 0.4/1000, and only 10% of these deaths are caused by cancer. Finally, while DES daughters conceive as easily as non-exposed women, they are 35% more likely to have a miscarriage, premature birth, stillbirth, or tubal pregnancy (Apfel & Fisher, 1984).

A recent review of the medical literature found a range of expert opinions about the long-term effects of DES on DES daughters. Some speculate that "what is currently known [is] 'the tip of the iceberg' " (Herbst & Bern, 1981, p. 1) and that DES daughters will be at higher risk of cervical, breast, and uterine cancer as they reach mid-life (Apfel & Fisher, 1984, p. 55). Others do not "take into account the possibility of other long term consequences" (Herbst & Bern, 1981, p. 1). In sum, the lack of clarity means that DES daughters live with medical uncertainty about the dimensions of risk associated with their prenatal exposure to this drug.

DES daughters live with uncertainty in another way too. Medical protocols for screening and treating DES-related problems have changed since 1971, when DES exposure was first linked to clear cell adenocarcinoma. One example of this involves treatment of adenosis. Today, experts recommend leaving it alone and observing it. In the early 1970s, however, they recommended treating it, and proposed a number of different approaches: partial removal of the vagina; cauterization of the vagina and cervix; cryosurgery (freezing); periodic removal of adenosis patches by punch biopsies (Apfel & Fisher, 1984, pp. 94–96). In the face of medical uncertainty, DES daughters must find ways to respond to and cope with long-term risk, changing medical knowledge, and the consequences of this changing knowledge for their interactions with the health care system. Ironically, DES daughters must return to medicine—the very source of their problems—for information and treatment.

Concomitantly, a growing body of research has been exploring the psychological dimensions of DES exposure. Results from a number of studies indicate that DES daughters may experience anxiety, grief, anger, or fear in response to learning that they have been exposed to the drug (Apfel & Fisher, 1984; Schwartz & Stewart, 1977). Psychiatrists Roberta Apfel and Susan Fisher argue convincingly that the reaction of DES daughters is characteristic of victims of trauma. Anke Ehrhardt and Heino Meyer-Bahlburg and their associates at the New York State Psychiatric Institute show that DES daughters "appear to be at risk for disorders of sexual desire, diminished sexual enjoyment, and (associated?) difficulties with sexual partners" (Meyer-Bahlburg, Ehrhardt, Endicott, Veridiano, Whitehead, & Vann, 1985a) and have increased rates of major depression (Meyer-Bahlburg et al., 1985a) (see also Vessey, Fairweather, Norman-Smith, & Buckley, 1983). There are several alternative explanations for these findings: they are the "direct effects of prenatal DES exposure on the developing central nervous system" (Meyer-Bahlburg & Ehrhardt, 1985); they are responses to the damage DES does to "the most private places in the body . . . namely, the sexual organs"; they are expressions of disillusionment with health policy makers, government regulatory agencies, and drug companies, such as occur with every large-scale public disaster (Apfel & Fisher, 1984, pp. 5, 68).

Perhaps as a consequence of these issues, DES has stimulated political activity on the part of women. In 1978, a national organization was founded by women's health activists to provide information and support for people exposed to DES. The origins of DES Action can be traced to a committee organized three years earlier by the Coalition for the Medical Rights of Women, a feminist organization that seeks "to make the medical system more responsive to the needs and concerns of women" (Coalition for the Medical Rights of Women, 1980). DES Action is one part of the women's health movement. As such, it is connected to a political effort to restructure health care: "to alter the quality, quantity, content, and control of obstetrical and gynecological services on the societal level, institutional level, and in face-to-face interaction with professionals" (Ruzek, 1979, p. 143). An "issues" oriented group (Ruzek, 1979), DES Action collects and distributes information, testifies at public hearings, and attempts to change laws and regulations regarding medical services for the DES-exposed. In its view, DES was not tested sufficiently before it was released for sale, nor did DES mothers give informed consent before they took it during pregnancy. Furthermore, the drug industry and medical profession supported its use in pregnancy even after controlled studies published in the 1950s showed that DES was ineffective in preventing miscarriage; they were also slow to take responsibility for locating, screening, and caring for people exposed to DES after the publication of a report in 1971 linking prenatal exposure to DES with adenocarcinoma (see DES Action Voice, volumes 1–5 and issues 22–28).

The present paper analyzes an interview with one DES daughter to explore how she has understood and responded to the uncertainties surrounding her DES exposure at different stages in her life and to show how her identity as a politically active woman has emerged during this process. The interview is one of a series of focused interviews (Merton, Fiske, & Kendall, 1956) that I conducted with DES daughters for a study of the social and emotional effects for young adult women of living with risk and medical uncertainty associated with their prenatal DES exposure. The interviews were designed to identify issues DES daughters introduce as meaningful in relation to their exposure to DES. My approach was to ask open-ended questions, listen with a minimum of interruptions, and tie my questions and comments to the DES daughters' responses by repeating their words in questions and comments wherever possible.

To demonstrate the making of a political woman, I interpret three stories that emerged during the course of an interview with this woman: one occurred at the beginning of the interview, a second about 15 minutes after the interview had started, and a third occurred towards the end. The interview contains more than three stories. However, these three are central to understanding how this woman has become politicized, and were chosen for this reason. I use the grammatical structure within and across the stories to explore what the stories are about and how they become meaningful. I argue that when interpreted together they show how one woman has come to understand and accept her status as a DES daughter, after first denying it, and the reasons for this change. They show how this woman has come to accept herself as different, and as a member of a group of DES daughters. In sum, the stories are about becoming political, and the role of DES exposure in this process.

METHODOLOGY

It is by now commonplace to assert that people make sense of their life experiences by narrating them (see Mitchell, 1980, 1981). Much less common is attention to the production and analysis of narratives appearing in research interviews. Elliot Mishler (1986b) summarizes a growing body of work that has been produced by scholars interested in how the form and content of single stories that are told during interviews shed light on the experiences of individuals. According to these scholars, since interviewers and respondents jointly construct interviews, respondents will recall and report some material in the form of stories if interviewers allow them to; this depends on how they negotiate their dual and shifting roles as interviewer/listener-to-a-story and respondent/narrator during the course of the interview (Paget, 1983). These stories can provide the basis for an analysis of an interview (see, for example, Mishler, 1986a; Paget, 1982, 1983; Riessman, this volume).

Even less common than the analysis of single stories appearing in research interviews is the analysis of sequences of stories appearing in them. My work draws from and extends story analysis by considering how sequences of stories can provide insight into personal experience. I argue that in in-depth interviews, people spontaneously tell stories to tie together significant events and important relationships in their lives, and to "make sense" of their experiences. Through linked stories, people explain how their experiences—and their interpretations of these experiences—have changed over time. These sequences of stories can be used as data to interpret interviews.

I define stories, as do many story analysts, as follows: A story consists of a number of structural elements. Minimally, it has a recognizable beginning (orientation), signalled by the narrator and listener, and consists of linked categories (episodes), connected to each other temporally and/or causally. The episode structure conforms to the needs of listeners who simultaneously encode and interpret the episodes. Narrative clauses animate the events in each episode and report these events in the same sequence in which they are interpreted as having taken place. Woven through the narrative clauses are evaluative comments, descriptions and elaborations which suspend the action and make meaning of the events. A story's ending (coda) is acknowledged by both narrator and listener (Labov, 1972; Mandler, 1984; Mandler & Johnson, 1977; Polanyi, 1981).

A systematic analysis of interviews using story analysis can proceed in the following manner (Bell, 1985). First, the boundaries of stories are identified. The stories are then parsed and interpreted, as individual units and in relation to each other. The thematic and linguistic connections between stories are identified. The meaning of each individual story is explored on the basis of the stories that precede and follow it. Together, they constitute a respondent's "narrative reconstruction" (Williams, 1984) or "account" (Scott & Lyman, 1968) of his or her lived experiences.

To communicate a story, a narrator has the task of finding a form that is compatible with the expectations of the listener. If she is unsuccessful, her points will not be heard. Fortunately, Sarah (a pseudonym) tells her stories in a way that I can understand. Her stories have a recognizable, patterned structure, typical of white, middle-class Americans (Gee, 1985; Michaels, 1981; Riessman, this volume). Each story is a "fully formed" narrative (Labov, 1972). Each begins with an *abstract* (a plot summary), contains an *orientation* (introducing place, time, characters, and situation), *complicating action* (narrative clauses), *evaluation* (interpretation), *resolution* (the result of the actions) and *coda*. In addition to finding an overall structure familiar to me, Sarah divides the stories into smaller chunks, or *episodes* (Mandler & Johnson, 1977). These smaller chunks are probably reflections of how Sarah has stored and remembered her experiences (Mandler, 1984). Each episode reports something that happens (the beginning), followed by a response (development), which in turn brings about some event or state of affairs completing the episode (outcome). Each story is more likely to be understood and remembered by me because it is told in connected episodes (Mandler & Johnson, 1977).

In the analysis that follows, I approach the stories in two ways. First, I reduce each of them to its core narrative, or skeleton plot. This reduction preserves the abstract, orientation, complicating action, resolution, and coda. It leaves out the evaluation and thus excludes a great deal of descriptive material that Sarah, like other narrators, introduces to expand upon and explain the meaning of the stories. This material consists of "flashbacks, comments that suspend the action, and descriptions of character and setting" (Mishler, 1986a, p. 236). In the core narratives of the three stories, we can see that Sarah is reporting, in temporal order, how she became politicized. The second approach restores the stories to their complete versions. In the full stories, we can see the introduction of two contrasting "voices," or ways of comprehending the world, by means of which Sarah explains why she became politically active (Mishler, 1984).

ANALYSIS

Sarah is a middle-class white woman in her early 30s. She is married, has a son ("David"), age two, and is employed part time in a professional capacity in the service sector. Her husband ("Mark") is employed by one of the Fortune 500 companies. They live in a suburb of a large city in the northeastern United States. When we first met, Sarah offered to talk with me about her experiences; I called her a few weeks later and went to her home to interview her. The interview lasted about one and a half hours and was tape recorded. The three stories about becoming a political woman emerged during the interview. They cover a period of about 12 years in her life.

The first story, which occurred at the beginning of the interview, reports how Sarah found out she was a DES daughter (her gynecologist told her when she went to him to get birth control) and what this was like (it was unremarkable). She "denied, almost everything about" it and "really put actively put it out of [her] mind."[1]

The second story was told about 15 minutes after the interview started and describes the circumstances that led her to become "much more, actively concerned" about DES and that brought DES to the "forefront" of her mind. During her first pregnancy she went into labor at 5½ months and delivered a baby who lived only eight hours. In the second story, Sarah describes her shock at having problems after an easy conception and smooth pregnancy, her distress at "losing the baby," and her struggle to make sense of this. Her struggle involved understanding the mechanism of how this happened, accepting its relationship to the DES her mother had taken, and living with the knowledge that she had lost a baby.

The third story emerged towards the end of the interview. In it, Sarah explains why she joined DES Action and then became actively involved in it. She got angrier about some of the things that happened to her; she wanted to help DES daughters be more assertive and to help obstetricians be more aware of problems associated with DES; and she wanted to help herself by being educated and staying on top of problems she was convinced would occur at middle age or menopause. In addition, she liked the people in DES Action. Taken together, the three stories show how this DES daughter has coped with and responded to her exposure to DES. She explains how cir-

---

[1] The transcripts preserve many features of the participants' manner of speaking but are not fully equivalent to the talk (see Mishler, 1984). Nonlexical utterances, false starts, hesitations and repetitions are retained in the text. Interruptions and overlaps between speakers are marked by a left-hand bracket, "[". Silences shorter than one second are indicated by a comma, ",". The length of longer silences is marked by "(2)", with numbers representing seconds. Nonverbal sounds are given in parentheses "(laugh)". If they occur during speech they are noted in parentheses directly above the words happening simultaneously. "N" in the left-hand margin refers to the narrator/respondent and "L" refers to the listener/interviewer. This level of detail helps to display how the story emerges, and how the narrator and listener construct it together. It also shows how cohesion is created and maintained. Copies of the complete transcripts of the three stories are available from the author upon request.

cumstances have changed, how her perceptions of events have changed, how her coping has changed, and how these changes are related to each other and to her evolving status as a political woman.

it sort of f'flitted in and out

At first (Story 1), Sarah reports that DES was not a major part of her life. The core narrative is reproduced below.

Abstract:
    002   L: how you found out you were a DES daughter,
    003   L: and what it was like
Orientation:
    006   N: when I was around, 19,
    008   I was in college
Complicating Action:
    009   and I went, to a, a gynecologist to get birth control
    011   he was, he knew that I was a DES daughter because I had adenosis (1) um,
    012   so he, told y'know he told me (2.5)
    016   I think shortly after that,
    017   [my mother] told me,
    018   um and I either said "I know already" or, (inhale)
Resolution/Coda:
    022   and I was so concerned at the time about getting birth control,
    023   that I think it sort of didn't, um,
    024   it never really, became the major part of my life
    025   it sort of f'flitted in and out (tch) (1.5)

Despite the scientific basis of her gynecologist's logic, Sarah did not take his conclusion seriously. He knew she was a DES daughter because she had adenosis. He saw the cells, identified them, and interpreted them by referring to an abstract body of knowledge. Adenosis is a common condition in DES daughters; it is uncommon in non-exposed women and therefore it is an indication of DES exposure. Her mother, too, told Sarah of her exposure to DES; this assertion is supported by her experience of taking DES when she was pregnant with Sarah. Sarah dismissed both voices: her gynecologist's and her mother's. She explains her lack of concern about DES by placing it in the context of her life at that time. She was interested in birth control, that is, being a sexually active young woman. At the time, she was a 19-year-old college student, concerned with becoming sexually active and growing up. In comparison to these concerns, the possibility that her reproductive and sexual organs might be damaged was unimportant. The idea merely "f'flitted in and out" (line 025).

um (1) and that's when I (1.2) um began to accept the fact (1.2)

Sarah became actively concerned about DES after she had a miscarriage (Story 2). At first, the connection between DES and her miscarriage made no sense, but then her physician drew a link for her: DES had caused her to have an "incompetent cervix"[2] and therefore she had had a miscarriage. In addition, Sarah's life concerns had changed. No longer was she an adolescent, exploring her sexuality. She was a married woman who had just lost a baby. In this context, she began to take her exposure to DES seriously. In order to protect future pregnancies, she would first need to understand how her reproductive organs were different from those of women not exposed to DES, and how these differences could lead her body to function improperly.

Abstract:
    202 I then had some problems around, pregnancy,
    203 that sort of brought the whole issue of DES (1.5) t'much more t'the
            forefront of my mind
    204 and has made me much more, actively concerned about it,
Orientation:
    207 but, ah I, my first pregnancy, um, I had problems, due to DES
Complicating Action:
    208 I got pregnant
    224 and in the, middle of the night one night
    225 my, membranes broke,
    226 and (1.2) y'know Mark r'rushed me to the hospital
    227 and I delivered a baby girl,
    228 (tch) who lived about eight hours
    229 but she died
    232 and even then, when the, resident the (1.5) (tch) doctor who was
            taking care of me
    234 um said, in the aftermath that maybe she thought it was due to DES,
    235 um, I didn't believe her (1)
    261 and then I went back
    265 um she re- she had really done a lot of research
    266 and sort of, presented me with a whole, scheme of how this could
            have happened

---

[2] An "incompetent cervix," is a medical term that *Dorland's Illustrated Medical Dictionary* defines as a cervix that "is abnormally prone to dilate in the second trimester of pregnancy, resulting in premature expulsion of the fetus (middle trimester abortion)."

267   and why she thought it was related to the DES
270   then it was clear that it probably was,
Resolution/Coda:
277   um (1) and that's when I (1.2) um began to accept the fact (1.2)
278   y'know once it made sense,

In the immediate aftermath of the miscarriage Sarah's physician—this time a woman—could not give a satisfactory account of its cause. She said "maybe it was due to DES" (line 234). Sarah's response was disbelief. The physician could not explain the connection between DES exposure and the miscarriage. Sarah's choice was to respond by believing or disbelieving her; to trust or mistrust her doctor's proposal. She responded with disbelief.

Subsequently, the physician did "a lot of research" (line 265) and "presented [Sarah] with a whole scheme of how this could have happened /and why she thought it was related to the DES" (lines 266–267). She had gathered more data, sorted through them, and ordered them. She linked DES and the miscarriage together and expressed her explanation in the voice of medicine: She knew that Sarah had had a miscarriage because Sarah had an incompetent cervix. The connection between DES and the miscarriage was Sarah's incompetent cervix. Thus, she accounted for Sarah's miscarriage by blaming it on her cervix. Her logic is similar to the logic used by the gynecologist in the first story:

	Story 1	Story 2
sign:	adenosis	incompetent cervix
cause:	DES exposure	DES exposure
consequence:	?	miscarriage

The doctor, and then Sarah, understood the connection. Sarah's response to this proposition was acceptance because "it made sense" (1ine 278).

With her acceptance, Sarah began to take her identity as a DES daughter seriously. She understood that her reproductive organs were damaged, that because of DES she had had a miscarriage, and that this could happen again because she had an incompetent cervix.

At the same time that Sarah became actively concerned about her DES exposure, she learned her miscarriage was iatrogenic ("it was related to the DES"), and heard that it was her fault ("I had an incompetent cervix"). Even though the term "incompetent cervix" is a medical term, the adjective "incompetent" has "negative and judgmental connotations" (Fox, 1983, p. 462). As a pediatrician wrote in a letter to the *American Journal of Obstetrics and Gynecology*,[3] "it is easy to see how a mother grieving over the death of her premature infant might be additionally upset by being told by her physician that the premature birth resulted from her 'incompetent cervix'" (Fox, 1983: p. 462). This medical term blames the victim for the problem.

As long as Sarah framed her understanding in the language and logic of medicine, she could neither locate the problem outside herself nor begin to draw a connection between her condition and that of other DES daughters. She remained isolated—blaming her body for the miscarriage and identifying it as incompetent. Instead of recognizing her similarity to DES daughters, she recognized her difference from other (normal and competent) women.

I no longer can be, blithe about it, and say not me

Over time, Sarah became politicized (Story 3). The "more removed [she] got from what had happened to [her]" and "the more that time went by," "the angrier [Sarah] got about some of the things that happened to [her]" (lines 329–330). The third story reports a sequence of actions that Sarah took to become a politically active member of DES Action. The story's point is that she joined DES Action because she grew angry about what had happened to her and wanted to help herself and other DES daughters.

Abstract:
301 L: how did you, come to get involved with DES Action
Complicating Action:
302 N: (3.5) (tch) (inhale) heard an ad on t.v. or the radio (1.5)
305   and I think I it if they had the tape number
306   and I called up
307   and asked for information
308   and they sent me their little packet
309   and I, joined
311   and then a while later
312   they sent me a card,
313   um that they were having a coffee one of the the one of those like the one that you went to,
314   um and I couldn't go to that
322   um, but then I sort of felt like I had made an obligation to meet these people

---

[3] I am indebted to Catherine Kohler Riessman for this reference.

Resolution:
323   and, so I went ahead and met them you know
324   and liked them
325   and thought I it was someing [sic] something that I wanted to be
          more involved in
Coda:
327   (1.5) and have stayed that way

In this story she recounts interactions between herself and DES Action. First, Sarah moved from becoming actively concerned about her DES exposure (Story 2) to acknowledging her connection with others exposed to DES ("heard an ad on T.V. or the radio . . . and I called up / and asked for information / and they sent me their little packet / and I, joined") (lines 302, 306–309).

Sarah's active concern about DES led her to contact DES Action. Her request for information was consistent with a central goal of DES Action: to let DES daughters know about the need for medical screening and follow-up care, to refer them to physicians familiar with DES-related problems, and to provide them with reviews of medical and scientific studies about DES. In turn, Sarah accepted DES Action's request that she join the organization. She thereby acknowledged that she had something in common with other DES daughters. They, like she, faced the risk of reproductive difficulties and cancer because of the physiological effects of DES.

At this point, Sarah was not ready to accept the proposal that she had concerns that were similar to those of DES Action. She was invited to become active, to go to a meeting and share her experiences with others, ("they sent me a card, / um that they were having a coffee") (lines 312–313). She "couldn't go to that" (line 314). She was not yet ready to talk about what had happened to her. Ruzek (1979) observes that women's discovery of common concerns over health and reproduction is a crucial stage in the women's health movement. Once these commonalities are discovered, women can organize. DES Action, for example, offers more than information and support to people exposed to DES. It wants "to help people understand the politics of the DES experience" (Coalition News, August 1978, p. 3). To become an active member of DES Action means becoming a feminist health activist. It means joining the women's health movement. Sarah was not yet ready to protest the abuses of medicine collectively.

Nonetheless, Sarah felt an "obligation to meet these people" (line 322) and so she did, found she liked them, and became more involved. She joined the women's health movement. For Sarah, this meant understanding and accepting the iatrogenic role of medicine in her experience. First, medicine had prescribed DES to her mother, which caused Sarah's adenosis. Then, medicine had provided inadequate care for Sarah when she became pregnant (this point will be discussed more fully later in the paper). In other words, becoming a member of the women's health movement helped Sarah to locate the source of her problems in the medical profession (rather than in her incompetent cervix) and to seek solutions through collective political action (rather than as an isolated individual). As a health activist, Sarah would join with others to change medical care. Exactly what this would entail is left implicit in the core narrative.

To summarize, one way that Sarah makes her experiences meaningful is through the core narratives of three stories. Taken together, the three stories cover a span of about 12 years, and show how Sarah has changed: from a passive patient to an active one, from an isolated individual to a participant in a woman's health organization.

Thus, one way of understanding the three stories is by reducing each of them to its narrative core. Analyzing this core shows that Sarah's account is about a change in identity. The stories are linked together through the narrative clauses themselves: each builds on the sequence of actions in the previous one to illuminate when and how Sarah became politicized. Through the stories, this narrator has explained central changes in her life.

And yet, there are gaps in each story as they have been examined thus far. The core narratives exclude descriptions, asides, interactions between the narrator and listener, and most of the evaluative material. The gaps in story structure lead to difficulties in the analysis. For example, Sarah reports that she began to take DES seriously (Story 2) because her doctor "presented [her] with a whole, scheme" of how the miscarriage had happened. Sarah, according to this account, accepted the explanation because it was scientific. Earlier, however (Story 1), she had rejected the status of DES daughter even though her doctor gave her a scientific explanation: he told her she was a DES daughter because she had adenosis. In this respect, the language of science both is and is not sufficient; scientific knowledge does and does not give her an account she finds satisfactory.

There is a second way that Sarah, like other narrators, interprets the three stories: she conveys the meaning of each story by modifying the complexity of the narrative clauses themselves with gestures and expressive sounds, by pausing or hesitating, by shifting into or out of reported speech, changing tenses, and repeating words or phrases. Such evaluation (Labov, 1982, p. 227) explains why a story is worth telling, why the events in it are "not ordinary, plain, humdrum, everyday or run-of-the-mill" (Labov, 1972, p. 371). Thus, a way of filling in some of the gaps left by the analysis of the core narrative is by restoring the stories to their complete versions and examining them once again.

Constructing Knowledge in Two Voices

Elliot Mishler (1984, p. 63), drawing from the work of Silverman and Torode, has recently proposed the concept of "voice" to represent "a specific normative order, a particular assumption about the relationship between appearance, reality, and language." He describes two voices, representing two ways of knowing about health, illness, and disease, which he calls the voice of medicine and the voice of the lifeworld. The voice of medicine seeks to understand and explain events within the framework of the biomedical model (Mishler, 1981). According to this voice, health and disease are universal to the human species. Diseases have specific etiologies and can be diagnosed in individuals on the basis of objective signs and symptoms. References to individual life experiences that do not specify objective indications of disease are superfluous to the voice of medicine. The effect of this voice is to "strip away" the social context of health and disease as well as to ignore patients' experiences and self-understandings of their problems (see Mishler, 1984, p. 120). Usually the voice of medicine predominates in the explanation of health and disease. It frames problems in the language of medical experts and increases their mystification, thereby decreasing the ability of lay people to understand these problems.

The voice of the lifeworld represents the understanding of health and disease within a social context (Mishler, 1986b, p. 143). According to this voice, events become connected and meaningful depending on a person's "biographical situation and position in the social world" (Mishler, 1984, p. 104). The self is the center of the lifeworld. Mishler argues that even though the voice of medicine is the usual explanatory framework, health, illness, and disease become truly meaningful to people only after they have been contextualized. Thus, there is a constant struggle between the two voices, both in medical interviews, when doctors and patients attempt to understand each other, and when people try to make sense of their problems outside of the medical world.

Within the three stories, both voices can be seen in operation. As we shall see, Sarah's perspective on the relative contributions of each voice to her comprehension of DES changes over time, and this change contributes to her politicization. In order to understand why she becomes a political woman, as well as the meaning of this transformation for her, it is necessary to explore the dialogue between the two voices within and across the three stories. The contrast between these two ways of knowing is represented by Sarah's doctor(s) and her mother.

Sarah explores two approaches to understanding DES by comparing her relationships with her mother and her doctor, and her negotiations with them about DES. Sarah's gynecologist knew of her sexual activity and she learned of her DES exposure from him.

Episode 1 (doctor) (lines 007, '009–012)
007 I we-
009 and I went, to a, a gynecologist to get birth control,
010 and I happened to be lucky with my first exam
011 he was, he knew that I was a DES daughter because I had adenosis
         (1) um
012 so he, told y'know he told me (2.5)

In contrast, her mother didn't know Sarah was getting birth control and, in turn, Sarah didn't learn from her mother that she was a DES daughter. Sarah's laughter in her comment to me that she doesn't remember "How it became clear between [her] mother and [her]" (line 013) adds to the sense of tension and discomfort conveyed by her words.

Episode 2 (mother) (lines 016–020)
016 I think shortly after that
017 she told me
018 um and I either said "I know already" or, (inhale)
019 um (1) but I didn't learn from her directly first
020 uh I learned it from this doctor (1.5)

The difference between the two relationships is underscored by the repetition of words describing her negotiations with them about DES in these two episodes:

	Gynecologist		**Mother**
012	he told me	017	she told me
020	I learned it from	019	I didn't learn it from

The voice of medicine dominates in the first story. Despite Sarah's failure to take this voice seriously (the knowledge it conveyed merely "f'flitted in and out of" her mind), her understanding of her DES exposure is framed in its language ("adenosis") and logic (the objective sign indicates DES exposure).

The importance of understanding the meaning of DES exposure is conveyed by Sarah beginning in the first story with the repetition of key words and phrases about knowing, learning, understanding, remembering, and thinking. In an aside at the story's beginning, Sarah says that the details are fuzzy in her "head" (line 004) and in the second coda (ending) reports that she "really put actively put [DES] out of [her] mind" (line 038) (see Bell, 1985). For the most part, she uses negatives to describe her understanding of DES at this time of her life; DES had little meaning for her. "I think" and "I don't remember" are each repeated twice (lines 005, 016; 013, 035). She explains that since she *"didn't* have anything, that [she] understood was wrong with [her]" (line 034) she "sort of, *denied,* almost everything about it" (line 036) (emphasis added). Sarah ends the first story as follows:

```
033   I'I would y'know (1) I thought about it somewhat,
034   but um, didn't (1.5) since I didn't have anything, that I understood
            was wrong with me,
035   um (1.5) I don't remember
036   I mean I sort of, denied, almost everything about it
038   and really put actively put it out of my mind
```

About 15 minutes later in the interview, Sarah begins the second story, reintroducing the theme of knowing and the dialogue between the two voices. She also explicitly ties it to the first story. In the abstract of the second story, she begins:

```
201   so (1) in any case, um (1.8)
202   I then had some problems around, pregnancy,
203   that sort of brought the whole issue of DES (1.5) t'much more t'the
            forefront of my mind
204   and has made me much more, actively concerned about it,
```

The abstract provides a connection between the two stories, through contrast. "Mind," "actively," and "concerned," appear in each story, as displayed below, but to describe contrasting responses:

	Story 1		**Story 2**
038	out of my *mind*	203	t'the forefront of my *mind*
038	put *actively* put it out	204	more *actively* concerned
022	I was so *concerned* at the time about getting birth control	204	*concerned* about [the whole issue of DES]

The repetition of words describing how the context and Sarah's response to it had changed, makes each story more powerful. Through the contrasts, Sarah underlines the extent to which her understanding and interest in DES had become transformed through her experiences.

In addition, with the phrase "the forefront of my mind", the second story continues the theme of knowing begun in the first story. This theme is first referred to in the negative ("I still didn't understand" [line 237], "I hadn't educated myself" [line 238]). In the aftermath of losing the baby, Sarah couldn't understand why it had happened. She didn't believe her physician's explanation because, as she says:

237 y'didn't I still didn't understand the mechanism of how all this happens (1.2)
238 and I hadn't educated myself as to (1) what was actually going on

In addition, her doctor couldn't make a convincing case for the link between DES and the miscarriage: "she was sort of going through a whole list of things that she thought it might be / and that was sort of one out of" (lines 243–244).

Right after she lost the baby, Sarah's mother also linked DES and the miscarriage, but Sarah rejected this account too:

248 I can remember when my mother said "Maybe this is due to the DES"
249 I said, "Now don't be ridiculous,"
250 L: mhm
251 um because I did
252 I mean she was feeling awful
253 L: mhm
254 She was really d-
255 I mean we were all distraught
256 but y'know, to have her think that she had something to do with my losing the baby
257 was more than I could tolerate,

In the aftermath, neither her doctor nor her mother could convince Sarah that her miscarriage was due to DES because she could not understand, believe, or tolerate it so soon after she lost the baby. Neither voice could penetrate Sarah's anguish; neither made sense to her.

A few weeks later, she accepted the connection. At this point the story contains phrases about knowing, now in the positive, instead of the negative, as it had earlier ("it made a lot more sense to me" [line

269], "then it was clear" [line 270], "it made sense" [line 278]). Sarah attributes her new understanding to the power of the voice of medicine. The doctor used the scientific method. She "had really done a lot of research" (line 265) "and really had, um, done some work on it" (line 268). She had amassed "the facts" (line 275) and presented "a whole, scheme" (line 266) to Sarah. Sarah understood and accepted the explanation because it was presented in the logic and language of science:

272   um, that I had an incompetent cervix
273   and that, the incident of that is (some ?) the incidence of that is so
       much more higher in, DES daughters
275   um, because all the facts of the, miscarriage, fit with incompetent
       cervix

Sarah repeats the words for emphasis: "incompetent cervix" (lines 272, 275) and "incidence" (line 273) are both repeated twice. Sarah never overtly acknowledges that her mother, too, was correct; in this story, she discounts the voice of the lifeworld.

The coda to the second story, however, suggests an interpretation more complicated than this. Sarah ends the story saying "um (1) and that's when I (1.2) um began to accept the fact (1.2) / y'know once it made sense" (lines 277–278). The transformation described in this story, from not knowing to knowing and accepting the serious consequences of exposure to DES hinged on Sarah's ability both to understand rationally what had happened, and why, and to experience a pregnancy and miscarriage. Sarah's use of the word "sense" eloquently ties the two together. For "sense" has two meanings. It refers to something that can be grasped, comprehended, and known as well as to the ability to receive mental impressions through the actions of a body's sense organs (sight, taste, smell, pain, etc.) or through changes in the condition of the body (*Webster's Third New International Dictionary*). Logic and reason were not sufficiently powerful to induce a change in Sarah's attitude, nor was experience alone.

Sarah could accept her identity as a DES daughter because she had "some problems around, pregnancy" and subsequently her doctor presented her with a whole scheme of how these problems had happened. The centrality of Sarah's miscarriage to this transformation is signalled not only by the actions themselves but by her use of intensifiers, pauses, and repetition to suspend the action in the story between the times that she says "I got pregnant (5)" (line 208) and her report of the outcome "and in the, middle of the night one night / my membranes broke" (lines 224–225). Sarah suspends the action, first pausing for five seconds, to describe how normal the pregnancy was for her:

208 I got pregnant (5)
209 well, sometime in the fall of, 19, David was born in 19XX so it must
       have been 19XX
210 L: mhm
211 um (tch) and was due to have the baby in July of 19XX
212 and when I was five and a half months pregnant
213 I didn't have any trouble conceiving, which is one of the problems
       that, DES daughters have but I
                                    [
214 L: excuse me you were planning to get
       pregnant
215 yes I was planning to get pregnant
      [
216 you were trying to get pregnant
217 and I got pregnant the first month that I, tried to get pregnant
                                                  [
218 L: mhm
219 and that, you know went perfectly smoothly
220 and had a wonderful p'pregnancy,
221 um (2) you know the-
222 I had absolutely no, nothing to complain about
223 until, I was five and a half pregnant five and a half half months
       pregnant
224 and in the, middle of the night one night
225 my membranes broke,

Sarah was planning to get pregnant, conceived the first month she tried, and had a perfectly smooth pregnancy until she was five and a half months pregnant. She uses intensifiers in this section of the story ("perfectly smoothly" "absolutely no, nothing") to characterize the pregnancy. I enter into and strengthen the sense of normalcy here with my question, "you were planning to get pregnant" and comment, "you were trying to get pregnant". The cumulative effect of these evaluative devices and their content to this point is to establish just how unprepared Sarah was for what happened and to direct my attention to the subsequent sequence of events reporting the miscarriage itself (Labov, 1972).

Not until Sarah had lost a baby, a loss for which she had been entirely unprepared, could she accept the possibility of risks associated with DES, regardless of how these risks were explained to her. This interpretation is supported by Sarah's actions in the first story: she had not taken her doctor's account seriously even though it was framed in the voice of medicine. In the second story Sarah adopts this voice and speaks in its language. In sum, she accepts blame for the miscarriage, voicing the blame in the language and logic of medicine ("I had an incompetent cervix").

It is in the full version of the third story that Sarah shows how, over time, she has been able to incorporate the doctors' findings into her lifeworld. She integrates them by giving them meaning grounded in her experience and by drawing causal connections beyond the technical explanations provided by her physicians. Her reasoning is as follows: Medicine had prescribed DES to her mother. Medicine had "caused" her miscarriage (by exposing her to DES and failing to warn her of reproductive risks associated with this exposure). Thus, medical logic is fallible. Further, medical logic is not the only voice that can explain her situation.

In asides, repetitions, pauses, and elaborations in the third story, Sarah draws the events of the other two together and criticizes the actions, logic, and power of medicine. She then offers solutions, consisting of education, changed power relations between doctors and patients, and integration of two voices into understanding and responding to the risks resulting from DES exposure.

In her criticism of her doctors' actions, Sarah focuses on the way her pregnancy had been handled and refers back to the second story. She begins to shift the blame for her miscarriage from herself to medicine:

329 (inhale), well, the more I had ti- the more removed I got from what had happened to me
330 and the longer it, the more that time went by then, the angrier I got about, some of the things that happened to me,
331 um, and the, I really felt like (4)
332 the fact that I that' that I shouldn't have lost that first baby
333 and that something different should have been done (1.5)

There is some ambiguity in this section of the third story. The phrase, "I shouldn't have lost that first baby," could refer to Sarah's own sense of responsibility for the loss. She had been "blithe," had "put actively put [DES] out of [her] mind" and had not "educated" herself. Yet, in the larger context of the story, her admonition could also refer both to the first error, when DES was prescribed to her mother, and to the second, when her doctor should have known that she was at a greater risk of having a miscarriage and protected her. Medicine should have been more aware of the consequences of DES exposure, then and now: "something different should have been done."

Next, Sarah refers back to the first story, and criticizes the logic of medicine:

341   you know and and the the little things along the way
342   like not being, like being advised, to take the pill (1)
343   that it most likely wouldn't hurt me (1.5)
344   you know it's not clear whether it wouldn' or it wouldn't
345   but prudence would say, use some other method of birth control (2.5)

There has been "considerable controversy" within medicine over the "most appropriate method of contraception" for DES daughters. There are, as yet, "no data [to] indicate that any contraceptive method carries a risk of ill effects among DES-exposed women greater than the risk in the unexposed population" (Noller, Townsend, & Kaufman, 1981, p. 95). According to the logic of science, it is appropriate to prescribe birth control pills to DES daughters. Sarah's physician had correctly applied a body of knowledge to Sarah's individual case when he had prescribed birth control pills to her. Nevertheless, the DES Task Force recommends that use of the birth control pills "must be viewed in a prudent fashion, and the decision to use them made only after careful consideration of alternate methods, patient preference, and medical judgment" (U.S. Department of Health, Education and Welfare, 1978, p. 16). After educating herself, Sarah had learned that her physician's advice, "to take the pill (1) / that it most likely wouldn't hurt [her]" (lines 342–343), while not wrong, omitted a step. He had been imprudent; he had not, apparently, explored the use of another method of birth control. He had not given her all the information so that she could reasonably decide for herself.

Sarah's use of the word "prudence" implies that she has become familiar with the literature on DES (Dutton, 1984). In addition, without speaking of her mother, Sarah uses her mother's logic (that of the lifeworld) and argues that her physician should have used it too. He should have used common sense (prudence) instead of adhering to the logic of science (if there is no statistical evidence that birth control pills are harmful, it is safe to prescribe them). Sarah is critical of her physician's advice and the way he made it. Ironically, her debt to her mother is unnoticed and unmentioned in her account. Her mother remains silent, although her mother's logic does not.

Finally, Sarah criticizes the power of medicine. According to her, "DES women are patronized, to some extent, ... by their medical care" (lines 348, 352). They "shouldn't be" (line 350). Medicine, she implies, does not inform women or educate them about the risks associated with DES. Medicine encourages women to be "blithe" about the risks. Instead of collaborating and educating, physicians most often act as counselors or technical experts, encouraging DES women to be passive and dependent.[4]

Sarah's alternatives to these three problems involve, first, education. She would "help, obstetricians, be more aware" (line 337), so that they wouldn't, out of ignorance, prescribe dangerous medications or fail to use precautions for DES women.[5] She would inform other women of specific problems associated with DES exposure, because "there are women out there who don't know (1) / that this is a problem" (lines 353–354). She would educate herself, because she is "more interested in, being educated about [DES]" (line 362). Despite the lack of scientific evidence about problems for DES daughters later in life, she is worried:

```
365   oh w'well I'I'm fairly convinced at this point
366   that we'll have problems, a'at each, age period
368   you know if not a m'm', middle age then through menopause
370   then some, something else some problems will occur along the way
          (1.5)
```

In sum, women and their doctors should be educated about medical knowledge and the limits of this knowledge, so that they can act reasonably and prudently, now and in the future.

Beyond education, however, changing the power relationships between doctors and patients is another alternative both in the present and future. Sarah wants to "help DES daughters be more assertive / and get better medical care (1.5) right away" (lines 335–336), and to help herself stay "on top of what the next step might be" (line 363). Sarah's use of pronouns in the third story (from "they" [line 305] and "these people" [line 322] to "DES daughters" [line 335] and "DES women" [line 355] and then to "we" [line 366]) underscores her connection to other women and the power embodied in this. The words with which she describes what has happened and might happen to her are no longer couched in the voice of medicine as they had been in the first two stories ("adenosis" "incompetent cervix"). Now she

---

[4] See Danziger (1981), for a discussion of different types of doctor–patient encounters during pregnancy.

[5] By being aware during the second pregnancy, her obstetrician prevented the loss of the second baby. This physician had taken a number of precautions because of Sarah's DES exposure and her "incompetent cervix." In addition, she had educated herself and found a physician who was an expert in caring for DES daughters during their pregnancies.

speaks in the voice of the lifeworld ("this is a problem" [line 354] "reproductive problems" [line 355] "problems" [line 370]). Her recommendations for change and the language that she uses in the third story express what change means in the relationship between doctors and patients: changes in thinking, doing, and speaking.

Sarah ends the third story by looking ahead to the future, by acknowledging the uncertainty and risk that lie ahead. She speaks in the voice of the lifeworld. Unlike some physicians who do not take into account the possibility of long-term consequences (Herbst & Bern, 1981), Sarah can no longer "blithely" think "that since [she] / was past the age where most people get cancer / that there was nothing more (1.5) for [her] to think about" (line 359–360). She emphasizes this point by repeating it: "I no longer can be, blithe about it, and say not me" (line 371).

For Sarah, being a DES daughter has come to mean accepting risk and uncertainty for the rest of her life. The uncertainty is not hers alone; she recognizes that it is shared by other "DES women" and shared by the medical profession too. The third story, thus, moves beyond the view of doctors as sole experts and embraces a new vision: to seek and to share the wisdom of the lifeworld alongside of the expertise and uncertainty of medicine. To accomplish this both depends upon and necessitates becoming political. For only in and through the women's health movement can the structural changes implied by Sarah's view be put into practice. Sarah, as I say in my comment at the end of the third story, has "come, full circle" (line 372).

The expanded versions of the three stories show how and why Sarah's identity changed. The stories provide a vehicle for her to tie together significant events and important relationships in her life. The stories enable her to make sense of what has happened: "to repair ruptures between body, self, and world by linking up and interpreting different aspects of [her] biography in order to realign present and past and self with society" (Williams, 1984, p. 197). Analyzing them enables us to see how she has come to understand and interpret the difficult experiences of her life.

DISCUSSION

In sum, for Sarah, these three linked stories show both how and why she became politicized, and what being political means to her. Sarah has accounted for her experiences through linked stories. Analysis of these stories has shown how she has come to terms with DES exposure, miscarriage, and the ever-present risk of cancer. The method of analysis preserves the structure she uses. By focusing on the core narratives and then the full versions of the stories, I have shown how this woman has responded to and coped with her DES exposure over time. Different aspects of the stories shed light on different aspects of her life; together the stories help us to understand her evolving political self.

First, Sarah shows that before she had problems, DES had no meaning for her. Following her experience of problems during pregnancy (losing the baby), she accepted her identity as a DES daughter; this acceptance depended upon understanding how DES had contributed to her difficulties. The combination of medical knowledge and life experience enabled her to accept this identity. Over time, however, she began to see more than this; her problem involved more than losing the baby. Multiple problems appeared. The loss could have been prevented; DES should not have been prescribed to her mother, and more than that, her physician should have known that she was at risk of a miscarriage, and prevented it. Furthermore, she should not have been prescribed birth control pills; according to the logic of common sense, they are contra-indicated for DES daughters. With this expanded vision, she is able to see that her problems are shared by other DES daughters and that the solution to them lies beyond the behaviors of individual doctors and patients. Her insight led her to join DES Action and become political. In this women's health group, she can become educated, staying on top of the situation, as well as educate physicians and DES women; and she can work to change the power relations between doctors and patients so that women will neither be patronized by medicine nor harmed by it. Membership in DES Action will, moreover, help her to deal with the future, by providing her with support and with information about the effects of DES at each age period. For Sarah, becoming political means balancing the voice of medicine with the voice of the life-world. Becoming a politically active member of the women's health movement means accepting the possibility of DES-related problems for the rest of her life.

Ironically, Sarah, like other DES daughters, must seek information and care from medicine, which is also a source of her difficulties. She has learned to respond to this irony in a collective fashion, instead of as an individual. Unlike many DES daughters, she has become politically active. The women's health movement offers a constructive alternative for her. It recognizes the need for medical services, but also the need for change in the system that organizes and provides these services. For this DES daughter, integrating risk and uncertainty has involved, over time, grief, anger and guilt, similar to patterns reported in psychological studies of DES (Apfel & Fisher, 1984). Rather than becoming overwhelmed and isolated by her experiences, however, she has directed her energies toward political change. Probably she will continue to need medical care for DES-related problems; realistically, she can join with other women to ensure that this care is offered and received prudently.

REFERENCES

Apfel, R. J., & Fisher, S. M. (1984). *To Do No Harm: DES and the Dilemmas of Modern Medicine*. New Haven: Yale University Press.

Bell, S. E. (1985). Narratives of health and illness: DES daughters tell stories. Paper presented at Sociologists for Women in Society Annual Meetings, Washington, D.C.

Coalition for the Medical Rights of Women. (1978, August). *Coalition News*.

Coalition for the Medical Rights of Women. (1980). *The Rock Will Wear Away*, San Francisco: Author.

Danziger, S. K. (1981). The uses of expertise in doctor–patient encounters during pregnancy. In P. Conrad & R. Kern (Eds.), *The Sociology of Health and Illness*. New York: St. Martin's.

DES Action Voice, Available from DES Action National, 1638B Haight Street, San Francisco, California 94117.

Dutton, D. (1984). The impact of public participation in biomedical policy: Evidence from four case studies. In J. C. Petersen (Ed.), *Citizen Participation in Science Policy*. Amherst, MA: University of Massachusetts.

Fox, H. A. (1983). The incompetent cervix: words that can hurt (letter). *American Journal of Obstetrics and Gynecology, 147,* 462–463.

Gee, J. P. (1985). The narrativization of experience in the oral style. *Journal of Education, 167,* 9–31.

Herbst, A. L., & Bern, H. A. (Eds.). (1981). *Developmental Effects of Diethylstilbestrol (DES) in Pregnancy*. New York: Thieme-Stratton.

Labov, W. (1972). The transformation of experience in narrative syntax. In W. Labov (Ed.), *Language in the Inner City*. Philadelphia: University of Pennsylvania Press.

Labov, W. (1982). Speech actions and reactions in personal narrative. In D. Tannen (Ed.), *Analyzing Discourse: Text and Talk*. Washington, D.C.: Georgetown University Press.

Mandler, J. M. (1984). *Stories, Scripts and Scenes: Aspects of Schema Theory*. Hillsdale, N.J.: Lawrence Erlbaum Associates.

Mandler, J. M., & Johnson, N. S. (1977). Remembrance of things parsed: Story structure and recall. *Cognitive Psychology, 9,* 111–151.

Merton, R. K., Fiske, M., & Kendall, P. L. (1956). *The Focused Interview: A Manual of Problems and Procedures*. Glencoe, Ill: The Free Press.

Meyer-Bahlburg, H. F. L., & Ehrhardt, A. A. (1985). A prenatal-hormone hypothesis for depression in adults with a history of fetal DES exposure. In U. Halbreich and D. M. Rose (Eds.), *Hormones and Depression*. New York: Raven Press.

Meyer-Bahlburg, H. F. L., Ehrhardt, A. A., Endicott, J., Veridiano, N. P., Whitehead, E. D., & Vann, F. H. (1985a). Depression in adults with a history of prenatal DES exposure. *Psychopharmacology Bulletin, 21,* 686–689.

Meyer-Bahlburg, H. F. L., Ehrhardt, A. A., Feldman, J. F., Rosen, L. R., Veridiano, N. P., & Zimmerman, I. (1985b). Sexual activity level and sexual functioning in women prenatally exposed to diethylstilbestrol. *Psychosomatic Medicine, 47.*

Michaels, S. (1981). 'Sharing time': Children's narrative styles and differential access to literacy. *Language in Society, 10,* 423–442.

Mishler, E. G. (1981). Viewpoint: Critical perspectives on the biomedical model. In E. G. Mishler, L. R. AmaraSingham, S. T. Hauser, R. Liem, S. D. Osherson, & N. E. Waxler (Eds.), *Social Contexts of Health, Illness, and Patient Care*. New York: Cambridge University Press.

Mishler, E. G. (1984). *The Discourse of Medicine: Dialectics of Medical Interviews*. Norwood, N.J.: Ablex Publishing.

Mishler, E. G. (1986a). The analysis of interview narratives. In T. R. Sarbin (Ed.), *Narrative Psychology: The Storied Nature of Human Conduct*. New York: Praeger.

Mishler, E. G. (1986b). *Research Interviewing: Context and Narrative*. Cambridge, MA: Harvard University Press.

Mitchell, W. J. T. (Ed.) (1980, 1981). *On Narrative*. Chicago: University of Chicago Press.

Noller, K. L., Townsend, D., & Kaufman, R. H. (1981). Genital findings, colposcopic evaluation, and current management of the diethylstilbestrol-exposed female. In A. Herbst & H. Bern (Eds.), *Developmental Effects of Diethylstilbestrol (DES) in Pregnancy*. New York: Thieme-Stratton.

Paget, M. A. (1982). Your son is cured now; you may take him home. *Culture, Medicine, and Psychiatry, 6,* 237–259.

Paget, M. A. (1983). Experience and knowledge. *Human Studies, 6,* 67–90.

Polanyi, L. (1981). What stories can tell us about their teller's world. *Poetics Today, 2,* 97–112.

Ruzek, S. B. (1979). *The Women's Health Movement*. New York: Praeger.

Schwartz, R. W., & Stewart, N. B. (1977). Psychological effects of DES exposure. *Journal of the American Medical Association, 237,* 252–254.

Scott, M. B., & Lyman, S. M. (1968). "Accounts." *American Sociological Review 33,* 46–62.

U. S. Department of Health, Education and Welfare. (1978). *DES Task Force Summary Report*. DHEW Publication No. (NIH) 79-1688.

Vessey, M. P., Fairweather, D. V. J., Norman-Smith, R., & Buckley, J. (1983). A randomized double-blind controlled trial of the value of stilboestrol therapy in pregnancy: Long-term follow-up of mothers and their offspring. *British Journal of Obstetrics and Gynecology, 90,* 1007–1017.

Williams, G. (1984). The genesis of chronic illness: narrative reconstruction. *Sociology of Health and Illness, 6,* 175–200.

CHAPTER 4

Ideology as Process: Gender Ideology in Courtship Narratives*

Sandra Silberstein

University of Washington

INTRODUCTION

> Customs of courtship vary greatly in different times and places, but the way the thing happens to be done here and now always seems the only natural way to do it.
>
> Herman Wouk, *Marjorie Morningstar*

Courtship patterns embody social relations fundamental to any culture. Kinship, gender, sexual practices, for example, are maintained through the institutions of courtship. Courtship storytelling displays speakers' membership in a community, their understanding of, and interaction with, these institutions. Accordingly, these stories provide striking examples of belief systems in process. With each (re)telling, these tales (re)create the world as it must be. Though always changing, the power of ideology is its capacity to represent cultural reality as natural.

This paper is about heterosexual courtship stories. It documents the complex, sometimes contradictory, ways in which speakers use

* I am most fundamentally indebted to the Blum/Meyer, McCloud/Brooks families for sharing life stories in the oral history project which provided the data for this study. I am grateful to the following friends and colleagues for discussions of the issues raised in this paper and/or for comments on previous drafts: Marcia Barton, Howard Brick, Douglas N. Brown, Sue Fisher, Anne Gere, Janis Butler Holm, Charlotte Linde, Alexandra Todd, Sharon Veach, and Evan Watkins. I am also indebted for many hours of discussion in feminist theory colloquia at the University of Michigan and the University of Washington. While this paper benefits from these associations, my colleagues and friends are, of course, unindictable for its shortcomings.

language to create and present themselves as gendered parties within institutions of courtship. I will argue that these stories evince an ideological process which creates and maintains gender as a social category.

The issue of ideology is central to those interested in the reproduction of gender. Every society develops a sex/gender system in which the fact of biological sex differences is invested with culturally determinate signification. Biological sex becomes socially constructed gender (Rubin, 1975). Ideological processes are necessary to gendered social relations.

For the purposes of this discussion I take the following to be axiomatic.[1] First, social relations exist in historically determinate times and places. The data I will be discussing, for example, comprises courtship stories told by white middle-class Americans of three generations. The structure of pressures and limits that channel these stories are historically specific. Second, I assume that social relations among cultural groups are never static; accordingly, ideology is always in process. The ideological categories of man and woman must be continually recreated. As Michele Barrett (1980) puts it, "ideology is a generic term for the processes by which meaning is produced, challenged, reproduced, transformed" (p. 97). Ideology is a complex phenomenon, a process through which cultural meanings and values are (re)produced.

Raymond Williams (1977) uses Gramsci's concept of *hegemony* to describe the process by which certain values and relations maintain dominance within a culture. Hegemony refers to the entire social process in which lived identities and relationships are saturated by dominant meanings and values. It is precisely this saturation of relations that feminist activists and scholars have sought to describe. In the early days of the modern Women's Movement, for example, Judy Syfers (1971) satirized what she took to be the dominant culture's view of women in marriage. In "I Want a Wife," women's subordination is presented as a natural element in every aspect of the marital relationship:

> I want a wife who will not bother me with rambling complaints about a wife's duties. But I want a wife who will listen to me when I feel the need to explain a rather difficult point I have come across in my

---

[1] The following discussion of ideology and hegemony is most heavily informed by the cultural theory of Raymond Williams (1977). Additional direct influences include L. Althusser (1971), K. Belsy (1980), M. Barrett (1980), T. Eagleton (1976), A. Gramsci (1929–1935/1971), and V. N. Vološinov ([1930] 1973).

course of studies. . . . I want a wife who is sensitive to my sexual needs, a wife who makes love passionately and eagerly when I feel like it, a wife who makes sure that I am satisfied. And, *of course,* I want a wife who will not demand sexual attention when I am not in the mood for it. . . . If, by chance I find another person more suitable as a wife than the wife I already have, I want the liberty to replace my present wife with another one. *Naturally,* I will expect a fresh, new life; my wife will take the children and be solely responsible for them so that I am left free. [Emphasis added.]

As illustrated by the Syfers piece, a lived hegemony is "continually resisted, limited, altered, challenged by pressures not at all its own" (Williams, 1977, p. 112). The hegemonic is not simply a static body of ideas to which members of a culture are obliged to conform. Rather, it requires a protean nature in which dominant relations are preserved while their manifestations remain highly flexible. The hegemonic must continually evolve so as to recuperate alternative hegemonies.[2] Individual members of a culture must come to actively identify with and reformulate dominant ideals. It is this ideological work—renewing, recreating, defining, and modifying the hegemonic—which is evident in courtship narratives.

THE DATA

From the point of view of data collection, courtship stories are particularly felicitous. Almost every adult has one, if only about a failed courtship. And the oral history interview proves a fertile context for collecting courtship narratives. As Linde (in press) points out, the interview technique is especially useful in eliciting types of speech sufficiently particular that one cannot simply wait for them to occur.

The stories discussed here were elicited in the course of oral histo-

---

[2] Barrett (1980) uses *recuperation* to refer to the "ideological effort that goes into negating and defusing challenges to the historically dominant meaning of gender in particular periods" (p. 111). Williams (1977) refers to hegemonic challenges as both *alternative* and *oppositional.* Oppositional hegemonies are easily recuperable as they exist still within the context of the hegemonic. Truly alternative hegemonies can themselves become hegemonic. Williams notes that in areas that impinge on significant areas of the dominant, there is strong pressure to convert the alternative to the oppositional. "I Want a Wife" illustrates this process of recuperation. Once a radical piece taught only in Women's Studies courses, its challenge has been defused through many anthologizings in college rhetoric texts. Once a potential challenge to the hegemonic, this piece has been rendered simply another example of expository prose. (See, for example, Kirszner and Mandell, 1986.)

ry interviews with each of 15 members of two multi-generational families. (Family trees for these six men and eight women will be found in the Appendix.) Each family consisted of a first-generation[3] widow (maternal grandmothers, Mrs. Blum and Mrs. McCloud), a second-generation couple, and a number of adult grandchildren and their partners.[4] My entree into each family was as a friend of a third-generation member; I conducted the interviews as a houseguest. While participants agreed to contribute to an oral history study, they did not understand its topic to be storytelling *per se*. Interviews touched on a wide range of topics, but, in each case, narrators described how they met and came to marry or live with their partners. In addition, interviewees were asked to relate, as best they could, their parents' and, in the case of the third generation, their grandparents' courtship stories. These narratives—personal courtship stories and those of progenitors—comprise the data examined here.

IDEOLOGY AS PROCESS: CHANGING IDEOLOGIES CONCERNING THE ROLE OF WOMEN

For those interested in the study of gender, it is tempting to imagine courtship stories as documentation of the gendered experiences of women and men. Certainly this is true to some extent. The institu-

---

[3] Generations have been designated first through third, with the oldest first. The term "first generation" should not be mistaken to mean first generation in this country, although this is true in Mrs. Blum's case. At the time of the interviews, first-generation narrators were over 70 years of age; second-generation narrators were aged 50–60; and third-generation narrators were aged 20–30. While all of these heterosexual partnerships were of at least four years duration, not all of the third generation couples were married.

[4] The families are quite similar except with respect to ethnicity. The Blum/Meyers are Jewish; the McCloud/Brooks are white Anglo-Saxon Protestants. The first-generation women each left college to marry their husbands, now deceased. Neither woman worked while she raised a family. The Blums had two daughters, the McClouds had three. The men did relatively well and left their wives comfortable in their old age. The women regularly visit their daughters almost all of whom live in different states.

The second-generation women both finished college. Both left the workforce in order to marry their husbands, both of whom had been in the service during the Second World War. These women raised families in the upper- middle-class suburbs which grew up after the war. Each woman had the same number of children as her mother. Each woman returned to the workforce "when the children were older."

All of the third-generation narrators completed college. Three of the five attended graduate school. One male from each family attended a highly ranked business school. One member of each family attended the University of Michigan where we became friends.

tions of courtship and bonding are fundamental to maintaining gendered social structures. Nonetheless, it would be difficult to know on what level oral narratives can be taken as documentary. History, including personal history, is created by narrative just as it documents it. Thus, we must assume that courtship narratives tell us, not necessarily "what happened" but rather what our speakers take to be narratively appropriate discussions of courtship. Most important, narrators' stated motives for their actions will be taken, not as statements about psychological reality, but as articulations within shared ideologies, or, to use C. Wright Mills' (1940) terminology, articulations of a shared "vocabulary of motive" with which communities of people explain their actions to each other.

In his article, "Situated Actions and the Vocabulary of Motive," Mills argues that motives do not exist "in" an individual, but rather "are the terms with which interpretation of conduct by social actors proceeds" (p. 355). So powerful is the need to conform to a shared vocabulary of motive, Mills points out, that people will actually refrain from doing something if they cannot locate a reason for it in their vocabulary of motive. Thus, the articulation of motives must be seen as a socially-determined phenomenon which tells us something of how social beings create mutually acceptable interpretations.[5] Though always in process, vocabularies of motive are, at any given point, conventionalized. This model does not deny individual agency, either in decision making or in text building. Rather, what is suggested is that, in order to be a member of a human community, one must describe one's actions in a fashion that displays that membership. Conventions ratify a point of view and render texts intelligible.

The data analyzed here present articulations within the vocabulary of motive of the courtship narrative. Across generations the most dramatic changes in that vocabulary of motive are seen in women's descriptions of their courtship decisions. These changes correspond to the evolution of 20th century ideologies concerning women's roles. (Note that we refer to middle-class ideologies, which correspond to the socioeconomic class of our narrators.) By documenting an ideological evolution, these narratives demonstrate ideology as process.

---

[5] Although his most proximate influence is Karl Mannheim, and Mills (1940) is professedly critical of Marxism in this essay, his formulation comes close to Marx and Engels' critique of ideology (*The German Ideology,* 1848/1947). In the course of a critical analysis of the practice of history, they warn that the ideas and conceptions of people about their actions should not be taken as the "sole determining, active force, which controls and determines their practice" (p. 30). Instead, they suggest that people articulate as motives the illusions of a particular epoch.

The similarities among narrators of the same generation reveal courtship storytelling as conventionalized.

The First-Generation Women

> [It] was the greatest love story that ever was written. I mean, ah, I adored him and he adored me and we had two beautiful children and a very good family life.
>
> Mrs. Blum

> Went one year to Kansas, [then to] Missoura. And, ah, met a lawyer . . . fell in love with him and married him.
>
> Mrs. McCloud

For the first-generation women, Mrs. Blum and Mrs. McCloud, husbands and families are described as the center of their lives. Neither woman expresses conflict over her decision to leave college before graduation in order to marry. Both women had small families, and neither woman worked for pay while raising them.

These descriptions show a striking correspondence to the feminine ideal portrayed to the middle classes of the 1920s and '30s—the decades in which Mrs. Blum and Mrs. McCloud were courting and raising children. The ideology is well-documented by contemporary scholars such as Barbara Ehrenreich and Deidre English (1978), and Ruth Schwartz Cowan (1976).

In her article "Two Washes in the Morning and a Bridge Party at Night: The American Housewife Between the Wars," Cowan argues that, contrary to popular notions, the "feminine mystique"—a middle-class ideal which centered women's lives on home and family—was not born in the baby boom of the 1950s. Rather, the concept was created in the context of the developing household technology which served increasingly servantless households of the 1920s and '30s.[6] Cowan uncovers the dominant ideology of these decades by examining the nonfiction sections of women's magazines. She explains:

> That mystique, like any system of cultural norms, was a complex and subtle affair, continuous with previous ideologies, yet clearly different from them. The mystique makers of the '20s and '30s believed that women were purely domestic creatures, that the goal of each normal woman's life was the acquisition of a husband, a family and a home, that women who worked outside their homes did so only under duress or because they were "odd" (for which read "ugly," "frustrated,"

---

[6] Ehrenreich and English (1978) make essentially the same point documenting the antecedents of this ideology at the turn of the century.

"compulsive," or "single.") and that this state of affairs was sanctioned by the tenets of religion, biology, psychology and patriotism (p. 148).

The modern housewife of the 1920s was "fairly well educated. . . . Her family was smaller than her mother's but more attention was lavished upon it" (p. 156). As Mrs. Blum reports, "In those days being a career woman was not considered the same as it is today."

This ideology, born when Mrs. Blum and Mrs. McCloud were young women, became more pervasive during the 1950s, when their daughters, Ellen Blum Meyer and Kay McCloud Brooks, were raising families. Cowan notes that,

> before that, it was a social ideology to which only the middle classes— perhaps only the upper middle classes—could possibly pretend. But the ideologies of the upper middle classes eventually percolate down to everyone else in our society and I would venture to guess that that is precisely what happened to the feminine mystique in the late '40s and '50s (p. 156).

As we trace the changing vocabularies of motive of the women I interviewed from three generations, we see interactions between two 20th century ideologies about women. We see first the feminine mystique described by Cowan. Then we see the impact of the second wave of the Women's Movement which surfaced in the 1960s.

Stories told by first-generation narrators require no justification for life choices made. The women completed raising their families during a period of some ideological consistency. Like the women in Cowan's magazines, they have small families, for whom they give up school and work. Brief summary should be enough to evoke all that we should know about this life: "Went one year to Kansas, [then to] Missoura. And, ah, met a lawyer . . . fell in love with him and married him."

In contrast, the stories of the second- and third-generation women acknowledge the ideals of the Women's Movement. The status of this potentially alternative or oppositional hegemony is the focus of the following two subsections. While the interaction of the hegemonic with the Women's Movement is still in process, the myth of the "superwoman" suggests that the hegemonic has had to find expression in new forms in order to maintain dominance. Courtship narratives from the second two generations exhibit an ideological process which has as its raw material a changing hegemonic and an oppositional ideology. Within these two generations we find different conventionalized solutions to this potential conflict.

The Second-Generation Women

> I had, ah, planned to go to graduate school. That's one of the reasons I was in the Navy. I had to pay off all the loans and debts that I had incurred when I was in school. And, um, it also was going to offer me educational opportunities. [Interviewer: The G.I. Bill.] Yeah, so . . . I was pointing toward that and I really was not, really did not expect to, ah, be diverted. . . . Eventually I decided that perhaps being diverted was something I was willing to be.
>
> Kay McCloud Brooks

> Many of my friends had gone to college to- to kill time or to look for husbands. I mean, that- that that never was considered, I mean I went to college, I intended to get a degree. So . . . I told him I couldn't even think about [his proposal], and I sent him home with the ring. And then I woke my parents up, and I thought about it, and I called him at seven o'clock in the morning and we were engaged that day.
>
> Ellen Blum Meyer

In the stories of the second-generation women, we begin to find conflict between public and private sphere participation. These women's stories are particularly interesting as they survey lives which span a significant ideological evolution. The women made life choices in the 1950s when the feminine mystique was strongest. They do not in any way imply that they regret the choices they made to place their families first. At the same time, the Women's Movement of the past 15 years has provided another vocabulary of motive which these women incorporate into their stories. Particularly when speaking with a younger female interviewer, second-generation women cite motives consistent with a developing feminist consciousness. Both of these ideologies are apparent when the second-generation women speak about their educational goals and workforce participation.

In her interview, Ellen Blum Meyer goes out of her way to tell me how important her college education was to her. When her husband proposed during the winter of her senior year, she couldn't think about his proposal, as she felt that any interpersonal turmoil might sabotage her academic performance. She emphasizes that, unlike many young women, she had not gone to college to find a husband; she had gone to get a degree. Within a day, however, she had accepted his proposal.

Kay McCloud Brooks tells a similar story. She stresses that she had joined the Navy so that the G.I. Bill might put her through graduate school. Her decision to accept Ed Brooks' marriage proposal was a decision for diversion. Both women, then, use the ideas of the current Women's Movement to stress the importance of education in their lives. It is the ideology born between the wars and flourishing in the 1950s that explains those decisions which place husband or family at the center of one's life.

This pattern is repeated when these women discuss their workforce participation. Elsewhere in our interview, Ellen Blum Meyer talks about her entry into the workforce in the 1950s. It seems that it took several years after her marriage for her to persuade her husband that it was proper for her to work. She notes that her college friends in the East were already working but that this did not yet seem appropriate in the Midwest. Ellen loved her first job but decided to give it up to help her husband in his business:

> It was a very hard decision for me to make because I had some identity and I was getting a lot of psychic income. . . . It was one of the few [part-time] jobs in retailing where you have some status. . . . So it was a very difficult decision for me to make. But I finally decided that our future was with his career.

Kay McCloud Brooks also gives up some options in the public sphere by putting family welfare first. In deciding to marry Ed Brooks, she postponed not only her graduate education but an academic career. For a good many years, raising three sons was a full-time job. In private conversations, I have found Kay to use the vocabulary of the Women's Movement when she speaks about academia. Decisions to be diverted rely on an earlier ideological perspective.

To be sure, both women have raised families they are proud of. And both women now have satisfying, remunerative work. What is significant here is that in similar ways Ellen and Kay provide reasons for their decisions which make some accommodation to a feminist vocabulary of motive. In so doing, they display and recreate the existence of dual ideologies.

The Third-Generation Women

> I actually did go up to Minneapolis . . . and had an interview . . . I wanted to have a job. I probably wouldn't have moved, I probably wouldn't have gotten married to him, if I hadn't had a job.
>
> Jean Meyer

> So I got both degrees . . . Bowling Green was one of the places that offered it and I didn't want to stay at Youngstown. It was either Miami or Bowling Green, but Miami really didn't have the program that I wanted.
>
> Linda Pierce Meyer

I unfortunately had decided that I wouldn't ever go out with a man again or get involved with one, even though he seemed really quite promising.

Rachel Simon

I had just moved to the San Francisco Bay area, had ah, had a new job, was very excited about being in a new place and establishing new contacts and new friends and quite frankly we were both very independent people, and neither of us had any desire at that point to try and solidify the relationship.

Laurel Williams

I just didn't want to get into another kind of unsatisfactory relationship cause I was just feeling very good about being on my own.

Colleen Simpson

In contrast to Ellen Meyer and Kay Brooks, aspects of feminist ideology are central to the vocabularies of motive of third-generation women. Each of these women stresses the choosing of a partner as consistent with, rather than a diversion from, her own goals. Ellen Meyer's daughter, Jean, asserts that she would not have married her (now ex-) husband and followed him to another city had she not received a job offer there in her field. Ellen Meyer's daughter-in-law, Linda Pierce Meyer, asserts that she decided to attend Bowling Green University, where her high school sweetheart Dan Meyer was already enrolled, because it was the only school in the geographical area which offered the program she wanted. Similarly the female partners of Kay Brooks' sons all assert they were independent and had fully-developed public-sphere identities at the time that they elected to share their lives with Jesse, Wyatt, and Matt Brooks.

In these stories we see the accommodation of a potentially alternative or oppositional hegemony. Each speaker participates in an ideological process in which a potentially radical ideology transforms a traditional story form: the courtship narrative. These stories by themselves do not allow us to judge these lives as fundamentally either radical or traditional. And these are lives still in process. By rendering these stories in the past tense, however, lives in process become finished products—products which are conventionalized even as they evince an ideological process. Lives and ideology in process seek mutually intelligible discourse.

IDEOLOGY AS PROCESS: UNCHANGING IDEOLOGIES CONCERNING THE ROLE OF MEN

Across generations, women's stories change to accommodate evolving perspectives on the role of women. One might expect a similar evolution as male storytellers accommodate changing perspectives on women and men. Interestingly, none of the men I interviewed spoke to these issues. Perhaps this should not surprise us.

First, men did not discuss women's changing roles. Presumably these middle-class men have been less affected by these changes than have their female partners. Men's structural position in these families has remained fundamentally unchanged. Second-generation men have been primary breadwinners while women stayed home to raise children. Women's later incomes provide opportunities for travel and a more secure retirement, but they do not threaten a lifetime of male economic dominance.

Like their fathers and grandfathers, the third-generation men can expect their earnings to substantially exceed those of their partners. Without comparable pay and affordable day care, women's economic dependence will be exacerbated by motherhood. Employed mothers tend to work a "double day" combining paid labor with provision of personal services in the home. To the extent that men's expectations of personal services are only slightly modified by women's paid employment, three generations of men may speak of their lives in very similar ways even as women find their roles substantially changed.

It is noteworthy, however, that none of the third-generation couples had children at the time of these interviews. Unlike the women who had already confronted competing ideologies concerning work and marriage, the men had yet to feel any concrete impact of a changing ideology concerning women's roles. The men may experience conflicts in the future when their spouses, then tired mothers, demand male private-sphere participation consistent with an emerging ideology. At this stage, however, the issue of women's changing roles is absent from these men's courtship narratives.

Although men's stories ignore changing female roles, one might have expected male storytellers across generations to reflect on changing male roles. In *The Hearts of Men: American Dreams and the Flight From Commitment,* Barbara Ehrenreich (1983) documents what she calls the collapse of the breadwinner ethic of the 1950s in favor of a male ethic of self-actualization and personal growth. According to Ehrenreich, in the 1950s

> there was a firm expectation . . . that required men to grow up, marry and support their wives. To do anything else was less than grown-up, and the man who willfully deviated was judged to be somehow "less than a man." This expectation was supported by an enormous weight of expert opinion, moral sentiment and public bias, both within popular culture and the elite centers of academic wisdom. But by the end of the 1970s and the beginning of the 1980s, adult manhood was no longer burdened with the automatic expectation of marriage and breadwinning. The man who postpones marriage, even into middle age, who

avoids women who are likely to become financial dependents, who is dedicated to his own pleasures, is likely to be found not suspiciously deviant, but "healthy" (pp. 11–12).

If we accept Ehrenreich's claim that masculinity has been redefined, we might expect to see the accommodation of competing ideologies across generations of male narrators. In fact, across generations men's narratives suggest no conflict between marriage and personal needs; moreover, we find no gender-specific shift in men's vocabulary of motive.

What we see instead in the third generation is a shift by both men and women to a self-actualized vocabulary of motive not unlike that documented by Ehrenreich. Male and female speakers structure their stories around the development of a relationship which narratively represents the fulfillment of personal needs. Narrators assure us that theirs were decisions based on compatibility and personal rapport. Six of the nine storytellers speak in terms of mutuality of decision making. Here are some examples.

When I first met him, and you know he told me what he wanted to do when he finished was . . . to be in academia. That really appealed to me in terms of the kind of lifestyle I wanted to be associated with . . . there was a bond . . . I had seen some indication of personal growth on his part.

Jean Meyer

During the first year we realized that we were very serious about each other. . . . we knew we wanted to get married, it was a question of when. Based upon our conversation, we realized . . . this would be the time to get married.

Dan Meyer

And so we became more and more kind of political comrades and close friends over the next . . . two and a half years. . . . so that- that was a period when we really became pretty tight on the basis of working together and we really work very well together. Ah- ah our styles and our different strengths really complemented each other at that stage which is something that- that we really- ah I was certainly was certainly very delighted to discover, and I think she valued it as much as I did.

Jesse Brooks

from day one um, as of that con-concert, we really hit it off and it grew from there . . . it's gotten a hell of a lot easier than when we were trying to maintain a relationship in two separate apartments.

Wyatt Brooks

We got along very, very well from the start . . . we just realized that-that this was the time to- to challenge ourselves essentially to live together.

Laurel Williams

but eventually . . . we just ended up being you know traveling companions . . . Colleen's just really good to travel with, I mean she really ah deals well with the ah world she's ah, she's real strong. . . . [I was thinking] I don't really know whether I want to complicate this with a sexual relationship as well. . . . if I want to add that dimension on top of the relationship. . . . I happen to be traveling with someone I enjoy traveling with um and I sort of value the friendship.

Matt Brooks

during that period of time we came to trust and rely on each other so much and- and found that we were such compatible traveling companions and that it was really rewarding being together, and that it was worth whatever costs there were for both of us.

Colleen Simpson

Women alone accommodate a changing ideology concerning the role of women; both women and men adopt a new vocabulary of self-actualization. While the latter represents a change in men's stories, it does not reflect a radical ideological transformation. Women's courtship stories change in significant ways across generations as they work to accommodate alternative ideologies. Men's stories are more similar than different as they reify the fundamentals of a hegemonic discourse.

IDEOLOGY AS PROCESS: NARRATIVE DEVICES SUPPORTING THE GENDERED ROLE OF WOMEN AND MEN

The preceding discussion interrogates responses to ideological change across generations. While women's stories accommodate a radical ideological shift, men's accommodations have been more modest. In the following section, the focus is on continuity. Across generations, we find remarkable gender-based consistency in the narrative devices employed by women and men. This continuity conserves fundamental elements of sex roles and helps to maintain gender as a social category.

The Women's Story

Deciding.

When I . . . had all these proposals at one time, I didn't know which way to turn, I asked my parents and they said, "You're the one that's gonna have to live with him, you have to decide.

Esther Blum

He asked me for a date, I'll never forget, ah, Monday and Tuesday, and then I got tired of saying no and I had a date with him on Wednesday night.

Eleanor McCloud

The first I decided I decided that Charles wasn't for me, and then, that was about all I had decided, and then I had a date with Paul . . . he presented me with a ring and I- I said I couldn't even think about it. . . . and then I woke my parents up, and I thought about it, and I called him at seven o'clock in the morning and we were engaged that day.

Ellen Blum Meyer

I had ah planned to go to graduate school. . . . I was pointing toward that and I really was not really did not expect to ah be diverted. . . . But ah, you know we continued to to go to the, to the dances and ah ((clears throat)) ah eventually decided that perhaps being diverted was something I was willing to be.

Kay McCloud Brooks

that whole two-week period is like crazy. I'm like trying to figure out you know like what do, I want to do and everything. I got- we got up the next morning, Peter went into the shower and I said to him well what the hell, let's just do it.

Jean Meyer

he reports . . . putting some thought into how to orchestrate a situation where it would be clear that I could ride in the cab with him. . . . I unfortunately had- had decided that um I wouldn't ever go out with a man again or get involved with one even though he seemed really quite promising. . .

Rachel Simon

The women's task in these stories is to decide. The kinds of decisions with which women of different generations were faced were quite different. First-generation women decided whether they wanted to go out with particular men. Sometimes they decided among suitors. And, when proposed to, each decided on a response. Second-generation women presumably had to decide how they felt about suitors, but they also had to decide the extent to which courting would interfere with their charted paths. In the third generation, the task of the women is to determine their relationship to men and to commitment. Whether the man is an aggressive suitor or a supplicant swain, the woman must decide. Sometimes the decisions are cited as being mutual; nonetheless, the woman must decide. In no story does a woman both initiate and orchestrate a relationship; in no story are the men described as reactive. Men are active. Sometimes women are active for periods, but, in the end, the need to decide—to react— defines the female story.

To be sure, it is not the case that women of any generation saw themselves as passive. They made their decisions actively, sometimes humorously or aggressively. Mrs. McCloud, at one point tells her Henry, "No you can't have any date; I haven't time for you." And Mrs. Blum must choose among five proposals.

In fact, the women stress their nonpassivity. The women spend a good deal of time assuring us of their spunkiness (first generation), their involvement in the public sphere (second generation), or their independence (third generation). The first-generation women stress that there was some hesitancy on their parts upon first meeting their husbands. The second-generation women stress how seriously they took their educations. And the third-generation women stress what- ever initiative they took, their independence, and their commitment to having careers.

To appreciate fully the significance of these gender-specific asser- tions, imagine a man assuring us that he wasn't particularly crazy about his wife when he met her. We might think him a cad. Imagine a man stressing, "I didn't go to college to meet a wife—I went to get a degree." Or a man assuring us that he wouldn't have followed his partner to another state without a job. In the end, the women's very assertions of perogative, strength, independence, "maleness", are what mark them as women.

Impression management: seeking assurance. The women in these families use different impression management devices than do the men. These are devices designed to control the impression of oneself that other participants will take away from a social interaction. While every social exchange can be said to involve impression man- agement—Clint Eastwood's silence can be as successful a tool as any other—these women employ devices not very often used by the men.

Women make explicit statements as to the kind of people they are.

I was a very conscientious person . . . and very sensitive and it both- ered me.

Esther Blum

Many of my friends had gone to college to- to kill time or look for husbands. I mean that- that that never was considered, I mean I went to college, I intended to get a degree.

Ellen Blum Meyer

I had just moved to the San Francisco Bay area, and ah, had a new job, was very excited about being in a new place and establishing new contacts and new friends and quite frankly we were both very independent people, and neither of us had any desire to try and solidify the relationship.

Laurel Williams

I just didn't want to get into another kind of unsatisfactory relationship because I was just feeling very good about being on my own.

Colleen Simpson

By and large, the women do not leave to chance the overall impression they will create. They tell the listener the kind of people they are, especially with respect to those issues about which they particularly care. Mrs. Blum assures us that she is a conscientious person and, elsewhere in our interview, refers to the difference between right and wrong which motivates her decisions. Mrs. Blum mentions several times that her behavior conformed to her moral code. The second-generation women tell us they are not the kind of women who take education lightly.[7] And, typical of the third generation, Wyatt Brooks' partner, Laurel Williams, assures me that she and her partner are independent people. In contrast, none of the men make explicit reference to the kind of person we are to take them to be.

Women cite opinions of others as motivation.

I said, "I'm not staying I'm leaving tomorrow." She said, "If you do," she said, "that is the meanest cruelest thing that anybody could ever do, how could you do that to such a wonderful boy?" . . . and I said ah, "I'm gonna leave." "Oh," she says "I thought I liked you when I met you, but," she says, "that is really cruel." . . . . So I called the other boy up and told him "I just can't do it. . ."

Esther Blum

---

[7] Throughout these interviews and in a pilot study with other women, I find it is the second-generation women who are anxious to tell me that they are not like other women. Remember Ellen Blum Meyer's assertion:

Many of my friends had gone to college to- to kill time or look for husbands. I mean that that that never was considered, I mean I went to college, I intended to get a degree.

Later she explains:

I generally find men easier to talk to. I ah, I think that's why I've always enjoyed working. I mean I- my forte was never the cocktail chatter.

But when Helen Rogers invited us out for dinner and she said, "Gosh," er you know the sort of standard thing, you know, "you make a nice couple," I said, "I really hadn't thought of it that way." . . . it really truly sort of changed my whole viewpoint . . .

Kay McCloud Brooks

Rather than relying on their own justifications for decisions, several women cite the opinions of others as a motivating force. Mrs. Blum cites the chastisings of another girl as her reason for not reneging on her first date with Jack Blum. Certainly, if she had not liked Jack, she would have broken her date and found another reason for her actions. Thus the decision is really hers, but the justification, or vocabulary of motive for it, is given, in part, as another's observation that she had "the best date in the house" and that she shouldn't "do that to such a wonderful boy." Similarly, Kay McCloud Brooks tells us that another woman's observation that she and Ed Brooks made a nice couple, "really, truly changed [her] whole viewpoint." And third-generation Linda Pierce Meyer explains that she did not want to cohabit without being married because she didn't know what her parents would think.

Women use moral content. The Blum/Meyer women in particular rely on a sense of right and wrong as a vocabulary of motive. Elsewhere in her interview, Mrs. Blum tells me,

If I had the power to influence children today . . . I would wanna teach 'em the basic principles and the difference between right and wrong. . .

Ellen Blum Meyer explains her unwillingness to risk sabotaging her academic performance in terms of her obligation to her parents: "My parents had sacrificed to send me to college." Her daughter, Jean Meyer, expresses a kind of moral indignation when speaking privately of the behavior of her ex-husband before they were divorced. Morality and obligation to family figure heavily in the stories of Blum/Meyer women.

The Men's Story

Orchestration.

I saw Ellen at a party and ah, you know, it was just like a chemical reaction occurs, and I felt that, wow, look at that girl. I'm gonna have this girl. . .

Paul Meyer

I'd actually proposed to her during the year but it was, to me, even though the proposal was there, the definite commitment to marriage wasn't cause I hadn't given her a ring.

Dan Meyer

Obviously the next move was mine and I had to figure out how to make this thing work, and I had to orchestrate something. . .

Jesse Brooks

So I followed up by going to see her at her office which was in the Public Inquiries Office um after I'd done some polite snooping to make sure that this wasn't somebody that my friend Dave Golden was in the process of taking out. Turned out not to be the case . . . so that left me wide open.

Wyatt Brooks

For that reason, you know, I was just not . . . ready to jump in with . . . anyone to travel with and I was going to be quite honestly rather particular, more particular about any woman I was going to travel with.

Matt Brooks

By and large, male stories are full of orchestration and male prerogative. Although women's narratives contain isolated instances of female assertiveness, we have no example of a woman orchestrating an entire relationship. We have many such instances in male stories. In fact, half of the men's stories involve some competition or conquest. It was in this context of male conquest or prerogative that women of all generations described their task as having to make a decision.

It is also in this context of conquest that we find the concept of gentlemanly rivalry for control of women. Second-generation Paul Meyer says of a potential competitor, "She came to the party with another gentleman . . . and I took her home." Third-generation Wyatt Brooks refers to "a gentleman by the name of Dave Golden," who invited him to the party at which he met Laurel Williams. Behaving like a gentleman himself, Wyatt "did some polite snooping to make sure that [Laurel] wasn't somebody that my friend Dave Golden was in the process of taking out." In both instances, male competition for the women is the context in which the concept of the gentleman is evoked.

In these stories, conquest is achieved through pursuit:

I went to put my arm around her, she jumped out the side of the car. . . . and then I met her [again] at this party and the chemistry took hold and

I pursued it from that point on. I was determined I was going to marry this girl.

Paul Meyer

She was . . . not nearly so interested and I was really very puzzled . . . and I said to myself . . . now you're really gonna have to figure out how to make this thing work.

Jesse Brooks

So that left me wide open. . . . I invited her to- for Thanksgiving dinner ah which she turned me down, she had other plans, but ah that was enough momentum. . .

Wyatt Brooks

We'd whistled at her, my roommate and I and caused her to go clipping down the street, ignoring us. . .

Ed Brooks

Initial rejection on the part of the women is not uncommon in these stories, providing an extra sweetness to male conquest. In fact, dating, like sports, is among the contexts our society provides for young men to learn to bear (occasional) instances of rejection and defeat. For this reason, and because of their eventual success, the men don't seem to mind sharing the fact that an initial date was turned down or that they overcame substantial misgivings on the part of the women. In first-generation women's stories, reporting initial misgivings on their part seems to be obligatory. In male stories, such reporting enhances their eventual success.

Reconstruction. While men's narratives illustrate their role in orchestrating a relationship, male storytellers are less certain about the details of courtship than are the women. Paul Meyer and his son Dan are both uncertain as to exactly which were their first dates. Ed Brooks is not sure how long he and Kay were engaged before they were married. And his son Matt Brooks is not sure exactly when and where he and his partner first made love. Uncertainty seems to be a male script. The result is that almost all the male narratives involve some reconstruction of what "must have" happened.

Jesse Brooks:
And then she came over here, then I think she came back there later and got me or something, but- or I was gonna drop by later, or something, in any event. . .

Matt Brooks:
We traveled for well ((sigh)) we must have left Caroico/Lapaz way some time around September, and I don't think, we didn't make love

for the first, it- think it was maybe in- It was in Paraguay which was probably end of October, maybe Novemberish.

Dan Meyer [phrases end with non-final rising intonation]:
I think I found her in the stand, and went up and sat with her, and then I- I think we went out to eat somewhere and there was, I had to give somebody else a ride home, so all three of us sat in the front seat, and I dropped somebody else off, and I- I don't remember, I think she may have. . .

Men are also far less certain of their parents' and grandparents' courtships, and these stories are a good deal shorter than those offered by the women. This uncertainty reinforces the impression that courtship stories are not a male domain. In fact, where possible, the men turn a courtship story into something else. Wyatt Brooks' courtship narrative follows the progression of a business deal, while Matt Brooks' story is a travel narrative. Their father, Ed Brooks, does not tell a story at all when asked how he met Kay McCloud Brooks. He volunteers little else but that they were introduced by friends. When I asked how long it was between the time they first went out and the time they were married, he responded, "Oh, I don't remember, I suppose ah, a year, year and a half, now Kay would be able to remember, I can't."

Impression management: male assurance. A colleague of mine notes what she calls the "assurance of audience" which she feels characterizes the male narratives in these families.[8] While her reaction was certainly subjective, I do not believe it to be idiosyncratic.

The Table indicates that the men speak more slowly than do the women, i.e. produce fewer words per minute. This is particularly significant as the number of fillers per minute—utterances such as *ah, um, oh*—is almost the same for both men and women. Since these fillers are accounted for in the calculation of words per minute, we discover that men not only speak more slowly but also produce more pauses. In part, then, male "assurance of audience" is created by their apparent assumption that a slower delivery with more pauses will not make them vulnerable to interruption—an assumption that seems to be correct.

Average Number of Words and Fillers per Minute

	Number of Words	Number of Fillers
Women	166	8.5
Men	135	8.6

[8] I thank Janis Butler Holm for this observation.

In two instances, the choice of vocabulary of motive helps to create an assured storyteller. Two of the men assert the logic or reasonableness of their decisions. Dan Meyer says, "It was somewhat of a logical decision" while Wyatt Brooks assures us that he made his decision on the basis of the fact that he and Laurel were "reasonable people."

Further displays of male assurance can be seen in the fact that they demonstrate the prerogative to be critical of their partners and yet to display a kind of gallantry.

Men can speak of women with irony or disapproval. Three of the men are ironic or critical when speaking of the women. All of the female narrators are quite careful about what they say of their partners. This may be class based. Many women of course speak ironically, even mockingly of their partners. But none of the women in these families did, not in tape-recorded accounts. In contrast, second-generation Paul Meyer and third-generation Jesse Brooks are quite humorous, and elicit a good deal of laughter from the interviewer when they describe their moment of conquest. Paul Meyer says in a carefully-paced delivery:

> She called me the next day at work and she wanted to know if I still had the ring. [S:voiced smile] I said, "Yes I still have the ring." [S:laughs] She said, "Would you bring it back tonight?" So I said, "Yeah, I'll bring it back."

Jesse Brooks says, again with timing that elicits interviewer laughter:

> I think she said something like . . . "I don't know whether you're really with anybody else at the moment," something like that, you know. And with considerable satisfaction [I] allowed as how no it was not inappropriate at all [both laugh].

Both men probably see this kind of teasing as a reflection of affection, nonetheless, in these interviews it is a teasing which seems to be solely the province of men. Matt Brooks is even openly critical of his partner at several points during our interview. He sums up his reaction to Colleen Simpson's handling of a situation when they were traveling together:

> "Jesus, how could you . . . say that," you know, I mean, "How long have you been in . . . Latin America?" This is a bit of a low point there in my estimation of Colleen.

Male storytellers are "gentlemen". At the same time, male storytellers are gentlemen. They may speak of their rejections by women, but they are careful not to mention women's most embarrassing moments, including rejection by the men. Linda Pierce Meyer, for example, tells us that Dan Meyer broke up with her during his senior year in college; he is far too gallant to mention this himself. And while Colleen Simpson mentions an assault in Latin America as the context for developing a rapport with Matt Brooks, he omits this. Perhaps he feels this would be a rather personal story to tell for someone else, but also he believes the assault to have occurred as a result of Colleen's poor judgment. In the case of both men, their vocabulary of motive precludes their detailing events which might seriously embarrass the women.

This same gentlemanliness generates a curious difference in the way the men use hedges as compared with the usage by the women. In these stories, men hedge when speaking for their partners. The women do not. Jesse Brooks says: "*I think* she said something like. . ."; "*I- I think* she valued as much as I did"; "It was pretty obvious to both of us *I think*. . ."; "That's the only circumstance *I think* that we would have considered [it]." Wyatt Brooks hedges: "*I suspect* that's cause we each wanted it to work." Matt Brooks hedges: "*I think* that we, certainly, I was, *I think* we were both fairly leary . . ." And Dan Meyer says, "*I don't think* there was any question in either of our minds. . ." (emphases added).

The women, on the other hand, never hedge when speaking for their partners. For the women, citing one's partner's feelings with confidence seems intended to indicate that the courtship stories are shared, that decisions have indeed been mutual. For women, as we have seen, citing the opinions of others is an important impression management device. In contrast, men show no need to invoke the authority of others. Hedging when speaking for the women allows men to appear gentlemanly and is consistent with male uncertainty in courtship stories. This same gallantry by which men omit mentioning women's defeats and hedge when speaking for women is simultaneously a mark of male stature and assurance.

CONCLUSION

These narrative strategies constitute conventionalized representations of gendered cultural positions. Women's protestations of assertiveness, and men's displays of same, mark them as gendered creators of narrative. It remains to consider implications.

It is worth reiterating the complex relationship between narrative and experience. On the one hand these stories are conventionalized. Individual storytellers live in diverse relations to the institutions of courtship and bonding about which their stories can be quite similar.

Nonetheless, storytelling is a lived experience which serves to recreate social relations. Courtship storytelling is surely part of the ideological apparatus that reproduces gendered individuals. Over and over again, through their expressions of both ideological change and continuity, these stories reproduce dominant meanings and values about courtship and gender.

On another theoretical front, the existence of gender-based narrative conventions suggests that language and gender socialization correspond. Socialization, after all, is a process by which one learns selective attitudes towards oneself and the social order. Part of language socialization involves learning to display one's narrative gender—a process which (re)creates gendered cultural positions. While studies of language acquisition and socialization have developed within separate research traditions, these data question the wisdom of maintaining this distinction.

Finally, it must be noted that gendered social positions are not neutral. Most women work outside the home; for most of these, paid labor has not significantly altered their traditional responsibilities within the home. Gender socialization which generates this "double day" contributes to a division of paid labor that maintains women's economic subordination. In North America today, women receive low wages in sex-segregated sectors of the labor force, and earn unequal wages in sexually integrated sectors. We live in a society where women and children are overrepresented among the poor, while women are underrepresented in upper echelons of most professions. These circumstances remind us that the process of learning to mark onself narratively as male or female is not an isolated cultural artifact. Rather, the ideological processes documented here are essential to the reproduction of particular economic and social power relations fundamental to our society.

APPENDIX: FAMILY TREES

The Blum/Meyer Family

Generation 1:

Esther Blum
+
[Jack Blum, deceased]
married: 1924

Generation 2:

Ellen Meyer
+
Paul Meyer
married: 1948

Generation 3: Jean Meyer Dan Meyer
+ +
[Peter Stein, divorced] Linda Pierce Meyer

The McCloud/Brooks Family

Generation 1: Eleanor McCloud
+
[Henry McCloud, deceased]
married: 1921

Generation 2: Kay McCloud Brooks
+
Ed Brooks
married: 1945

Generation 3: Jesse Brooks Wyatt Brooks Matt Brooks
+ + +
Rachel Simon Laurel Williams Colleen Simpson

REFERENCES

Althusser, L. (1971). Ideology and ideological state apparatuses. *Lenin and Philosophy and Other Essays.* London: NLB.

Barrett, M. (1980). *Women's Oppression Today: Problems in Marxist Feminist Analysis.* London: Verso.

Belsey, K. (1980). *Critical Practice.* New York: Methuen.

Cowan, R. S. (1976). Two washes in the morning and a bridge party at night: The American housewife between the wars. *Women's Studies, 3,* 147–172.

Eagleton, T. (1984). *The Function of Criticism.* London: Verso.

Eagleton, T. (1976). *Marxism and Literary Criticism.* University of California Press.

Eagleton, T. (1975/1978). *Criticism and Ideology.* London: Verso.

Ehrenreich, B. (1983). *The Hearts of Men: American Dreams and the Flight From Commitment.* Garden City, NY: Anchor Press.

Ehrenreich, B., & English, D. (1978). *For Her Own Good: 150 Years of Experts' Advice to Women.* Garden City, NY: Anchor Press/Doubleday.

Gramsci, A. (1929–1935/1971). *Selections From the Prison Notebooks.* Edited and Translated by Q. Hoare & G. N. Smith. New York: International Publishers.

Kirszner, L. & Mandell, S. (1986). *Patterns in College Writing* (Third Edition). New York: St. Martins.

Linde, C. (in press). *The Creation of Coherence in Life Stories*. Norwood, NJ: Ablex.

Marx, K., & Engels, F. (1848/1947). *The German Ideology*, R. Pascal (Ed.). New York: International Publishers.

Mills, C. W. (1940). Situated actions and vocabularies of motive. *American Sociological Review, V*, 904–913. [Reprinted in J. G. Manis & B. N. Meltzer, Eds., (1967). *Symbolic Interaction: A Reader in Social Psychology* (pp. 355–366).] Boston: Allyn and Bacon.

Rubin, G. (1975). The traffic in women: Notes on the "political economy" of sex. In R. R. Reiter (Ed.), *Toward an Anthropology of Women* (pp. 157–210). New York: Monthly Review Press.

Syfers, J. (1971, December). I Want a Wife. *Ms, 1*

Vološinov, V. N. (1930/1973). *Marxism and the Philosophy of Language*. New York: Seminar Press.

Williams, R. (1977). *Marxism and Literature*. Oxford: Oxford University Press.

Wouk, H. (1955). *Marjorie Morningstar*. New York: Doubleday.

CHAPTER 5

Worlds of Difference: Contrasting Experience in Marriage and Narrative Style*

Catherine Kohler Riessman

Laboratory in Social Psychiatry
Harvard Medical School, Boston, MA and
Smith College School for Social Work,
Northampton, MA.

There is now deep appreciation for the fact that women's experience—in virtually every aspect of their lives—varies depending on sociocultural context. While initially feminists were criticized for their middle-class bias, feminist scholars now attend closely to what is common and what is different among women (Geiger, 1986), an orientation strongly reflected in studies of marriage (Rubin, 1976). Knowledge about diversity can be extended further if attention is paid to the variety of linguistic forms women use to talk about their marriages, for styles of telling can illuminate the different cultural contexts of marriage and, consequently, the similarity and diversity of women's experience in it.

Narrative methods provide a useful approach for this analysis, as individuals often narrate personal experience in research interviews,

* The study on which this paper is based was jointly conducted with Naomi Gerstel. Besides the overall collaboration, she gave helpful comments on an earlier draft, as did Susan Bell, Jack Clark, Elizabeth Gelfand, Peter Guarnaccia, Elliot Mishler, Marianne Paget, and the editors. Special thanks to the narrative group at Harvard Graduate School of Education for their insights about "Marta's" narrative. The research was supported by a fellowship from the National Institute of Mental Health (5 F32 MH09206). Direct all correspondence to Catherine Kohler Riessman, Laboratory in Social Psychiatry, 74 Fenwood Road, Boston MA 02115.

even when investigators do not explicitly ask for such detailed accounts (Mishler, 1986). Although typically analyzed as stories (see Bell, this volume), there are a variety of other forms of narrative that individuals use to convey personal experience. Polanyi (1985) notes some of the various genres of narrative we recognize in interaction (such as reports, generic and hypothetical narratives, as well as stories) and has begun to specify their distinctive features. Other research is beginning to suggest that forms of telling may vary with class and cultural background. For example, we know from recent research in education that the black and white children use different narrative structures and that white classroom teachers have difficulty "hearing" narratives of black children because of the way they are organized (Michaels, 1981; Michaels & Cazden, 1986). In the research interview, as in the classroom, it is likely that "lack of shared cultural norms for telling a story, making a point, giving an explanation and so forth can create barriers to understanding" (Michaels, 1985: p. 51). In interpreting interviews with women, failure to attend to different narrative styles is particularly consequential for it limits understanding of diversity, and may accentuate the class and cultural divisions between women that feminists have tried so hard to diminish.

This paper will compare two women's narratives about marriage and its dissolution—one told by an Anglo and one by a Puerto Rican—and show how similarities and differences in experience are encoded in contrasting narrative styles. Neither woman tells a story, in the linguistic sense of that term. The Anglo woman tells an habitual narrative and the Puerto Rican woman tells an episodically structured one. As I argue, these linguistic choices are well suited to what each woman is trying to say about her experience. Significantly, although both are highly competent narrators, only the Anglo woman is understood by the interviewer. (This last point is developed in another paper. See Riessman, 1987.)

These two interviews are part of a study of gender differences in the experience of separation and divorce. One hundred and four women and men were interviewed who had been separated up to three years using a structured interview schedule. The interviews, conducted in the respondent's homes, were taped and transcribed. The interviewer asked each interviewee "to state in your own words the main causes of your separation." This question and subsequent probes provided the "scaffolding" (Cazden, 1983) for the telling of the marital history. Two thirds of the cases were located through probate court records of the divorced in two counties of a northeastern state; a third came from referrals.

The Anglo woman's response is typical of the form of temporal organization that most interviewees used and, in its themes as well, is similar to many other women's accounts of their marriages. The Puerto Rican woman's narrative was selected because it was different, in both form and content. Although other Hispanics also used the episodic form, we cannot generalize as to its typicality because of the small number of Hispanics in our sample. Nor can we separate the effects of social class and ethnicity in shaping narrative style. Despite uncertainty about which populations the two interviews represent, there is evidence that these two styles of narrating are used by contrasting groups in other settings (Michaels, 1981) and thus illustrate alternative forms for telling about personal experience more generally.

In both cases, gender roles are the fulcrum around which the women describe their marital conflicts. At the same time, each marriage is embedded in a sociocultural context that has unique imperatives and dynamics, beyond the gender issues. These social structural differences are mirrored in the narratives the two women tell. Thus, an analysis of their narratives can illuminate when and how women's experience is the same and different.

SUSAN'S NARRATIVE

Susan is a 36-year-old, college-educated, white divorced woman who lives with her three children (ages 10, 8, and 5). She has been living apart from her husband for almost three years. Currently unemployed and looking for a job, she receives regular support payments from her ex-husband and still lives in the house, in a middle-class neighborhood, that her mother helped them buy. Nevertheless she experiences considerable financial strain, for her income is barely half what it was when she was married and the costs of raising her growing children have increased. Typical of many women in her situation, divorce was a financial catastrophe (Weitzman, 1985).

Susan's narrative about the history of her marriage is an archetypal account of the oppression traditional marriage brings to women, with the accompanying feelings of powerlessness, passivity, and victimization that many women report. (For the full transcript see Appendix A in Riessman, 1987.) As the following excerpt reveals,[1] Sus-

---

[1] Transcription notations are as follows: lines are numbered sequentially from beginning of answer to question about causes of separation; "N" and "I" designate whether narrator or interviewer is speaking; "(p)" signals a long pause of four seconds or longer; "[ ]" indicates interviewer's non-lexical utterances during narrator's speech; words in italics indicate marked increase in loudness or emphasis.

an begins her narrative by telling us that she married her husband because she got pregnant; in fact, she mentions this fact three times, perhaps to excuse her responsibility for the marriage and therefore its failure (Scott & Lyman, 1968):

```
08  N:  Mm, let's see (p) I was twenty-five when I was married
09      and I was pregnant
10      and there wasn't um (p)
11      didn't really have my head on very well I guess I
12      I kind of decided I should get married
13      I was pregnant
14      I didn't really give it that much thought
15      I don't think I would have married Bill if I had not been pregnant
16      I think we would eventually would have gone off our own ways
```

At the time, Susan had few choices besides marriage for abortion was not legal. Once married, her experience was like many other middle-class women of her generation. She describes the gender-based division of labor that characterized her marriage and the burden she felt caring for three children with little help from her husband, who occupied himself with his job:

```
20  And basically I had the children um
21  from day one (can't hear)
22  uhm he did not help out
23  it was not a give and take
24  I really carried 99% of the brunt of everything that had to be done
25  and I resented it [uhm]
26  you know the years went by
27  and I built up this resentment [uhm]
```

She goes on to describe how they didn't talk about their problems, how she "buried" her needs. Their emotional estrangement led to sexual disengagement, with separate beds and then separate bedrooms. Finally, the anger "surfaced" and they realized the marriage was over.

In its form, Susan's narrative is organized by time. It begins with the decision to marry, recounts the birth of the children, progresses through the years of the marriage, and ends with the separation. This temporal ordering of events into a narrative is a classic form in which individuals remember and recapitulate past experience (Labov, 1982; Mandler & Johnson, 1977). Although by no means the only one, such narrative sequencing is generally available as a form of telling in our culture.

TABLE 1

Line No.	Utterance
08	I was 25 when I was married
20–21	I had children from day one
26	the years went by
44–45	we stopped talking early on in our marriage
54	we continued to have children
59–60	we had more children/ that took up a lot of time
74	there was no sex
76–77	we slept in separate bedrooms/ that started out really early in our marriage
79–81	when we lived in Providence/ right after Nancy was born/ she was born in '74
99–100	so then I suggested single beds . . . which is what we did
101	and then the *follow*ing year in '75
114–115	then when we moved up here/first thing we did was to redo the attic
116	and then he moved up there as soon as that was done

In Susan's use of time as the organizing principle for her narrative, nothing is out of order (see Table 1.) The narrator also has a strong sense of place, for she locates the changes in the sleeping arrangements within the context of the family moves; they lived in Providence in 1974 (where they changed from a double to single beds), they moved to her mother's house in 1975 and then into their own house the following year (where her husband slept on the third floor), and, finally to the residence in which the interview takes place (where he had lived in an attic apartment). Susan is very clear in her mind about the order in which things happened and she guides the listener through the five year period recapitulated in the narrative, relating the decline in intimacy to changes in the marital residence and associated sleeping arrangements over time. Note in Table 1 her repeated use of the phrase "and then," which temporally orders the events she is describing. Through the use of time as a linguistic device, Susan brings order to her memories of her marriage. Yet there is an incongruity in the narrative; the events described first (notably having children) and the events described later (not sleeping together and not having sex) are contemporaneous. Thus the events as narrated may not be as "real" or "objective" as the form suggests (Mishler, 1986: appendix).

Besides using time to order and thereby structure her narrative, Susan also employs time in still another way. Although stories are told in the simple past tense (Labov, 1982), Susan uses other verb forms to construct her habitual narrative. For example, in describing her husband's lack of involvement in the home she says:

```
46   um and he spent more and more time at work
47   he didn't want to come home
48   he'd come home and
49   and then I would say
50   'I'd like you to spend a little time with the kids' and he
51   he'd just wanted to go up and read a book, kind of thing.
52   We just didn't communicate really.
```

She conveys the feeling of blurred time by the use of verb tense ("he'd come home and then I would say . . ."),[2] suggesting the repetitious nature of her husband's unavailability. Later in her narrative, Susan returns to her perception of blurred time during the marriage:

```
123   I guess (p) I don't know as I look back it's amazing that
124   that you accept things and you just
125   you know that they're wrong
126   but you just kind of go along and
127   take each day and
128   and the days become weeks
129   and the weeks become months
130   and suddenly you have three children and
131   you're communicating less and less
132   but you're just kind of existing
133   we were just existing
```

She makes artistic use of verb tense as well as repetition to communicate the experience of "just existing" through time. Here she also changes pronouns from the personal "we," "I" and "he" which she used earlier in the narrative to the general "you" and then back to "we" at the end. These shifts, and especially the use of the impersonal "you" to describe a distinctly personal perception, communicate her alienation at the time of the marriage from her self as she knows it now. The use of the impersonal voice also expresses her sense of passivity or inability to bring about any change over the many years of her marriage and, perhaps, her growing identification with women in similar situations.

Susan's narrative is not merely a personal statement about marriage, but a cultural one as well, both in its form and content. Al-

---

[2] For an analysis of how a child uses aspect marking, or verb changes, to develop a narrative line, see Gee (1985).

though it does not meet the criteria of a story, the form of the narrative nonetheless relies on forward sequencing and values the precise timing of events. Its use of time as an organizing device displays the sacred value that the clock and calendar have in Western middle-class culture (Agar, 1980). It is culturally rooted in its content, as well, for it describes how one woman experienced the ideology of domesticity—an historical and class-specific (at least initially) vision of marriage (Degler, 1980). The taken-for-granted aspect of the companionate ideal allows Susan to use it as a standard for marriage, thereby legitimating her divorce. Contrary to the ideal, Susan experienced the absence of sexual and emotional companionship, as well as the burdensome conditions of domestic life for women. Her account is also embedded in notions of love particular to American culture (Swidler, 1980). Like those of other middle-class women, it pivots on issues of intimacy, sharing, and communication in marriage (Rubin, 1976). It is a deeply women-centered account of the costs of the gender-based division of labor in traditional marriage.

In fact, Susan graphically describes her growing awareness of what Friedan (1963) has termed the "problem with no name." She grew resentful that she "carried 99% of the brunt of everything that had to be done [in the home];" she expected that marriage would involve more than a relationship between "roommates;" and finally, she became conscious of the fact that she was "just existing," implicitly contrasting this mode of being with her ideal model. She repeatedly uses the phrase "give and take" to describe her expectations about marriage. Not only did she expect help with child care, she also expected emotional reciprocity. Heavily influenced by the culture of psychotherapy, living fully for her involves talking about emotions and problems. Instead, she found herself married to a man who "didn't give a lot" and whose "idea of having an argument was not to discuss it at all." Instead of life—as defined by emotional sharing and reciprocity—Susan experienced a deadness in her marriage. To communicate this, she invokes images of death in her repeated use of the theme of burial, as Table 2 displays. Susan visually depicts the idea that her true self was submerged in the marriage. Finally it "surfaced" in the anger that was the proximate cause of the separation.

Susan's linguistic choices assure that the meanings she intends will not be missed. There is a relationship between what she is trying to say about her experience in marriage and the narrative structures she chooses. Her understanding is that her marriage disintegrated over many years. There was no critical incident which brought the

TABLE 2

Line No.	Utterance
56	you bury yourself in the things that have to be done on a daily basis
68	I buried all of what I needed for myself
94	I'd bury everything
136	the anger was all buried

decision to divorce to the fore. By contrast, many others in the study cited specific incidents which turned the tide, typically constructing stories to convey the importance of these critical events in their decisions about divorce. But for Susan, the slow downward spiral of her marriage over time is the point she is trying to convey—an understanding that is well suited to the habitual narrative form, but would not have been suited to a story, for example. Through the choice of genre and imagery, she achieves her communicative aim and conveys what was missing in her marriage.

MARTA'S NARRATIVE

Marta is a 24-year-old, dark-skinned Puerto Rican woman who lives with her two children (ages 6 and 3) in a small apartment on a lively but shabby street. Separated from her husband for two years, she is not employed and lives on public assistance, supplemented by child support payments from her ex-husband. Currently attending a community college, Marta anticipates that her financial situation will improve in the near future, after she gets her degree and a job. She hopes to be a parole officer some day.

Marta's narrative is not organized temporally,[3] nor does its content pivot on issues of intimacy. Unlike Susan, Marta does not start at the beginning and recount the events of the marriage in chronolog-

---

[3] Some might argue that Marta's account is not, strictly speaking, a narrative at all but rather an argument or listing because it is not structured by time and becauses it relies so heavily on generic thematic abstractions and not instances or specific events. There is considerable disagreement in the literature about the definition of narrative (see Mitchell, 1985). The most restrictive is Labov's (1982) notion of a story which encodes specific past time events. Yet respondents also use ordered event clauses which do not encode specific events, such as in habitual and hypothetical narratives. The point is that there are a variety of genres which we recognize in interaction. See Polanyi (1985) on narrative genres and Riessman (1986) for a discussion of the relationship between genre and meaning in accounts of marital failure.

ical order, beginning with the reasons for the marriage, what the marriage was like, and the reasons for the separation. Instead, time as well as place change repeatedly throughout Marta's narrative, starting with her opening statement:

```
01  I:  Can you state in your own words what were the main causes of
        your separation?
02  N:  I guess the mental abuse.
03  I:  What do you mean?
04  N:  (p) I find it very painful (p) to be treated (p)
05      like I was treated when I was living with my mother uh
06      no communication
07      he was very irresponsible
08      I mean, he could have a job but yet (p)
09      it didn't matter much. (p)
10      To him it was like well
11      if it happens it happens and if it don't it don't.
12      With me I like to work.
13      I've made, I have made sacrifices
14      where I didn't, I didn't spend much time with my children due to
        you know, working and whatnot but
15      someday I know my children will accept it
16      and they will respect me for it.
17      But no, I do, eheheh, if you were about to ask if I I resent any of
        the things I have done
18      no, I don't. Uhm
```

The narrator begins in the present (line 4), moves to the far past (line 5), to the recent past (line 7), back to the present (line 12) and then back to the past (line 13), to the future (line 15) and then to the present (line 17). These multiple shifts in time foreshadow what is to come and suggest that precise timing of events is not critical in Marta's understanding of her marriage. Substantively, Marta faults her husband in her opening statement for not being a steady worker—an issue she shares with other working-class women (Rubin, 1976). As with Susan, there is the suggestion of conflict in the marriage over gender roles. Despite this important similarity, both the form of Marta's discourse and its content suggest a markedly different experience of marriage.

Marta uses an episodic frame to structure her account of marital failure. Unlike Susan, who tells a linear and temporally ordered narrative, Marta's account displays the complex development of a theme through a series of related episodes. Each incident restates the theme in a different way. In this genre, time, place, and characters shift across the major episode boundaries, with an important overall

theme developed by seemingly distinct episodes. The connections between the individual episodes are implicit and must be inferred by
the listener. This narrative structure is not unique to Marta; it has
been observed, in a less developed form, in the stories minority children tell in classroom situations (Michaels, 1981; Michaels & Cazden,
1986). In Marta's case, the form is particularly suited to what she is
trying to say about her marriage.

A structural analysis of the narrative led to the understanding that
Marta's narrative is about cultural conflict. Each episode provides an
instance of such conflict, which I discovered only after repeated listening to the tape and repeated readings of the transcript. Put differently, I understood the content of the narrative only through a close
analysis of its form. The points at which the interviewer became
confused were particularly instructive. These examples of break-
down in the discourse illuminated "the interactional work that usually goes unnoticed in smooth exchanges" (Michaels, 1985: p. 37).
(See Riessman, 1987, for an analysis of the interaction in this interview and for the complete transcript.)

Marta introduces the theme of her narrative quite early when she
says:

21 He had more growing up to do than I did.
22 I was too advanced for him in a lot of ways.

While she tells us here that she and her husband were different on the
dimension of "growing" and "advancement," the precise meaning of
these phrases does not become clear until later. Like an abstract of a
narrative (Labov, 1982), the two lines hint at and summarize but do
not fully explicate. The narrator goes on to develop her theme in the
first of five related episodes.

The first episode—superficially about going out and staying
home—approaches the theme of cultural conflict in the marriage in
an oblique way.

24 N: O.K., like (p) he did not mind dedicating a lot of time to his
        sports
25   his friends, the softball league, and things like that.
26   And if I asked just to go like to a movie with the children
27   or go out to dinner at a restaurant
28   just *one* day
29   he couldn't understand *why* I wanted to do that
30   when I could do it at home
31   just sitting down watching TV or
32   just having a family dinner

```
33        which would be the same going to a restaurant
34        and you, the cost is the same
35        except that you don't do the dishes afterwards, you know.
36        Not that I didn't mind doing them
37        it's just that
38        I just wanted for us to go out
39        and be sociable.
40        he didn't like the idea of being surrounded by one too many
          people, person.
41        And, uh, [uhm] (p) I really don't know
42        it's very difficult. (p)
43        I guess it was outgoing versus not outgoing.
```

Here, Marta tells us that she and her husband had different ideas about how to spend their leisure time together. She wanted to "go out" to a restaurant or movie and "be sociable" whereas he either wanted to go out with his friends alone or stay at home with the immediate family. At one level, Marta is decrying the gender-segregated leisure patterns characteristic of working-class marriages (Halle, 1984; Rubin, 1976), a problem that Susan apparently did not experience, perhaps because the sociocultural context of her marriage was so different. However, this episode takes on additional meanings because the marital partners are not only working class but also migrants from Puerto Rico. In this cultural context, we begin to sense that "going out" versus "staying home" may be a metaphor for something broader—acculturation, perhaps. Marta wants to participate in the public world whereas he wants her to remain in the private.

Marta proceeds to continue to develop what she means by "outgoing" in a second episode.

```
45   N:   No, I really, to him the excuse was always
46        "well we don't have the money
47        we don't have a car"
48        uh, when it came to a movie, "I don't know if I want to put the
          time in."
49        But yet when it came to a softball game on a Sunday afternoon
50        "well why don't you come along with the kids"
51        and I would please him then.
52        Also because I liked, I enjoyed watching the games [mhm]
53        not just because he was in it
54        or because he liked them so much
55        but because I also enjoyed them.
56        There were a lot of my friends there along with
57        as much as his
```

58   and we all had a great time.
59   But when it came to things *as a family*
60   there were always (p) *obs*tacles.
61   I just couldn't under*stand* it.
62   He would, he was, he was more happy just staying at home not doing anything
63   or doing something around the house
64   than just going out
65   and just doing something just for each other
66   and our children and ourselves.

The theme of cultural difference is given its second rendering in the topic of doing things "as a family" in this episode. The issue is not merely going out or staying home, as the first episode suggests, but the kinds of things that count as shared leisure. We find out that Marta's husband was not entirely a homebody, as she portrayed him in the first episode. He was active in a weekend softball game. Although she says she "enjoyed watching the games" and admits that "we all had a great time," this type of outing is not what Marta defines as doing "things as a family." She concludes this episode with a return to the topic of "going out."

Upon closer inspection, we begin to sense that "his" and "her" leisure activities, as portrayed in Marta's account, are not only gender- and class-based but also cultural, as well. Softball games are a major arena for male socializing in Puerto Rico and this tradition has continued with migration, even in urban neighborhoods in the United States. Although women and children are encouraged to watch, and to socialize with their friends at these events, playing the game is a distinctly male activity. It continues the socializing patterns of the Island, as going out with male friends and being with family do. By contrast, going out to restaurants and to movies are more Americanized leisure pursuits.

The narrator develops the theme of differences in degree of acculturation in the third episode of her narrative, also on the topic of socializing.

70 N: Well, he felt threatened when I asked him if
71   "can I have one night off
72   and just go out with the girls, from work"
73 I: [can't hear]
74 N: yes, or uh if my girlfriends or relatives asked me out to dinner
75   he didn't like that very much
76   he couldn't understand why.
77   Uh, anything dealing with friends or relatives
78   or anything work related
79   he felt threatened by it. [hum]

For Marta "going out" also means doing things without her husband, such as dining out with friends and relatives. She tells us that "he didn't like that very much" and in fact, felt "threatened by it." Cross-cultural studies suggest that Marta is probably correct in her assessment (Nash & Safa, 1980). Especially in working-class Puerto Rican families, married women are expected to remain in the home when they are not at their jobs. Certainly, socializing in public places without the company of the husband is not approved behavior for married women. In contrast to Marta, Susan does not mention these issues in her narrative, suggesting that she was not constrained in these ways in her marriage and that her husband was probably not "threatened" if she socialized without him.

The scene of conflict shifts in the fourth episode of the narrative. After a long pause, Marta introduces the topic of her employment— an issue that never comes up in Susan's account:

80		Uh (p) I guess the one things that did it most
83		was when I got hired to work at the Fire Department
84		and uhm (p) he felt, he really, to him,
85		I, I didn't feel I was trusted.
86		I was surrounded *by* men
87		and the demands came *from* men
88		where I was cons- I had to do my job.
89		Period. That's all I was doing.
90		He didn't like it very much.
91		I guess the friendship of *those strange men*
92		didn't appeal to him very much.
93	I:	And, he wanted you to quit.
94	N:	He didn't quite admitted it
95		but he would have liked it
96		if I would have, you know, quit, my job.

She intimates that it was not the fact that she was employed that bothered her husband. Historically, a large percentage of Puerto Rican women have worked to supplement the family income, as Garcia-Preto (1982) notes. Rather, it is the type of job she had and her psychological investment in it that threatened him. She worked as a dispatcher in the Fire Department, with men. As she states, "I guess the friendship of *those strange men* didn't appeal to him very much." Her employment might have been acceptable if it had been women's work. Instead, she had entered the male world of power and authority. Marta aspired to a career in corrections and, earlier in the narrative, she stressed how she liked to work and contrasted this with her husband's lack of commitment to his job. Marta is completing college, surpassing her husband in education as well. As a point of contrast, in Susan's marriage the traditional hierarchy prevailed; he had more education than she and he was the breadwinner. Because this form of inequality is taken for granted in Susan's cultural context, it is not seen as an issue in the marriage. In Marta's, however, the asymmetry does become an issue, for it reverses the usual status difference between husband and wife. Marta's ambition has led her to "go out" into the world to better her situation. We now understand why her husband "felt threatened" and why he may have placed such an emphasis on staying home. Through education and employment, Marta has stepped outside the traditional role for women in Puerto Rican culture. She is achievement-oriented and acculturated whereas her portrait suggests that her husband resists Americanization and clings to Island ways, including some of the negative aspects of machismo (De La Cancela, 1981). His marginality may also be due to harsh socioeconomic conditions (Bonilla & Campos, 1981).

In the coda or ending to this fourth episode in the narrative, Marta explicitly states the conflict: her husband's allegiance to traditional beliefs about women's proper role in Puerto Rican culture and her growing involvement in the new American culture of women's self actualization. Speaking in the voice of her husband she says:

    98   Yes, definitely yes.
    99   Just quit in general and just stay home
   100   take care of the children
   101   take care care of my house
   102   and him
   103   and never mind what my, my wants, desires were.

In adopting his voice, Marta recreates the overt and conflictual interactions in the marriage concerning what her husband expected her to do with her life. In contrast, Susan does not use her husband's voice in this way, suggesting that women's proper role was not an overt area of conflict in her marriage. Instead, Susan uses this linguistic device to convey her efforts to get her husband involved in child care (line 50: "I'd like you to spend a little time with the kids"), whereas Marta uses reported speech in the excerpt above (and again later) to depict her husband's and his family's efforts to keep her confined to the home. This comparison of the details of the talk in each woman's narrative suggests that they share a struggle over gender roles. Yet it takes a very different form in the two marriages.

In the fifth and final episode of Marta's narrative, the contrast between the two women's experiences in marriage is most vividly displayed. Here, Marta explicitly articulates and develops her theme of culture conflict, depicting a variety of marital problems related to kin that are entirely absent from Susan's account of her marriage.

```
107  N:  Um hum. And when it came to family
108       (p) uh (p) his family and my family are two different people.
109       My family were city-oriented
110       his family was more Island-type-oriented people.
111  I:   What is, what is, how does?
112  N:  O.K. Even though both of our parents came from the same place
113       my family
114       not only did the majority of the children were born out here in
               the United States
115       we had a more easy going fast type living while
116       (p) his family only knew the slow pace (p) [uhm] type living
117       very old fashioned
118       more so than my family
119       I guess I could say that
```

Marta introduces this last episode by harking back to the topic of family. Here, however, she means family of origin and not the conjugal family. She introduces the episode with an abstract of the content which will follow—"his family and my family are two different people"—suggesting that the families are from two different cultures. She begins to specify the ways in which they are different, saying his family is "Island-type-oriented" and hers is "city-oriented." The interviewer is totally lost (line 111); she does not see the relevance of this material on urban/rural differences between the families to the question she asked about the causes of the separation. As a white, middle-class woman, she lacks the necessary intuitive schema or background knowledge (Agar, 1980) to properly grasp the acculturation contrast which is at the core of the last episode. Marta adeptly provides the background knowledge, a further indication of her ability to move back and forth between cultures. She contextualizes what she is saying, including in the narrative her analysis of what the listener needs to know to understand it. In a lengthy response (see Riessman, 1987), Marta tells that her family and her husband's family were different on a variety of dimensions. In a passage replete with hesitations and apologies, she describes her mother-in-law:

```
138  his mother was (p)
139  uhm (p) overly sociable to a point where
140  she was a very friendly loving person, O.K.
141  don't get me wrong
```

142   but she was also cruel (p)
143   she was, uh huh huh (p) oh, how do I describe her
144   (p) selfish (p) she was the
145   not a one man woman type thing
146   she would go for whatever came along type thing.
147   Uh she was, she cohabitated
148   she fornicated
149   she, every, uh she committed adultery
150   every sin in the book she did. [uhm uhm]

She contrasts this manner with her own parents, who were more conventional in their sexual behavior. Later, she describes how the two sets of parents differed in their conduct in her home:

175   I did not approve of them [his parents] coming into *my* home
176   uh, very loud type of behavior
177   intoxicated
178   uh, certain behaviors that they had I did not approve of.
179   My home is my home
180   and it should be respected
181   I have rules and regulations along with everybody ah ah like everybody else.
182   (p) My family, yes, they're loud and everything else
183   but they cooperate with me.

In presenting the series of contrasts, Marta makes her point, depicting the two families as polar opposites. Table 3 summarizes the contrasts. The descriptors she uses suggest that, beside class, a core element differentiating the families is cultural. In Marta's family, the

TABLE 3

His Family	Her Family
island oriented (110*)	city oriented (109)
children born in Puerto Rico (114)	children born in U.S. (114)
slow (116)	fast (115)
old fashioned (117)	modern** (126–133)
immoral (146–153)	
dead marriage (154–155)	active marriage (156)
loud and intoxicated (176–177)	loud but cooperative (182–183)
accusatory and rejecting (184–187)	accepting (184–187)
no feeling of togetherness (190)	always stuck together (189)
light skinned** (204–205)	dark skinned (205)

*line number in transcript
**implicit in text

children were American-born and thus spent their formative years in the United States before they returned to Puerto Rico, placing her family further along on the continuum of acculturation than his family, who migrated when the children were grown (Mizio, 1974). Pace of living and family values follow from these differences. Marta's earlier comments about her husband's orientation to "staying home" and her desire to "go out" take on added meaning in light of these family differences. A further contrast she draws between the families is racial, only here there is a contradiction. Typically, lighter skin is associated with more advantaged class standing among Latins. Marta is darker skinned than her husband, but she intimates that her family was of a higher class than his.

Contradictions are at the core of this episode, as well as at the core of Marta's account more generally. Both the form and the content of the discourse reveal the complexities and paradoxes contained in Marta's perceptions of the irreconcilable cultural differences between the two families—an issue that is entirely absent from Susan's account. Marta describes her family as having "a more easy going fast type living." She describes his family as "very old fashioned," but she disparages his mother's sexual freedom. She describes her father as "very passive" and yet "the strength" of the family. Nonetheless, the marriage failed, she suggests, because of a clash in cultures—a clash that resonates within her, as well as between her and her ex-husband, and between the families.

The cultural opposition between the two families is manifested in their contrasting attitudes towards women's work outside the home. Marta's parents, like many urban, middle-class Puerto Ricans, have greater sympathy for female autonomy whereas her ex-husband's parents, like the rural agricultural class from the Island, have more traditional views. For this latter group, the roles of husband and wife are clearly defined, with the husband having the authority to control his wife and children (Garcia-Preto, 1982). In her narrative, Marta communicates the opposition of the two views about women's autonomy by adopting the voice of each set of parents. Through role playing and use of reported speech, she conveys to the listener the contrasting families' prescriptions about how she, as a married woman, should lead her life:

121   "Well, why can't she stay home more often"
122   "she should take more care of the house"
123   "children come first, so does husband"
124   "those are first priorities." [ahh]
125   My mother says "yes" or my father

126   "yes children have to be taken care of
127   and yes a home has to be looked after
128   but the wife also has things that she needs to do for herself
129   we're only human beings"

Marta's in-laws think that a woman's role is solely to care for her house, children and husband whereas her parents understand that this work may not be sufficient for a woman. We now understand the meaning of Marta's comment in the first episode of her narrative. By progressive American standards, she *was* more "advanced" than her husband, and his family as well. He (and they) have "more growing up to do."

Near the end of the fifth episode Marta introduces a new character into her narrative, the girl from Puerto Rico:

207   I guess what I'm saying is
208   they already had picked out the girl
209   they would have preferred to see him married to

In this excerpt, Marta moves back in time to the period of her courtship. She changes place as well for the events she reports took place in Puerto Rico, where Marta grew up. The heart of the final episode is contained in the emotional retelling about the girl her husband was supposed to have married:

212   this was the girl that that that that
213   caused a lot of heartaches (p) and a lot of
214   (p) bitterness I guess on my part

The narrator's pauses, repetitions, and choice of language all flag the significance of this passage. Marta tells of the continuing psychological presence of this other woman. Her thoughts return again to her husband's family and she says poignantly:

223   I never knew what it was they saw in her
224   not that I was Miss Perfect
225   I do have my faults but
226   I don't know (p)

In preferring the girl from Puerto Rico over her, Marta tells us that her husband's family rejected her. Given the significance of family in Puerto Rican culture, this may well have been the death blow to the marriage. For at the same time as Marta disparaged the lack of acculturation of her husband's family, she also wanted to be accepted by them. Divorce from the family was the price Marta paid for being "too advanced." She tells us of the pain of things that can't be changed—her skin color, his family's rejection of her—at the same time as she celebrates her change and growth.

Again we see the contradictions at the core of the narrative. In a variety of ways, Marta suggests that an intracultural tension exists not only in the two families, but within herself as well. For example, she stresses over and over the similarities between the families ("both of our parents came from the same place" and "we're both being Spanish"). At the same time, however, she emphasizes the differences in traditions and values. Her hurt about the girl from Puerto Rico suggests she wants to be accepted by her husband's family and yet she ridicules their backwardness. The birth of two children outside of marriage when she was quite young belies Marta's identification with the new American woman. Consensual unions are common among *less* acculturated Puerto Ricans (Fitzpatrick, 1981), yet Marta implies her family was *more* acculturated than his. Finally, Marta displays ambivalent feelings about the patriarchal Puerto Rican family. Marta blames her husband for not being responsible and not providing for his family but she later deprecates his "male chauvinistic type attitude" toward her college aspirations. Marta no longer sees machismo as a desirable characteristic, as traditional Puerto Rican culture does, but she is ambivalent about criticizing it.

At many levels, the clash of cultures within Puerto Rican culture and how this manifested itself in her marriage is the theme of Marta's narrative. The complex development of this theme is achieved by a narrator who constructs her "point" by using a series of interconnected episodes, each of which bears on the essential conflict. The genre Marta used to tell her account—an episodically structured narrative—is exquisitely appropriate to the theme she tries to convey. It is both dramatic and persuasive precisely because she gives us this scene and that scene, this instance and that instance, present time and past time, thereby underscoring the deep nature of the conflict. Further, the episodic form of the discourse is reflective of Marta's life which, rather than linear and progressive as Susan's was, has been a mosaic of seemingly disjointed events: birth and youth in the United States, adolescence on the Island, return migration to the mainland for early adulthood. Typical of many Puerto Ricans, this back and forth migration is associated with a pattern of dismantling and reconstruction of familial and community ties (Garcia-Preto, 1982). Just as the trajectory of Marta's life has been different so, too, is the style of her discourse.

CONCLUSION

This paper has analyzed the marital life histories of two women from contrasting backgrounds—histories revolving around gender issues in differing cultural contexts. While their marriages were difficult, the analysis showed the highly competent, but different way each organized her account into a coherent narrative. Both women were active speaking agents who mulled over and evaluated their experiences in the very process of telling them.

Instead of worlds of pain, this analysis has emphasized the worlds of difference in each woman's experience of marriage which, in turn, is reflected in her mode of discourse. Both narratives depict culturally embedded and contextualized understandings of what marriage is like. Yet there is a major point of convergence, for both women's struggles pivot on gender role issues. It is a taken-for-granted assumption that both Susan and Marta, as women, will care for house, husband, and children. Both women found domestic life confining and challenged the expectation that they put their own needs aside in marriage. Yet because each woman worked out the role issues in a different sociocultural context, the experience of marriage and the particular gender role issues within it varied markedly. From her vantage point, Susan tells of the years she spent as a homemaker, raising children with little help from her husband, and the growing alienation which accompanied her social and emotional isolation in the home. Her account stresses the absence of intimacy and domestic sharing in her marriage. From her vantage point, Marta describes the tension between her aspirations for achievement in the larger world and the expectations of traditional Puerto Rican culture about what a wife should be. Her account stresses the absence of shared leisure and other issues that arose because of the clash in cultural values in her marriage. In each case, the constraints of class, ethnicity, and family history and structure distinguished their perceptions and experiences, contextualizing and particularizing the gender conflicts.

Linked to the content of their accounts, cultural difference is reflected in each woman's discourse. They use different narrative genres, each characterized by a definite style and structure. Susan tells an habitual narrative, using the easily recognized form of temporal ordering to describe how she was gradually worn down by her marriage. Marta tells an episodic narrative, with a series of topics loosely stiched together by theme rather than time. Elsewhere I have analyzed how Marta's account was not understood during the interview because of its lack of temporality (Riessman, 1987). Although narrative analysts have tended to treat time as critical (thereby displaying the preoccupation in Western culture with forward sequencing), Marta vividly shows how other deep structures beside time order experience in narrative. Similarly, although previous investigators have focused on the story as the prototypic form of narrative (Labov, 1982; Mishler, 1986; Polanyi, 1985), Susan and Marta display how individuals reconstruct and interpret personal experience using a variety of other narrative genres as well.

While there is evidence from other sources that narrative style may be related to cultural background (Michaels, 1981), I have not argued that Susan's and Marta's choices of narrative form were primarily culturally determined. It is not simply that Puerto Ricans tell episodic narratives and Anglos tell temporally ordered ones. Such a conclusion is impossible based on the analysis of only two cases and runs the further danger of stereotyping. Rather, I have suggested that the genre each woman chose was related to meaning. There was a relationship between narrative form and life experience. Each woman conveyed her distinctive understanding of marital events through the particular linguistic choices she made, including the choice of narrative genre. Each expressed through her way of telling what her experience of marriage was like.

Although culture did not determine narrative form, it did play a role in how each narrative was constructed, as well as in the content that each narrator deemed appropriate to include. For example, both Susan and Marta include kin, in sharp contrast to the marriages depicted in Rubin's work (1976), yet the prominence of kin varies markedly in the two narratives. Marta places kin relations in the center of her drama. In Susan's, the actors she draws upon are conjugal family members and, very residually, her mother, whereas in Marta's account the cast of characters is much more extensive, including two sets of parents, the girl from Puerto Rico, Marta's male colleagues at her job, and others. This contrast in the number, type, and importance of particular characters speaks to broader issues differentiating the two women's realities. In Puerto Rican culture, marriage is not a dyadic relationship but much more explicitly a union of two families (Fitzpatrick, 1981). As Marta explains in her narrative, the marriage failed because the two families' values, and subsequent pressures, could not be reconciled. Thus she answers the question about the causes of the separation by telling the *family* history, within which the *marital* history is embedded. In contrast, Susan answers the question by giving a chronological history of the marital relationship only. Susan and Marta also use other linguistic strategies to convey their culturally distinctive understandings of marriage. Susan invokes images of death to convey her experience of contraint in the domestic sphere. Marta communicates the theme of cultural tension in her marriage through vivid use of contrasts and juxtapositions—between herself and her husband, between her and his family, and between the traditional and the emancipated woman within herself.

This paper has suggested that, aside from a "his" and "her" marriage (Bernard, 1972), there is similarity as well as considerable diversity in women's perceptions of marriage, as expressed through the narrative forms they use to reconstruct their experiences. More work is clearly needed on how contrasting groups of women narrate their marital histories. If we are to take women's accounts of marriage seriously, we need to grant their narratives the kind of meticulous attention that can allow both the similarities and the differences among women to come to the fore. As the analysis of Susan's and Marta's narratives has tried to suggest, differences in the experience of marriage are embedded in the *form* of telling, not merely in the *content* of what is told.

REFERENCES

Agar, M. (1980). Stories, background knowledge and themes: Problems in the analysis of life history narrative. *American Ethnologist, 7*, 223–39.

Bernard, J. (1972). *The Future of Marriage.* New York: World.

Bonilla, F., & Campos, R. (1981). A wealth of poor: Puerto Ricans in the new economic order. *Daedalus, 110*, 133–76.

Cazden, C. (1983). Peekaboo as an instructional model: Discourse development at school and at home. In B. Bain (Ed.), *The Sociogenesis of Language and Human Conduct: A Multi-disciplinary Book of Readings* (pp. 33–58). New York: Plenum.

Degler, C. N. (1980). *At Odds: Women and the Family in America from the Revolution to the Present.* New York: Oxford University Press.

De La Cancela, V. (1981). Towards a critical psychological analysis of machismo: Puerto Ricans and mental health. *Dissertation Abstracts International, 42*, 368–B.

Fitzpatrick, J. P. (1981). The Puerto Rican family. In C. H. Mindel & R. W. Habenstein (Eds.), *Ethnic Families in America: Patterns and Variations* (2nd ed. (pp. 189–214). New York: Elsevier.

Friedan, B. (1963). *The Feminine Mistique,* New York: Dell.

Garcia-Preto, N. (1982). Puerto Rican families. In M. McGoldrick, J. K. Pearce, & J. Giordano (Eds.), *Ethnicity and Family Therapy* (pp. 164–186). New York: Guilford.

Gee, J. P. (1985). The narrativization of experience in the oral style. *Journal of Education, 167*, 9–35.

Geiger, S. N. G. (1986). Women's life histories: Method and content. *Signs, 11*, 334–351.

Halle, D. (1984). *America's Working Man: Work, Home, and Politics among Blue-Collar Property Owners.* Chicago: University of Chicago Press.

Labov, W. (1982). Speech actions and reactions in personal narrative. In D. Tannen (Ed.), *Analyzing Discourse: Text and Talk* (pp. 219–247). Washington DC: Georgetown University Press.

Mandler, J. M., & Johnson, N. (1977). Remembrance of things parsed: Story structure and recall. *Cognitive Psychology, 9*, 111–151.

Michaels, S. (1981). 'Sharing time:' Children's narrative styles and differential access to literacy. *Language and Society, 10*, 423–42.

Michaels, S. (1985). Hearing the Connections in Children's Oral and Wirtten Discourse. *Journal of Education, 167*, 36–56.

Michaels, S., & Cazden, C. (1986). Teacher–child collaboration as oral preparation for literacy. In B. B. Schieffelin (Ed.), *Acquisition of Literacy: Ethnographic Perspectives* (pp. 132–154). Norwood, NJ: Ablex.

Mishler, E. (1986). *Research Interviewing: Context and Narrative.* Cambridge, MA: Harvard University Press.

Mitchell, W. J. T. (Ed.). (1981). *On Narrative.* Chicago: Chicago University Press.

Mizio, E. (1974). The impact of external systems on the Puerto Rican family. *Social Casework, 55*, 76–83.

Nash, J., & Safa, H. I. (1980). *Sex and Class in Latin America.* New York: Bergin.

Polanyi, L. (1985). *Telling the American Story: A Structural and Cultural Analysis of Conversational Storytelling.* Norwood, NJ: Ablex.

Riessman, C. K. (1986). 'It's a long story:' Women and men account for marital failure. Paper presented at XI World Congress of Sociology, New Delhi, India.

Riessman, C. K. (1987). When gender is not enough: Women interviewing women. *Gender & Society,* Vol. 1, 172–207.

Rubin, L. (1976). *Worlds of Pain: Life in the Working Class Family.* New York: Basic Books.

Scott, M. B., & Lyman, S. M. (1968). Accounts. *American Sociological Review, 46*, 46–62.

Swidler, A. (1980). Love and adulthood in American culture. In N. J. Smelser, & E. H. Erikson (Eds.), *Themes of Work and Love in Adulthood* (pp. 120–147). Cambridge, MA: Harvard University Press.

Weitzman, L. (1985). *The Divorce Revolution.* New York: Free Press.

PART III

Institutional Discourse

CHAPTER 6

The Obstetric View of Feminine Identity: A Nineteenth Century Case History of the Use of Forceps on Unmarried Women in Ireland

Jo Murphy-Lawless

Department of Sociology
Trinity College, Dublin

OBSTETRIC DISCOURSES AND THE ISSUE OF CONTROL

Although childbirth is a significant personal experience for women, it is also a social event bound up with the maintenance and reproduction of social order. That birth is circumscribed by ideologies about women, about children, and about the requirement for social reproduction is manifest in the context which has signaled the advent and growth of male-controlled childbirth since the 18th century. The displacement of a female-controlled system of childbirth management and the institution of professional male control over women in labor were the key features during the 18th century in the move to convert birth into a medical specialism.[1]

With increasing conflict between women and obstetricians about how birth is managed, during the very recent past feminists have challenged the obstetric view that childbirth must be a medical event.[2] The feminist critique of current obstetric practice points out

---

[1] On the history of male-controlled childbirth, see Ehrenreich and English (1973); Oakley (1976); Donnison (1977); Rich (1977); Wertz and Wertz (1977); and Versluysen (1981).

[2] See for instance Brook (1976), Kitzinger (1979), Beels (1978), and Inch (1982).

that at the core of the debate is the issue of who controls women in birth, and feminists have demanded both an end to unnecessary medical intervention and a return to women-centered and women-controlled reproductive care (Arms, 1975, 1977; Oakley, 1976, 1980).

However, in positing a "golden age" of women-controlled childbirth which we must now try and regain (Macintyre, 1977), the feminist argument fails to examine the nature and extent of obstetric power. In speaking simply of a male takeover from women, the argument fails to examine the crucial role obstetric discourse played in achieving male control over women giving birth. Using discourse, obstetric science created an ideology about laboring women which was then imposed through clinical practice. While necessarily contesting the ideology which makes up the obstetric view of women, the feminist critique has paid insufficient attention to the importance of obstetric discourses as the source of that ideology. It has not examined how these discourses were able to link ideology and practice and what the resulting impact was on women's identities as childbearers. The ideology of male-controlled childbirth and its effects on women in labor warrant a detailed analysis. I want to explore this area, using a series of clinical reports compiled during the 1870's, at the internationally renowned Rotunda Hospital in Dublin, in which the use of forceps, particularly on unmarried women, was advocated as an acceptable clinical practice. This incident of the 1870's exemplifies what the ideology of male-controlled childbirth made possible.

The establishment of male-controlled childbirth throughout Europe and the United States during the 18th century involved far more than the ousting of women midwives from their traditional role as birth attendants. In constructing a science of childbirth to secure their professional ambitions, men midwives invented a new object of attention in their discourses, that of the poor suffering woman in labor. As a result women experienced a radical break in the social practices surrounding childbirth. The new science gave rise to the institution of the lying-in hospital. Crucial to the way that lying-in hospitals were to function, and to the power than men midwives came to exercise over women in labor, were their discourses on childbirth.

Over a period of more than 200 years these medical discourses have argued that women, by their very nature, are incapable of negotiating the hazards of childbirth both as reproducers and as managers, and thus require male intervention and control.

During the 18th century, men midwives, as they called themselves, advanced new theories about women in childbirth, based on an account of female sexuality which declared that women had certain essential or basic qualities. This "essentialist" account, also reflected in the philosophical works of the period, maintained that women were endowed with a complex of physical characteristics, principally the softness and feebleness of their reproductive organs from which their psychological traits of dependence and passivity developed (Bloch and Bloch, 1980; Jordanova, 1980; Easlea, 1981; McLaren, 1984). These qualities of softness and dependence were seen as the essence of female nature. It was this essential female nature which rendered women physically and emotionally incompetent to undergo labor. Rather than defining female reproductive organs as being pliable and elastic, men midwives interpreted a woman's "soft parts," as muscular feebleness. Using the sexual metaphor of the conquest and penetration of female nature common to the scientific discourses of the period, men midwives spoke of the (male) foetus in its descent of the birth canal as acting like a battering ram against a woman's "soft parts."[3]

Childbirth was then defined as an overwhelmingly dangerous and painful natural practice which, given the inherent weakness of women, threatened their lives. Thus Fielding Ould, an eminent Irish man midwife wrote: "In the most favourable labours poor women endure as much pain as mortals are well able to undergo" (Ould, 1742: p. 49). Another Irish man midwife, Frederick Jebb, in describing the course of labour, said

> We cannot sufficiently admire the intention of Providence in thus ordering the matter . . . in the period between the pains, the woman is perfectly in repose . . . were the whole labour one continual state of pain, how few would live to see the end of it. And amongst the few that might possibly outlive the operation, I believe scarcely one would recover from the enfeebled state to which such horror must reduce the strongest constitution. (Jebb, 1770, p. 9)

In his *Treatise of Midwifery,* Ould insisted "that the course of pain and danger which women undergo from the time of pregnancy till some time after birth is very considerable" (1742: p. 70), on which he based his conclusions that the proper course of action for the man midwife was to "hasten labour" and "lessen pain." By deploying these premises about women's natural physical incapacity to deal

---

[3] Given that the baby's head moves down the birth canal stretching the perineum only very gradually, there is no logical rationale for this image of a battering ram. See Mehl, Peterson, and Brandsel, "Episiotomy, Facts, Figures and Alternatives" in D. and L. Stewart (eds.) *Compulsory Hospitalization or Freedom of Choice in Childbirth?* NAPSAC Publication, 1979. ch. 15.

with labour, the medical discourses in the eighteenth century turned childbirth into a continuing problematic event which then required the scientific practice of the men midwives to see it through to a successful conclusion. With their invention of "the poor suffering woman" as Ould always referred to women in labor, men midwives raised the argument about the pain and danger of labour to the status of a scientific truth, and their conceptual framework about women shaped the evolution of the science of childbirth.

There were strong links between the new science of childbirth and political practices which enabled the setting up of lying-in hospitals. The construction of the female body in labor as a problem was connected with the economic function of birth, a theme pursued in the general philosophical and economic discourses of the period. Classic mercantilist arguments which concentrated on the political mathematics of the population issue weighed reproductive outcomes in economic terms and contributed to the interest in childbirth and in the management of women as childbearers. The medical discourses which designated the female body as an important source of scientific inquiry mirrored the growing awareness of the body's potential as the ultimate source from which time and labor could be extracted.

This is the point that Foucault (1977, 1979a, 1981) has made in looking at how the female body became a medical object. Foucault has isolated the female body as one of the four central targets in eighteenth century discourses on sexuality. It was during this period that sex was progressively systematized in the move to secure control over population. Sex was perceived to be the phenomenon at the heart of the political problem of population. Foucault argues that the proliferating series of regulatory mechanisms and apparatuses of power, which emerged during this period, can be traced to the explosion of discourses on sexuality. These discourses formed the juncture at which changing concepts about the body, both the individual body and the social body, produced new sets of power relations around the body. The process of fracturing and dividing the body, and its subjection to multiple apparatuses of power, as segments of the population were differentiated according to their usefulness to society as a whole, make up what Foucault has termed "bio-politics." The regulation of sex in all its manifestations was crucial to bio-politics, being the point of access, as Foucault says, to "the life of the body" and "the life of the species" (1981, p. 146).

Men midwives made constant reference to their role in preserving the "life of the species." Fielding Ould, for instance, wrote that midwifery was not "the meanest province in the medicinal Commonwealth, but much on the contrary, as on it depends not only the preservation of the species but the various methods of relieving distressed women from extraordinary pain and torture, innumerable disorders and death . . ." (Ould, 1742: p. 2). In this context, lying-in hospitals were seen as life-preserving institutions for women. According to Bartholomew Mosse, the man midwife credited with founding the Rotunda Hospital in Dublin, it offered shelter and skilled care to women otherwise "destitute of attendance, medicine and often proper food, by which hundreds perish with their little infants and the community is at once robbed of both mother and child" (Browne, 1947: p. 3). However, lying-in hospitals also provided the setting where theories about women and childbirth could be practiced on a specific population. The power of men midwives to control women in childbirth lay in their ability to postulate a connection between the individual body and the needs of the social body.[4]

THE CONTRADICTORY EFFECTS OF BIO-POLITICS

The Rotunda Lying-in Hospital, begun in 1745, was the first lying-in hospital in the British Isles. At that time, the contemporary perception that poverty was far greater in Ireland than elsewhere in the British Isles provoked great concern about the country's economic development. In the documentation which supported the Rotunda's establishment, the relief of poor lying-in women was seen to have a strategic function. Mercantilist opinion held that greater numbers of manual and agricultural workers would increase national wealth. If the Rotunda took on the task of overseeing the labors of women from the working classes, it would contribute to the national economy because "the increase of inhabitants most to be desired is amongst the lowest ranks."[5]

The "poor suffering" women in labor of the men midwives' discourses were thus conflated with the "laboring poor" and the lying-in hospital was regarded as a new form of charity. As Ould remarked

---

[4] Foucault discusses medical practice emerging as part of the apparatus of collective control of the body in "The Politics of Health in the Eighteenth Century" in *Power/Knowledge* C. Gordon, ed. See also "The Confessions of the Flesh," ibid.

[5] This opinion, expressed by a well-known Dublin preacher, Dr. Lawson, in his sermon to mark the opening of the chapel to the Rotunda in 1759, was the main reason for the public support the Rotunda received from the outset. See its *Royal Charter, 1756.* That women from the class of the "labouring poor" were assigned a pivotal role as reproducers is clear from the large amount of state aid granted to the Rotunda by the Irish House of Commons throughout the 18th century. For perceptions about poverty in 18th century Ireland, see C. Maxwell, *Dublin Under the Georges 1714–1830* (1956) and L. Cullen, *An Economic History of Ireland Since 1660* (1972).

in his Treatise "the poor who are by much the greater number (are) most subject to misfortunes in childbearing" (Ould, 1742, p. 79). The social fact of poverty was added to the argument about women's natural incapacity to justify the existence of a lying-in hospital to monitor childbirth. The poor also provided a continuing source of clinical material, an advantage to themselves of which the men mid-wives were well aware.[6]

The Rotunda was written up by contemporaries as a novel charita-ble effort providing shelter and medical supervision for poor women in labor, the benefits of which would accrue to the entire community. Women applying for admission to the Rotunda were expected to be "fit objects of charity," according to its Royal Charter. The Rotunda remained the only lying-in hospital in Ireland until 1824, after which the rapidly increasing numbers of men midwives were responsible for the founding of five more lying-in hospitals. In terms of numbers of women admitted, the Rotunda remained the largest single lying-in hospital in Ireland through much of the 19th century and was also the only hospital which would admit women regardless of both their economic and marital status, and of their place of origin.

This adherence of the Rotunda to its self-appointed role as a char-itable refuge had both positive and negative effects on its obstetric practice. Its charitable bias meant that unmarried women could ap-ply to the Rotunda for admission when they were on the point of giving birth. Although illegitimacy rates appear to have been sub-stantially lower in Ireland during the 19th century in comparison with the rest of the British Isles, at least 5% of total births in any given year did involve single women.[7] The Rotunda would accept

---

[6] Irish scientists in the eighteenth century saw the expansion of medical practice as a way of establishing a reputation at international level they did not otherwise possess because of their colonial status in relation to mainland Britain. In 1757, the Medico-Philosophical Society exhorted doctors to take up "their duty to publish the results of their experiences for the benefit of others in the fields of anatomy, physiology, surgery, and midwifery." See *Transactions, Medical and Philosophical Memoirs*, Volume 1, 1757, Medico-Philosophical Society.

[7] Historians have asserted that post-Famine Ireland adhered to a remarkably strict code of sexual behaviour, tied to the use of marriage as a predominantly economic mechanism in a rural society obsessed with the value of land and property. But the increasingly restrictive nature of Irish marriage after the Famine did not involve a radical climb in the rate of illegitimacy. See K. H. Connell's earlier work on peasant marriage in the *Economic History Review* (1962) and most recently, D. Fitzpatrick and S. J. Connolly's articles on pre- and post-Famine marriage patterns in *Marriage in Ireland* A Cosgrove, ed. On British rates of illegitimacy in the 19th century, see the chapter "Sexuality and the Labouring Classes" in J. Weeks' *Sex, Politics and Society*. On the situation of women in general in post-Famine Ireland, see Joe Lee's account "Women and the Church since the Famine" in *Women in Irish Society*, M. MacCurtain and D. O'Corrain, eds. (1978) pp. 37–45.

them if they were forced to seek the shelter of an institution to have their babies. Accepting every woman who was "a fit object of charity" led to high rates of admission. The Rotunda also undoubtedly benefited from the men midwives' refusal to practice away from an urban base. As a result, rural areas were consequently underserviced, more especially as schemes to train women midwives to fill the gaps thus created were consistently underfunded and downgraded.[8]

A further positive effect on the Rotunda of this concentration of numbers was a wealth of clinical material. Clinical records were kept from 1786 onwards. Up to then, the hospital registry had noted the number of women admitted and the number of children born alive, that is, information related to how many people the hospital had assisted as a charity. With the inception of clinical records, the emphasis shifted from statistics on poor laboring women to the process of labor itself. The records can be seen as chronicles for how men midwives objectified a woman in labor. She was fragmented into symptoms, cases, and complications. By the middle of the 19th century, even though the Rotunda was still a charitable institution, the detailed clinical records were evidence of the hospital's primary function as a medical establishment.

When Sinclair and Johnston, two assistant masters of the Rotunda, published their *Practical Midwifery* in 1858, the text exemplified the clinical approach. They preferred the obstetric outcomes of 13,748 cases as proof of the success of the Rotunda's approach to childbirth management. Sinclair and Johnston wrote in detail about the surveillance that had evolved around women in labor so that dress, diet, management of the stages of labor, position for birth, length of bedrest, and the timing of discharge were all standardized norms imposed on women at the hospital's discretion. Obstetric management decreeing how women should labor and for how long was the crucial layer of authority over the "fit objects of charity" because it had the power to direct women's bodies in labor in accordance with the perceptions of men midwives.

In the main, Sinclair and Johnston used maternal mortality statistics to make their point about the Rotunda having a superior system in comparison with other lying-in hospitals. They collated their figures so as to present the most optimistic profile. The earliest clinical records had distinguished between maternal deaths related to the "efforts of nature" and deaths from the "efforts of art" that is, inter-

---

[8] Schemes for what were termed "nurse pupils" to provide women midwives in the more rural areas existed from 1770 onwards. By 1854 however, even though individual county boards had been urged to contribute to the cost of training women midwives, a mere 656 women nurse pupils had passed through the Rotunda in comparison with 2,875 male medical pupils.

ventions by the men midwives. Sinclair and Johnston in an equally arbitrary but more politic use of categories divided deaths into three categories: the first were those deaths from "accidents" of puerperal fever which they claimed were beyond their control. Puerperal fever was the dangerous, life-threatening infection which could set in after a woman had given birth. In the second category they included all other deaths which did not arise from the "effects of labor," according to them, and finally in the third category were the deaths which they thought did arise from the "effects of labour."

The aim was to have as few cases as possible in the third category, on which men midwives rested their reputation. Sinclair and Johnston listed the 163 deaths out of 13,748 cases as being in the proportion of one in 84 1/3. Subtracting those who died of puerperal fever, death being "accidental," the proportion of maternal deaths from all other causes was shifted to read one in 148.75. Again subtracting deaths the men midwives attributed to women's general weakness, unrelated to the "effects of labour," Sinclair and Johnston arrived at a "true" rate of maternal mortality, those deaths which were calculated to have resulted from labor, as being one in 295 2/5 proportionately of the 13,748 women delivered. The laboring woman had been turned into a process and reduced to a fraction.

This play with numbers and categories of maternal deaths was a significant discourse of the period. Lying-in hospitals were alert to the need to secure their reputations professionally and politically, and the maternal mortality rates were a highly sensitive indicator on both counts. Assertions about successful systems of childbirth management were based on these statistics; the lower the rate that could be recorded, the better proof of superior management. These figures came to dominate medical journals in the 19th century as men midwives throughout the British Isles expounded their theories and techniques in competition with one another, each using his connection with a lying-in hospital as the source of his clinical material.

A higher rate of maternal mortality also had immediate political repercussions, particularly when an increase was traced to puerperal fever. For though Sinclair and Johnston tried to classify it as an accident, puerperal fever was firmly identified by the nineteenth century with lying-in hospitals.[9] In the period before sepsis and anti-

---

[9] The Wertzes in their history of childbirth management in America speak of puerperal fever as a "classic example of iatrogenic disease" (1977: p. 128). Oakley (1976) and Rich (1977) echo this view, Rich describing in detail the ignominious end of Semmelweis's career as a medical practitioner, after his findings on the cause of puerperal fever had been rejected by his colleagues. The lying-in hospital where Sem-

sepsis were understood, and before the advent of antibiotics, what was clear to men midwives was that puerperal fever flourished in the hospital setting, an unintended consequence of the institutionalization of childbirth. Because women could be affected by an outbreak, the fever had a disastrous impact and the only method of containing it was to close down wards where it occurred.

Puerperal fever undermined the rationale of lying-in hospitals to preserve the lives of poor women as reproducers. The funding of the hospitals, either by benefaction or by the state, was dependent on the success which they were seen to have in achieving their aim. Too high a number of maternal deaths led to public concern. The Rotunda itself faced closure four times in the nineteenth century because of puerperal fever epidemics. Yet even when both hospital and public authorities were sufficiently alarmed as to post notices around the city asking women to remain at home to give birth, destitute women were still presenting themselves at the door of the hospital seeking shelter where they could give birth.[10]

The existence of puerperal fever exposed men midwives to the negative aspects of the breadth of clinical material they otherwise enjoyed. Firstly, they were confronted with the failure of their science. They could name the fever, dissect its victims, describe it, but in no way control it. Yet they and their hospitals seemed to set it in motion. Secondly, the women who came to the Rotunda were highly susceptible. They often suffered from the cumulative effects of poverty and malnutrition. Some had travelled a great distance, arriving at the Rotunda in an exhausted condition, sometimes already in labor. They were ill-equipped to deal with the consequences of an infection which ran rife in the hospital with contamination spread by men midwives.

Originally in setting up the Rotunda, men midwives had claimed a

---

melweis worked in the mid-19th century was reputed to have a maternal mortality rate from puerperal fever five times higher than the Rotunda. See Sir William Wilde's account of the hospital, Chapter XI in his *Austria; its Literary, Scientific and Medical Institutions*, Dublin, 1843.

[10] Unlike London, Paris, and many of the German cities, Dublin never had the resource of a trained corps of women midwives even before the advent of men midwives. The limited provision the Rotunda made for training women as nurse pupils meant that the only skilled help available in Dublin was hospital-based and male-controlled. During a severe epidemic of puerperal fever at the Rotunda in 1819, the master, Dr. Labatt, recorded that though he had sent around circulars about the epidemic to discourage women from coming to the hospital, many women still sought admission "saying that they would rather run the risk of fever in the hospital, where they would have food and attendance, than remain at home destitute of both." See F. Churchill, *Collected Essays on Puerperal Fever* (1849), p. 18.

dual authority over the lives of women, first as arbiters of a charity whose function was to regulate and preserve the lives of the poor, and also as practitioners whose control of the female body in labor was the basis for the definitive science of obstetrics they were constructing. These two roles were increasingly thwarted because of the unexplained prevalence of puerperal fever. The Rotunda's status as an asylum for women seemed to men midwives a growing theat to its status as a scientific establishment. Puerperal fever was perceived by them as a malady afflicting poor women in the main and only occasionally affecting middle class and upper class women whom men midwives assisted in giving birth at home.[11]

In seeking to resolve the problems set in motion by the fever, the medical authorities in the Rotunda sought an answer at the expense of the women coming to the hospital. Men midwives had always contended that labor was complicated by the physical and psychological incompetence of women. They now extended this explanation to a hypothesis about puerperal fever. The fever seemed to be most prevalent among women carrying illegitimate babies. It was claimed that the disturbed psychological state of these women encourged the fever to take root. In this way, men midwives concocted an answer to the charge that they fostered puerperal fever: women were forced to bear the responsibility both for their marginalized social status and for their deaths in childbirth.[12]

PUERPERAL FEVER, SEDUCTION, AND THE USEFULNESS OF FORCEPS

Sinclair and Johnston's attempt to present the lowest possible maternal mortality figures by disclaiming responsibility for deaths from puerperal fever did not stem the growing public disquiet about the

---

[11] An early master of the Rotunda, Dr. Joseph Clarke, claimed he had never encountered a case of puerperal fever in any of his private patients over 35 years.

[12] "There are two main sources of mortality in the Rotunda Hospital. One large source arises from the number of unmarried women . . . the other is the immense number of primipararous cases" (first-time mothers), Dr. McClintock, a former master of the Rotunda, stated in 1872. He argued that because it was a charity, the Rotunda was forced to accept a disproportionate number of women in these two categories. See "Clinical Report of the Rotunda Lying-in Hospital, 1871." The medical opinion that most deaths could not be attributed to hospital practices but to the physical and emotional state of women prior to their entry was repeatedly aired in discussions about puerperal fever. Another former master of the Rotunda, Dr. Denham sketched in this picture of the train of events which led to women dying in childbirth: "When a girl

issue. From 1851 to 1861, the number of admissions to the Rotunda fell by almost a quarter while the rate of maternal mortality increased to 2.4% of annual admissions (by comparison with the maternal mortality rate for 1829–49 of 1.34%). Puerperal fever was rampant and a further investigation by the Public Health Commissioners in 1856 ended with a recommendation that the Rotunda establish immediately an external department from which men midwives would go out and supervise births for women in their homes, thus reducing the numbers of hospital admissions. In 1863, the hospital closed with another epidemic.

In 1867, a former master, Evory Kennedy wrote to the Board of Governors at the Rotunda quoting figures on the large drop in admissions. Acknowledging competition from other lying-in hospitals, he nevertheless attributed the drop principally to the public fear about puerperal fever:

> Puerperal fever . . . is known to haunt our lying-in hospitals as its peculiar habitat, and so great are its ravages . . . and such the proportion of victims swept away by it . . . that there are physicians and philanthropists who even question whether lying-in hospitals, as generally constructed, do not prove rather a curse than a blessing to the lying-in patient. (Kennedy, 1867, p. 516)

The ravages of the fever had given rise to the now "prevalent idea of recoveries being better at their own homes than in hospital" said Kennedy, which notion accounted for the drop in admissions. To preserve the opoportunities for midwifery practice, Kennedy suggested that the main body of the hospital no longer be used for lying-in women, that a series of chalets be built to one side which could accommodate some women and that the external department be extended so that many more women could be dealt with at home. The main building could be used to extend the teaching facility of the hospital concentrating on gynecological practice so that the Rotunda as the location for a "school of instruction" need not be abandoned.

The hospital governors rejected Kennedy's proposals but he returned to his criticism of the large hospital system which he saw as responsible for puerperal fever, with a paper delivered to the Dublin Obstetrical Society in 1869. Kennedy was not the first to point out

---

comes up from the country and flies away from her friends, and perhaps gets into some miserable lodging, she, after remaining there for a considerable time in a state of semi-starvation, falls into bad company, and then comes into the hospital for her confinement; it is important to bear these facts in mind." Also quoted in "Clinical Report of the Rotunda Hospital for 1871."

that puerperal fever seemed less of a problem in small cottage hospitals in Ireland. But as a former master of the Rotunda, Kennedy aroused a great deal of anger amongst men midwives attached to the Rotunda. The ensuing discussions about his views amounted to more than 200 pages in the Society's journals. Kennedy was universally derided by his colleagues for his views which were taken as an attack on the scientific ethos of obstetrics and also on what they considered their personal integrity. Several of the men midwives said that they could not possibly be responsible for carrying infection from one patient to another.[13]

By 1869, Johnston was master at the Rotunda and felt under particular attack about puerperal fever. Anxious to avoid any charge of mismanagement, he introduced a new line of argument in his first annual clinical report, in 1869, where he listed 25 maternal deaths. It was here he first advanced the rationale that those women who had contracted puerperal fever had done so because as victims of "seduction," they were already weakened by "remorse and fretting." Thus they had been unable to withstand the rigors of childbirth and consequently developed the fever. His opening remarks were a defense of the hospital system in general. He claimed that any infectious fevers which appeared in the hospital were ones for which women had a propensity because of where they lived and which they brought in with them.

How much rather should we look for these diseases in the localities from those seeking admission emanate, in the narrow, filthy, unswept streets, the courts and alleys in too many instances reeking with the pestilential effluvia of half-putrid offal and ordure, which by imperfect sewage or no sewage at all, allows the noxious gases escaping therefrom to pervade the overcrowded, small unwashed, ill-ventilated apartments, their bedding, if possessed of such a luxury, saturated with filth and dirt; the unfortunate occupants frequently in a weak, emaciated state, from want, penury, starvation, and disease . . . in fact everything most likely to engender the malady we all have so much to fear. (Johnston, 1869, p. 102).

The conditions in which working class women lived did not cover all the instances of puerperal fever, so Johnston supplemented it with

---

[13]Although men midwives readily viewed unmarried women's social circumstances as a moral issue which entailed physiological consequences, they refused to examine whether they themselves had any personal culpability in causing puerperal fever. Their status as professionals left them above suspicion, they argued. The same Dr. Denham when master of the Rotunda rejected Semmelweis's opinions about medical students and doctors carrying the disease, saying that "We have students always with us, puerperal fever only sometimes." (Browne, 1947: p. 127).

inferences about the deadly consequences of promiscuous sexual behaviour. In his list of maternal deaths, he made entries under the heading "Cause" like:

Pyaemia   Victim of seduction, remorse and fretting extreme
Peritonitis   Ditto
Mental Shock   Ditto
Mental Shock   Seduction, great mental depression.

The fuller case notes added this detail:

No. 4   25 years of age, her first pregnancy and died of pyaemia, 15th day after delivery. She was admitted from a distant county, the victim of seduction, and her remorse and fretting from the moment of coming in was extreme and most distressing to witness.

No. 35   34 years of age. She also was the victim of seduction, distress of mind and remorse no doubt being the cause of the fatal illness.

No. 12   28 years of age, second pregnancy, unmarried, caught cold in a railway train coming up from County Meath, was lying in a lodging house for a week . . . Peritoneal symptoms set in immediately after delivery, between which and distress of mind she sank on the fourth day. (Johnston, 1869, p. 108)

The phrase "she sank" sounds quite gentle yet it neatly obscured the horror of a death from puerperal fever in which women endured agonizing pain while remaining conscious and articulate until their last few moments alive.

The etiology of puerperal fever was simple enough.[14] What men midwives described as puerperal fever or peritonitis (they used these terms interchangeably) they associated with only the one symptom of a distended and extremely painful abdomen. In fact their definition of puerperal fever was only one manifestation of an enormous range of illnesses like pyaemia, erysipelas, and phlebitis, which, beginning with obstetrically induced infection in the uterus, often ended in women's deaths. Bacteria would spread from the initial site of infection in the uterus either into the abdominal cavity, or into the bloodstream, or would trigger the formation of infected clots in the pelvic

---

[14] I am indebted to Shorter for his substantive account of puerperal fever. Although he has attacked the feminist perspective on childbirth, he deals well with what he calls the doctors' "fudging" of the figures for puerperal fever in all its guises, and argues that to avoid a dramatically misleading undercount of maternal deaths due to obstetric infection, the assumption in assessing the 19th century records should be that all infections occurring within a month of delivery were obstetric in origin. See his *History of Women's Bodies* (1982), pp. 103–138.

veins, or inflame pelvic connective tissue. These serious peurperal infections frequently overwhelmed the body's defenses and ended in death. There were three sources of obstetrically induced infection. The first was the septic environment of the hospital itself, a far greater threat to women than the slums.[15] Secondly, there were the hands of the men midwives as they examined women which spread infection to the uterus either from other women or from the dissecting room. The third source of infection comprised the torn and bruised tissues of the cervix and vagina in the wake of a mechanical obstetric intervention like a forceps delivery.

What is clear is that at least 23 of the 25 maternal deaths which Johnston recorded in his first annual report were attributable to obstetrically induced infection. The clinical records reveal the process whereby the cause of death was filtered through the pre-existing model of women that men midwives had created. When women died after childbirth from infectious disease, that disease was seen to have a causal relationship to the model of how women were thought to function rather than to their management by men midwives. Men midwives disclaimed responsibility by explaining that death in childbirth was part of the physical susceptibility of being a woman. Further disclaimers could be attached to poor women coming in from the slums, that they brought the disease in with them. But a novel extension of the incompetent female model was Johnston's labeling of unmarried women as being most susceptible to fever. In his subsequent clinical reports, Johnston wrote at length about the women he called "innupta," that is unmarried, saying that such women were "admitted in a state of great mental distress from seduction." It was a "notorious fact," he commented, "that whenever they found feverish symptoms occuring after delivery, they constantly traced them to mental anxiety, caused either by seduction or by the husband having deserted and beaten his wife." (Johnston, 1872, p. 207).

The common perception of the process of labor amongst men midwives was that it should always be in their control. They cited overwhelming pain, the baby acting as a battering ram against the "soft parts," and women's general tendency to disease as reasons why they should intervene. So despite the individual pattern of each woman's labor, all were made to conform to an invariable rule. If first stage labor, when the cervix was dilating, was slower than men midwives

---

[15] Again, Shorter makes the point that maternal mortality was far less common in homes no matter how unfavorable the conditions, because working class women acquired a degree of immunity to their own bacteria whereas the hospital exposed them to "spectacular insalubrity," pp. 127–8.

wished, thex forced the pace by employing both manual dilation of the cervix with their fingers and a mechanical dilator. The expulsive second stage they could terminate with forceps. Such interventions also introduced the opportunity for infection. Thus a woman who labored slowly for whatever reason was particularly at risk in contracting puerperal fever as a result of her management by men midwives.

Johnston became convinced that these slow labors were more likely to occur amongst unmarried women because of their overwrought emotional state, and that in instances such as these, he should use the forceps to terminate labor rapidly.[16] He reasoned that this would protect women from inflammation and fever:

> Why should we permit a fellow-creature to undergo hours of torture when we have the means of relieving her within our reach? Why should she be allowed to waste her strength and incur the risks consequent upon the long pressure of the head on the soft parts . . . one of the fertile causes of puerperal fever (is) the labour being allowed to continue till inflammatory symptoms appear. (Johnston, 1872, p. 185)

The application of the forceps he argued was a "timely interference" which would bring benefits to both women and babies, lowering mortality rates. In his annual account for 1872, he reported that he had used the forceps on 131 women, nine of whom had died from puerperal fever. On 35 of these women, he had employed the forceps when they were as little as two-fifths dilated, that is, when the cervix was less than half open. Claiming this as a new practice not reported before in midwifery annals, Johnston wrote that he had adopted it after a case in which a woman who had not fully dilated had nevertheless exhibited "symptoms . . . such as to induce him to deliver with the forceps." "She went on favourably until the third day when on going round the wards," he found her "in a state of collapse and she passed away." The post-mortem revealed that the cervix had become completely detached and had been sloughed off. However, Johnston did not interpret this as a consequence of his

---

[16] In *Practical Midwifery,* Johnston had made the distinction between "tedious" labors which were simply slow according to the men midwives, and "difficult" labors where the forceps or other instruments had to be used because labor was clearly impeded by gross pelvic deformity, for instance, as the result of rickets. Johnston had merged the two categories by the time he became master, so that a slow labor, a common enough occurrence with first-time mothers, became classed as dangerous. Hence Johnston was inclined to treat first-time married mothers as he did unmarried women.

hasty forceps operation but said that the woman's case "had induced him to adopt the practice he had followed ever since (of applying the forceps before full dilation) and he found it attended with the greatest advantage, both as to the safety of the mother and the child" (Johnston, 1872, p. 207). To prove his point about the efficacy of the forceps, he described in detail another case in which he delivered a woman by forceps before she was fully dilated. When he found he could expand her cervix with his finger, he did not hesitate to use the forceps. Her death shortly thereafter was free of any uterine symptoms, he wrote. Johnston's reasoning about using forceps is a prime example of the male medical model about women. He was able to view the deaths as extraneous detail, unconnected with his intervention, because he had fulfilled his task of rescuing women from the danger of labor.

A master of the Rotunda holds office for seven years in which time he lays down the obstetric policy of the hospital. By the time Johnston completed his mastership in 1875, the number of forceps deliveries was higher than at any other point in the 19th century. He had sanctioned their use on 752 women out of 7,862. 554 of these were first-time mothers. 123 women had had the forceps applied to them before full dilation had occurred, of whom 44 had been subjected to the forceps when only two-fifths dilated. The mortality rate was greatest amongst the women who had been least dilated when the forceps were applied. Johnston's statistics indicate that the woman who was allowed to labor without forceps had one chance in 233 of contracting puerperal fever in comparison with a woman delivered by forceps who faced a one in 15 chance.

Altogether, 48 women of the first-time mothers subjected to forceps died after they gave birth, from puerperal fever. Of these 48, Johnston wrote that 28 developed puerperal fever because they were unmarried women suffering as a result of their seduction.

In his summary clinical report on the use of forceps, presented to the Dublin Obstetrical Society in 1878, he maintained that delivery by forceps especially before full dilation was "perfectly safe and its use justifiable for it . . . in great measure secures the safety of the mother . . . by obviating the danger produced by prolonged pressure of the foetal head on the maternal soft parts, and all of its evil consequences." (Johnston, 1879, p. 47).

Working from the incompetent female model, Johnston had employed an obstetric technique which actually substantially increased the risk of maternal mortality. The practice, based on this model, determined the adverse birth outcomes of the women subjected to a forceps delivery.

THE INVENTION OF WOMEN'S IDENTITY AS CHILDBEARERS

In examining how power and knowledge function through discourse, Foucault has written that medicine surrounds itself with a "solid scientific armature" (1980, p. 109). Yet at the same time medical discourse, playing a key role in bio-politics, has been profoundly implicated in the production of social relations. This medical armature enabled the forceps policy to be carried out in the Rotunda. The scientificity of Johnston's clinical accounts served to disguise how women were subjected to a set of power relations which they could not challenge.

By the 1870's, the Rotunda had enjoyed an international reputation in obstetric practice for more than 100 years. Its clinical records were treated as an ongoing authoritative source of the hospitals' teaching on the management of childbirth. Johnston himself was praised by his colleagues for being a skillful, earnest clinician who exercised careful judgement along with manual dexterity. He was not an aberration outside the medical paradigm but worked from solidly within it. His ideas were not new amongst men midwives. The attribution of a death from puerperal fever to a woman's emotional state, citing her presumed grief and shame about her pregnancy, had been advanced before.

Nor was it unheard of to apply the forceps to women when they were only partially dilated. Despite his boast, Johnston had been preceded in advocating this practice by the British man midwife, Smellie, 125 years earlier.[17]

The power of men midwives to impose practices arbitrarily stemmed from their theoretical discourses. Once these discourses had secured expression through the institution of the lying-in hospital, it was inevitable that men midwives would invent the necessity for obstetric practices without having to question their effects on women.

---

[17] Obstetric history is rife with similar examples. In American hospitals, De Lee's system of "prophylactic" forceps deliveries, in combination with the notorious drug scopolamine, enjoyed great popularity from the 1920's onwards. See (J. De Lee, "The prophylactic forceps operation," *Am. J. Ob. Gyn. 1:* p. 34–44. October, 1920. Also see Kitzinger (1985: p. 212). For an account of De Lee's influence on obstetric practice in America, see W. Arney, *Power and the Profession of Obstetrics* (1983). For 19th century examples of American medical arguments on women's emotional instability in childbirth, see G. J. Barker-Benfield, *The Horrors of the Half-Known Life* (1976). He has an excellent account of Marion Sims, the so-called "architect of the vagina" who specialized in aggressive operative gynecology on the grounds that women's emotional state could be controlled through a modification of their sexual organs.

Johnston's policy on forceps is one example of how this power worked. He was able to sanction the use of forceps on a wide scale, trying it to his theory about women and seduction, and the need to absolve the hospital from any responsibility in creating puerperal fever epidemics.

After Johnston gave his final paper on forceps deliveries to the Dublin Obstetrical Society in 1878, his colleagues debated the issue almost exclusively in terms of whether the increased use of forceps would lower maternal mortality rates and so advance the hospital's teaching reputation. When referred to in the debate, the objects of this practice, the women, appeared most frequently as numbers, averages, and fractions of the many statistics presented to 'prove' lower mortality, emphasising how essential demographic techniques and a numerical discourse were to the politics of male midwifery.

In both Johnston's clinical reports and the debates on them, women were treated as a distinct population presenting a series of technical problems which were dealt with by breaking them down into subcategories of cases and characteristics, all of which were specified by men midwives. The numbering and categorizing of pregnant women was one of the mechanisms of objectification around which the power relations were organized within the lying-in hospital. Like the staff at the French penitentiary, Mettray, whom Foucault describes as "technicians of behaviour" (1979b: p. 294) the men midwives also created a set of power relations through an interlocking series of techniques and discursive mechanisms to produce docile bodies. In a similar manner, the clinical reports of the Rotunda functioned as a discursive mechanism.

Johnston's colleagues never questioned the central premise about the weakness of women in childbirth, and his seduction theory was an acceptable explanation of death from puerperal fever amongst the group of unmarried women. Throughout Johnston's mastership, the only hesitation in classifying women as having been seduced was whether prostitutes might be masquerading as genuine victims of seduction in order to seek shelter in the hospital when giving birth.

The forceps era in the Rotunda provides a graphic illustration of the continuity of power relations which have enmeshed women in childbirth since the eighteenth century. In this instance, unmarried women were made into a specific medical problem and labeled as victims, which resulted in their being further victimized with, for them, disastrous consequences.

In examining male ideologies about women, MacKinnon (1982) observes that the elements which compose the female stereotype reflect male sexual power. The imputed quality of female passivity for example, reflects the male expectation of a lack of resistance which is reinforced by social practices. So also, female incompetence summons up male support albeit on male terms. An examination of obstetric discourse reveals the process of male ideology about women's bodies in the making. From the time when male medical discourses first defined the female body in labor as problematic, women were mapped out as a territory where obstetric practices could be endlessly rehearsed and a discourse was further developed to legitimate these practices. Men midwives laid claim to the territory of the female body through the invention of their theory about female incompetence.

It has meant that women undergoing childbirth have been subject to a definition of themselves which originated within male medical discourse. This definition has had concrete effects on women and continues to permeate obstetric thinking.[18] Obstetric theory and practice have modified both the identity of women as childbearers and their birth outcomes. Freud wrote in "Dora": "I will simply claim for myself the rights of the gynecologist—or rather much more modest ones." It is little wonder that Freud aspired to even some of the unlimited power than men midwives had. Their ability to dominate the female body in labour by means of the obstetric view of feminine identity has led to their total control of women's reproductive care.

REFERENCES

Arms, S. (1975). *Immaculate Deception*. Boston: Houghton Mifflin.
Arms, S. (1977). Why women should be in control of childbirth. In D. Stewart

---

[18] Obstetric discourse has consistently been able to take on new technologies while employing the same rationale for their use. The discourse continues to resist any challenge by deploying the theory of female incompetence. In the current variant of Johnston's argument, the Rotunda Hospital argues that its high rates of induction and epidurals are necessary because it deals with a greater proportion of women from the lowest socioeconomic group, and that 16% of its patients are unmarried mothers ("The Year of the Baby" *U*, May, 1982, Vol. 3., No. 7, pp. 56–7).

For current examples of the argument about women's feebleness in pregnancy, see the eminent British obstetrician, Bourne, "Advice to Pregnant Women" in *Pregnancy* (1975). Bourne cautions women not to take on physical exercise "more vigorous than scrubbing a floor or even polishing a table." A telling instance of women's objectification appeared in the 1985 annual report for St. James Hospital in Dublin: as reported in the *Irish Medical Times*, January, 1986, "St. James is indebted to the Coombe Hospital for taking a number of very premature in utero transfers of babies." The pregnant women who were moved from one hospital to another are here referred to only by the phrase "in utero," as passive baby carriers.

& L. Stewart (Eds.), *21st Century Obstetrics Now* (no. 1977, pp. 73–88). Marble Hill: NAPSAC.

Arney, W. R. (1983). *Power and the Profession of Obstetrics*. Chicago: University of Chicago Press.

Barker-Benfield, G. J. (1976). *The Horrors of the Half-Known Life*. New York: Harper and Row.

Beels, C. (1978). *The Childbirth Book*. Great Britain: Turnstone Books.

Bloch, J. H., & Bloch, M. (1980). Women and the dialectics of nature in eighteenth-century French thought. In C. MacCormack & M. Strathern (Eds.), *Nature, Culture and Gender* (pp. 25–41). Cambridge: Cambridge University Press.

Bourne, G. (1976). *Pregnancy*. London: Pan Books.

Brook, D. (1976). *Naturebirth: Preparing for Natural Birth in an Age of Technology*. Harmondsworth: Penguin.

Browne, T. D. O. (1947). *The Rotunda Hospital 1745–1945*. Edinburgh: F. and S. Livingstone.

Churchill, F. (1849). *Collected Essays on Puerperal Fever*. Dublin.

Cullen, L. (1972). *An Economic History of Ireland Since 1660*. London: B. T. Batsford.

Connell, K. H. (1962). Peasant marriage in Ireland: Its structure and development since the famine. *Economic History Review, 500–523.*

Connolly, S. J. (1985). Marriage in pre-famine Ireland. In A. Cosgrove (Ed.), *Marriage in Ireland*. Dublin: College Press.

De Lee, J. (1920, October). The prophylactic forceps operation. *American Journal of Obstetrics and Gynecology, 1, 34–44.*

Donnison, J. (1977). *Midwives and Medical Men*. London: Heinemann.

Dublin Obstetrical Society. (1869, August and November). 'Reports' (Debate on E. Kennedy's paper on zymotic disease). *Dublin Quarterly Journal of Medical Science, XLVIII, 225–429.*

Easlea, B. (1981). *Science and Sexual Oppression: Patriarchy's Confrontation with Women and Nature*. London: Wiedenfeld and Nicholson.

Ehrenreich, B., & English, D. (1973). *Witches, Midwives and Nurses: A History of Women Healers*. Old Westbury, N.Y.: Feminist Press.

Fitzpatrick, D. (1985). Marriage in post-famine Ireland. In A. Cosgrove (Ed.), *Marriage in Ireland*. Dublin: College Press.

Foucault, M. (1977). Power and sex. *Telos, 32, 152–161.*

Foucault, M. (1979a). Interview with Lucette Finas. In M. Morris & P. Patton (Eds.), *Power, Truth and Strategy* (pp. 67–76). Sydney: Feral Publications.

Foucault, M. (1979b). *Discipline and Punish: The Birth of the Prison*. Harmondsworth: Penguin.

Foucault, M. (1980). Truth and power. In C. Gordon (Ed.), *Power/Knowledge: Selected Interviews and Other Writings* (pp. 109–133). Brighton: Harvester Press.

Foucault, M. (1980). The politics of health in the eighteenth century. In C. Gordon (Ed.), *Power/Knowledge: Selected Interviews and Other Writings* (pp. 166–182). Brighton: Harvester Press.

Foucault, M. (1980). The confessions of the flesh. In C. Gordon (Ed.), *Power/Knowledge: Selected Interviews and Other Writings* (pp. 194–228). Brighton: Harvester Press.

Foucault, M. (1981). *The History of Sexuality Volume One: An Introduction.* Harmondsworth: Penguin.

Freud, S. (1977). *Case Histories I "Dora" and "Little Hans".* Harmondsworth: Penguin.

Inch, S. (1983). *Birthrights: A Parent's Guide to Modern Childbirth.* London: Hutchinson.

Irish Medical Times. (1986, January).

Jebb, F. (1770). *A Physiological Enquiry into the Process of Labour and an Attempt to Ascertain the Determining Cause of It.* Dublin.

Johnston, G. (1870, February and May). Clinical report of the Rotunda Lying-in Hospital for the year ending 5th November 1869. *Dublin Quarterly Journal of Medical Science, XLIV,* 101–112.

Johnston, G. (1871, February and May). Clinical report of the Rotunda Lying-in Hospital for the year ending 5th November 1870. *Dublin Quarterly Journal of Medical Science, LI,* 155–177.

Johnston, G. (1872, January and June). Clinical report of the Rotunda Lying-in Hospital for the year ending 5th November, 1871. *Dublin Quarterly Journal of Medical Science, LIII,* 160–180.

Johnston, G. (1873, January and June). Clinical report of the Rotunda Lying-in Hospital for the year ending 5th November 1872. *Dublin Quarterly Journal of Medical Science, LV,* 180–208.

Johnston, G. (1874, January and June). Clinical report of the Rotunda Lying-In Hospital for the year ending 5th November 1873. *Dublin Quarterly Journal of Medical Science, LVIII,* 177–204.

Johnston, G. (1875, January and June). Clinical report of the Rotunda Lying-in Hospital for the year ending 5th November 1874. *Dublin Quarterly Journal of Medical Science, LIX,* 124–166.

Johnston, G. (1876, January and June). Clinical report of the Rotunda Lying-In Hospital for the year ending 5th November 1874. *Dublin Quarterly Journal of Medical Science, LXI,* 256–295.

Johnston, G. (1879, January and June). Clinical report of 752 cases of forceps delivery in hospital practice. *Dublin Quarterly Journal of Medical Science, LXVIII,* 43–65.

Jordanova, L. J. (1980). Natural facts: A historical perspective on science and sexuality. In C. MacCormack & M. Strathen (Eds.), *Nature, Culture and Gender* (pp. 42–69). Cambridge: Cambridge University Press.

Kennedy, E. (1867, August and November). Important letter from Dr. Evory Kennedy to Governors of the Lying-In Hospital. *Dublin Quarterly Journal of Medical Science, XLIV,* 514–521.

Kennedy, E. (1869, February and May). Zymotic diseases as more especially illustrated by puerperal fever. *Dublin Quarterly Journal of Medical Science, XLVIII,* 269–306.

Kitzinger, S. (1979). *Birth at Home.* Oxford: Oxford University Press.

Kitzinger, S. (1985). *Woman's Experience of Sex.* Harmondsworth: Penguin.

Lee, J. J. (1978). Women and the church since the famine. In M. MacCurtain & D. O'Corrain (Eds.), *Women in Irish Society: The Historical Dimension*. Dublin: Arlen House.

Macintyre, S. (1977). Childbirth: The myth of the Golden Age. *World Medicine, 12*(18), 17–22.

MacKinnon, C. (1982). Feminism, Marxism, method and the State: An agenda for theory. In N. Keohane, M. Rosaldo & B. Gelpi (Eds.), *Feminist Theory*. Sussex: Harvester Press.

McLaren, A. (1984). *Reproductive Rituals: The Perception of Fertility in England from the Sixteenth to the Nineteenth Century*. London: Methuen.

Maxwell, C. (1956). *Dublin Under the Georges, 1714–1830*. London: Faber and Faber.

Medico-Philosophical Society. (1757). A proposal for furthering the intentions of the society. *Transactions, Medical and Philosophical Memoirs, I*, 300–310.

Oakley, A. (1976). Wisewoman and medicine man: Changes in the management of childbirth. In J. Mitchell & A. Oakley (Eds.), *The Rights and Wrongs of Women*. Harmondsworth: Penguin.

Oakley, A. (1980). *Women Confined: Towards a Sociology of Childbirth*. Oxford: Martin Robertson.

Ould, F. (1742). *A Treatise of Midwifery in Three Parts*. Dublin.

Rich, A. (1977). *Of Woman Born: Motherhood as Experience and Institution*. London: Virago.

Rotunda Hospital. (1756). *A Copy of His Majesty's Royal Charter for Incorporating the Governors and Guardians of the Hospital for the Relief of the Poor Lying-In Women Dublin*. Dublin.

Rotunda Hospital. (1759). *A Sermon Intended to Have Been Preached at the Publick Opening of the Chapel of the Lying-In Hospital in Great Britain Street*. Dublin.

Shorter, E. (1983). *A History of Women's Bodies*. London: Allen Lane.

Sinclair, E., & Johnston, G. (1858). *Practical Midwifery: Comprising an Account of 13,748 Deliveries which Occurred in the Dublin Lying-in Hospital During the Course of Seven Years Commencing November, 1847*. London: J. Churchill.

Stewart, D., & Stewart, L. (Eds.). (1979). *Compulsory Hospitalization or Freedom of Choice in Childbirth?* Marble Hill: NAPSAC.

The year of the baby. (1982, May). *'U' Magazine, 3*(7).

Versluysen, M. (1981). Lying-in hospitals in eighteenth century London. In H. Roberts (Ed.), *Women, Health, and Reproduction* (pp. 18–49). London: Routledge and Kegan Paul.

Weeks, J. (1981). *Sex, Politics and Society: The Regulation of Sexuality Since 1800*. New York: Longman.

Wertz, D., & Wertz, R. (1977). *Lying In: A History of Childbirth in America*. New York: Free Press.

Wilde, Sir W. (1843). *Austria: Its Literary, Scientific and Medical Institutions*. Dublin.

CHAPTER 7

The Rhetoric of Heterosexism

Susan J. Wolfe

The University of South Dakota

DEFINING HETEROSEXISM

In her pioneering work *The Second Sex,* first published in 1949, de Beauvoir explored the myth of the feminine, and the social and economic forces which have shaped individual women's lives so that each would become an image of that myth. A feminist existentialist, she saw the process as one by which society established a woman as Other:

> One is not born, but rather becomes, a woman. No biological, psychological, or economic fate determines the figure that the human female presents in society; it is civilization as a whole that produces this creature, intermediate between male and eunuch, which is described as feminine. Only the intervention of someone else can establish an individual as Other (de Beauvoir, 1952, p. 249).

Since the publication of de Beauvoir's book, numerous feminist works have emerged analyzing the ways in which women have been socialized to fulfill the roles which society, or men, expect of them. The roles of the mass media, of literature, of childrearing and education have all been examined. Sexism has come to be seen as an organizing principle for most cultures, an ideology giving rise to the institutions which support it (such as institutionalized motherhood; see Rich's *Of Woman Born* [1976] for an extensive treatment of motherhood as an institution).

Yet not until the 1970's was heterosexuality perceived as a like institution by gay activists and lesbian feminists. Theorists within both movements, however, have come to realize that the sexual politics which assure the dominance of male over female work equally effectively to assure the dominance of heterosexuals over gay men and lesbians. As Altman (1982) has observed, a thorough study of the repression of gay men and lesbians must deal not only with obvious private and public discrimination and violence and with the state action which permits them, but with the ideology which renders repression possible—heterosexism. Drawing on Millett's view of sexual politics as a form of "herrschaft," a relationship of dominance and subordination, Altman (1982, pp. 110–111) defines heterosexism as "that ideological structure that assumes heterosexuality as the norm and homosexuality as deviant and, indeed, despicable." Heterosexism differs from homophobia, an irrational fear and hatred of homosexuality and/or gay men and lesbians, for it, like sexism, is supported by institutions—local, state, and federal law; military regulations; marriage, and the family.

Rich (1986) terms heterosexism "the bias of compulsory heterosexuality, through which lesbian experience is perceived on a scale ranging from deviant to abhorrent or simply rendered invisible" (p. 26). In arguing for a feminist critique of compulsory heterosexual orientation for women, she demonstrates that heterosexism functions to oppress all women as surely as it oppresses lesbians and gay men, since male power is grounded in the control men exert over women's sexuality and productivity. In fact, Rich adapts an essay by Gough on the relationship between the family and sexual inequality, demonstrating that the characteristics of male power which produce sexual inequality also enforce heterosexuality. Among the characteristics of male power are the power of men

1. to deny women [their own] sexuality—[by means of clitoridectomy and infibulation; chastity belts; punishment, including death, for female adultery; punishment, including death, for lesbian sexuality; psychoanalytic denial of the clitoris; strictures against masturbation; denial of maternal and postmenopausal sensuality; unnecessary hysterectomy; pseudolesbian images in the media and literature; closing of archives and destruction of documents relating to lesbian existence]

2. or to force it [male sexuality] upon them—[by means of rape (including marital rape) and wife beating; father–daughter, brother–sister incest; the socialization of women to feel that male sexual "drive" amounts to a right; idealization of heterosexual romance in art, literature, the media, advertising, etc.; child marriage; arranged marriage; prostitution; the harem; psychoanalytic doctrines of frigidity and vaginal orgasm; pornographic depictions of

women responding pleasurably to sexual violence and humiliation (a subliminal message being that sadistic heterosexuality is more "normal" than sensuality between women)]

3. to command or exploit their labor to control their produce—[by means of the institutions of marriage and motherhood as unpaid production. . .]

4. to control or rob them of their children—[by means of father right and "legal kidnapping"; . . . seizure of children from lesbian mothers by the courts. . .] (Rich, pp. 36–38, excerpted)

Rich argues that a complex system of forces compels women to identify with men, to place male needs above their own, and to believe that heterosexuality and marriage are inevitable. Gay activists like Altman may differ on the perceived roots of heterosexism and the strategies most likely to be successful in its elimination, but would agree that its prejudices include the belief that homosexual behavior is unnatural, immoral, or "sick"; the belief that it is contagious— that is, that exposing others, especially children, to gay men and lesbians will cause them to become homosexual; the belief that gay men and lesbians are neurotic, maladjusted, or unstable; the conviction that gay men and lesbians cannot provide adequate role models as parents and teachers.

LANGUAGE AND PREJUDICE

Feminists who have analyzed language have by and large subscribed to the Sapir-Whorf hypothesis, arguing that "it is language which determines the limits of our world, which constructs our reality" (Spender, 1980, p. 139). Language serves as a symbol system, a means of classifying the world, and once humans have a specific language as a means of classification, we tend to see reality in terms of that system. Far from being objective, our perceptions and knowledge are shaped by language.

Feminist analyses of language often contend, moreover, that men have been the originators of language because men have wielded the power in most cultures (see Daly, 1973; Miller & Swift, 1977; Spender, 1980; Stanley, 1977). Language reinforces theories of male superiority and hence serves to support male domination. In English, for example, terms which refer to women frequently pejorate, taking on negative and even obscene connotations, while corresponding terms referring to men do not; "courtesan" and "courtier," "master and mistress" are illustrative of many such pairs (Schulz). In turn, the fact that so many terms for women have negative and sexual associations reinforces the identification of women as sexual objects available to men.

In a similar manner, labeling gay men "queer" or "sissies" associates male homosexuality with deviance and effeminacy (the latter equating homosexual orientation or practices with gender confusion, and reinforcing a dominant stereotype of gay men). Likewise, the use of the term "straight" as an antonym for "gay," when "straight" also denotes "honest" and "forthright" and serves as an antonym for "drug user" and "criminal," also supports heterosexist beliefs that gay men and lesbians are at once perverted from normal practices and deserving of punishment. And, while "gay" itself has been coined by gay men to capture the gay experience, or the attitudes of those who identify primarily with their own sex (versus "homosexual," with its clinical and psychoanalytic associations), it, too, is likely to pejorate in the usage of heterosexuals, as terms for women have pejorated—simply through their association with members of a subordinate, repressed group.

The rhetoric of heterosexism, the language and discourse strategies adopted to enforce compulsory heterosexuality, has been encoded as law at every level of American government. It continues to figure in adjudicating cases involving lesbians and gay men, and justices' opinions are shaped by it even as they provide new instances of it. Heterosexist rhetoric and court rulings based upon it reinforce in turn the heterosexism of the heterosexual majority—whose prejudices and beliefs have been captured by the rhetoric which convinces them.

LEGAL INTERPRETATIONS AND NORMATIVE STANDARDS: HOMOSEXUALITY AS IMMORAL/UNNATURAL

Though it can be successfully argued that Christianity has played an important role in Western heterosexism, the source of judicial precedent concerning homosexuality must be traced to English common law. Often cited in contemporary cases is Blackstone's condemnation of homosexuality as a crime so horrible that Christians ought not to name it:

> I will not act so disagreeable part, to my readers as well myself, to dwell any longer upon a subject the very mention of which is a disgrace to human nature. It well be more eligible to imitate, in this respect, the delicacy of our English law, which treats it in its very indictments as

crime not fit to be named: 'pecatum illud horrible, inter Christiano non nominadum. . .' This the voice of nature and of reason, and the express law of God, determined to be capital. Of which we have a signal instance, long before the Jewish dispensation. (quoted from Bowers v. Hardwick, 1986, pp. 215–216)

Chief Justice Burger, though willing to mention the word "sodomy" in concurring with the Court on its ruling in Bowers v. Hardwick, cites Blackstone as well as "Judaeo-Christian moral and ethical standards" and Roman law, as a precedent:

As the Court notes, ante at _____, the proscriptions against sodomy have very "ancient roots." Decisions of individuals relating to homosexual conduct have been subject to state intervention throughout the history of Western Civilization. Condemnation of those practices is firmly rooted in Judaeo-Christian moral and ethical standards. Homosexual sodomy was a capital crime under Roman law. . . During the English Reformation when powers of the ecclesiastical courts were transferred to the King's Courts, the first English statute criminalizing sodomy was passed. 25 Hen. VIII, c. 6. Blackstone described "the infamous crime against nature" as an offense of "deeper malignity" than rape, an heinous act "the very mention of which is a disgrace to human nature," and "a crime not fit to be named." (Blackstone's Commentaries *215.) The common law of England, including its prohibition of sodomy, became the received law of Georgia . . . To hold that the act of homosexual sodomy is somehow protected as a fundamental right would be to cast aside millennia of moral teaching (Bowers v. Hardwick, 1986).

Few feminists would agree with Blackstone that the apparently victimless crime of consensual homosexual sodomy, an act committed by Hardwick in his own home, is of greater "malignity" than rape. Indeed, the ranking of these felonies by Blackstone seems as much an indication of gynophobia as homophobia. The Georgia statute challenged by Hardwick, however, ranks a single private, consensual act of sodomy among its more serious felonies, for it carries a penalty of up to 20 years in prison, a sentence equal to that which may be imposed for aggravated battery (Bowers v. Hardwick, 1986).

The willingness of the Supreme Court to buttress an opinion by appealing to Judaeo-Christian moral standards is neither new nor surprising; such appeals may be readily traced to English common law, as has been shown. Moreover, in ruling on the behavior of others, justices base their opinions on their view of the "prevailing social mores" of the community as well as legal precedent—the normative rationale.

In determining what constitutes normal or moral behavior, judges rely on the opinion of other experts. Mental health practitioners may provide information about what is considered normal; a dictionary may be consulted to define the boundaries of morality when no legal definition of a term exists. Yet standards of mental health, too, are culturally determined: in many cultures, entire households have been expected to follow a master in death, a mass suicide which would be regarded as unbalanced and illegal in the United States in the twentieth century. Likewise, most lexicographers record common usage, the "everyday" word usage of the majority. When psychiatric classifications and dictionary definitions capture the heterosexism of much of the American public, and when courts in turn render judgments based in part upon these "expert" views and in part upon their own prejudices, their rulings serve as future precedents and as evidence to the majority that heterosexism is justified.

Since the 1960's, gay and lesbian employees, military personnel, and students have been increasingly willing to challenge laws and regulations restricting their behavior. Gay activists have succeeded in altering the classification of homsexuality in the American Psychiatric Association's Diagnostic and Statistical Manual of Mental Disorders (DSM), and thus presumably eliminated one of the arguments for discrimination on the basis of sexual orientation. Homosexuality, classified as a *sociopathic personality disturbance* in the 1952 edition (a designation for those who failed to conform to cultural norms), was characterized as a *personality disorder* (a disorder distinguished by "deeply ingrained maladaptive patterns of behavior") in 1968; homsexuality was removed as a category in 1973 (only those in conflict with their sexual orientation remained classified as disturbed [Slovenko, 1985, pp. 448–450]). Nonetheless, assumptions that homosexual acts are "unnatural" as well as immoral prevail in many courts, as the opinion offered by Burger above indicates.

The courts have responded to some extent, as in the case of Norton v. Macy, wherein the court articulated a principle which appears to provide public employment protection for lesbians and gay men: a public employee may be fired for homosexuality "only if all immoral and indecent acts of an employee have some ascertainable deleterious effect on the efficiency of the service" (Hoffman, 1978, pp. 338–339). Yet the language of the principle, at least, prevents us from hailing it as an example of judicial tolerance; first of all, all homosexual acts are termed "immoral" and "indecent."

Moreover, the breadth of interpretation permitted by "some ascertainable deleterious effect on the efficiency of the service" has allowed many justices to uphold the dismissal of gay public employees on the basis of their own speculations about what might detract from the efficiency of a school or a police department. In general, they have cited the "common knowledge" that homosexual acts are immoral, obscene, unnatural, and disgusting, and thus offensive to co-workers and damaging to the image of public institutions.

In Schlegel v. United States (1969), for example, a case in which a civilian had been dismissed from the Army for having participated in off-duty homosexual acts, the Court of Claims upheld his dismissal. Although off-duty misconduct warranted dismissal only if "detrimental to the efficiency of the service," the plaintiff's superiors testified that Shlegel's presence would have impaired office morale. The ruling captures the judge's opinion of homosexual activity and of the plaintiff who had dared to object to his dismissal:

> Any schoolboy knows that a homosexual act is immoral, indecent, lewd, and obscene. Adult persons are even more conscious that this is true. If activities of this kind are allowed to be practiced in a government department, it is inevitable that the efficiency of the service will in time be adversely affected.

In addition to ridiculing Schlegel for his presumed naivete or stupidity, the judge has implied that the plaintiff will engage in homosexual acts in the office, though no charges had been brought to this effect—"If activities of this kind are allowed to be practiced in a government department." He also assumes that the plaintiff's having engaged in such "activities" will in and of itself affect efficiency. We can perhaps construe that heterosexual activities, even if occurring in a government department, have no impact on efficiency.

The courts have rendered many similar opinions, basing them upon the "prevailing social mores" of a given community (Hoffman, 1978), upon dictionary definitions of terms, and upon the expert testimony of psychiatrists. But heterosexist beliefs underlie all of the above. Heterosexism maintains the contradictory premises that homosexuality is at once unnatural, immoral, and hence repugnant, yet so attractive that it may be contagious; that heterosexuality, though the only natural expression of human sexuality, requires for its maintenance that all role models for the future generation be heterosexual. (Of course, the probability that 10% of the individuals in a population may have a homosexual orientation already is either ignored, or considered as evidence of the increased threat of a homosexual role model.)

The case of Gaylord v. Tacoma School District No. 10, occurring in 1977 after both the reclassification of homosexuality by the American Psychiatric Association and Norton v. Macy, illustrates that a gay high school teacher need not be accused of overt homosexual activities (either sexual or activist) to be barred from public teaching. Heterosexism alone provides sufficient grounds. In this instance, Gaylord, a teacher with 12 years of unblemished service at Wilson High, lost his job after counseling a homosexual student who subsequently informed the vice-principal that he "thought Gaylord was a homosexual." When confronted, Gaylord conceded his homosexuality; his dismissal followed within two months.

School board policy allowed discharge for "immorality," but the Supreme Court lacked a legal definition of the word. They chose to use the "ordinary, common, everyday meaning" of the term, and concluded that "homosexuality is widely condemned as immoral and was so condemned as immoral during biblical times." The concurring judges also noted the trial testimonies of a psychiatrist and a sociologist which "proved" that homosexuality was socially unacceptable, because "adults in this country react negatively to homosexuality" or find it "frightening." That Gaylord had failed to seek psychiatric help to change his sexual orientation provided evidence of his immorality—he had made a voluntary choice to remain homosexual. The American Psychiatric Association's manual, which by then had removed homosexuality from its list of disorders, served to condemn rather than to excuse him: since Gaylord would have been suffering from a disorder only if he had a desire to change his sexual orientation, he was immoral rather than "sick." The objection other teachers and administrators might have had to his sexual activities was thus adequate grounds for his dismissal.

Furthermore, the court concluded that Gaylord's presence might foster homosexual activity among high school pupils, who would equate his retention with adult approval of homosexuality:

> Gaylord's homosexual conduct must be considered in the context of his position of teaching high school students. Such students could treat the retention of the high school teacher by the school board as indicating adult approval of his homosexuality. It would be unreasonable to assume. . . [that this] creates no danger of encouraging expression of approval and of imitation.

The assumption that the mere presence of a teacher known to be gay might shift the sexual orientation of high school students is an appeal to the myth of contagion. It seems particularly odd in a trial whose discussion included West's (pp. 10–11) remark that "The thought of intimate contacts with their own sex disgusts many persons," supporting the contention that co-workers would find Gaylord's presence disruptive.

The court's conclusion that Gaylord must have been guilty of illegal and immoral acts (sodomy and lewdness) simply because he identified himself as homosexual illustrates another heterosexist assumption: the notion that gay men and lesbians are by nature promiscuous, victims of uncontrollable sexual appetites. Gaylord did not identify himself as a latent homosexual; thus, he was found to have admitted to being a practicing or overt homosexual, and, in turn, to have committed sodomy because "sexual gratification with a member of one's own sex is implicit in the term 'homosexual.'"

Without even circumstantial evidence of Gaylord's sexual activities, the court held him responsible for the common definition of the term. As is evident in the 1976 edition of the *American Heritage Dictionary* (AHD), *homosexuality* denotes sexual activity unless limited by a modifier like *latent:*

> homosexuality n. 1. Sexual desire for others of one's own sex. 2. Sexual activity with another of the same sex.

The term *heterosexuality* is not listed separately in the same dictionary; it is listed simply as a noun under heterosexual, but its meaning may be inferred:

> heterosexual adj. 1. Characterized by attraction to the opposite sex. 2. Of or pertaining to different sexes.—n. A heterosexual person.

Homosexuality also has negative connotations; its definition has been loaded to imply a baser, indeed, somatic sexual response. *Desire* has *craving, sexual appetite,* and *passion* as its synonyms in the AHD; by contrast, *attraction,* the more rational emotion experienced by heterosexuals, is defined as an interest in or admiration for another person because of some "quality or action." *Desire* is an emotionally-charged term hinting at lack of control; thus, the first definition of homosexuality leads to the second—driven by a craving or appetite, the gay man proceeds to "sexual activity with another of the same sex."

These definitions remain in the 1982 edition of the AHD, so we may assume they are still in force. To say that one is homosexual assumes that one engages in homosexual acts, usually construed as acts of sodomy. And sodomy, outlawed in all states until 1961, is still illegal in half of them.

Lasson (1985, p. 648) observed in 1985 that in "most jurisdictions one has the right to be homosexual, but he or she has no right to participate in homosexual activity." However, the courts construe the term "homosexual activity" as broader than "sexual activity with another of the same sex." A 1981 Oklahoma statute provided for suspension or dismissal of teachers for "advocating, . . . encouraging or promoting public or private homosexual activity" as well as for the "crime against nature" (National Gay Task Force v. Board of Education, 1984. Struck down for being "overbroad" by the Tenth Circuit Court of Appeals in 1985, it was defended by dissenting Judge Barrett:

> Sodomy is *malum in se,* i.e., immoral and corruptible in its nature without regard to the fact of its being noticed or punished by the law of the state. It is not *malum prohibitum,* i.e., wrong only because it is forbidden by law and not involving moral turpitude. It is on this principle that I must part with the majority's holding that the "public homosexual conduct" portion of the Oklahoma statute is overbroad.
>
> Any teacher who advocates, solicits, encourages or promotes the practice of sodomy "in a manner that creates a substantial risk that such conduct will come to the attention of school children or school employees" is in fact and in truth inciting school children to participate in the abominable and detestable crime against nature.

There is widespread concern among gay activists that the 1986 Supreme Court sodomy ruling will be used to justify discrimination against homosexuals (Levin, 1986, p. 34). Given the fact that there is "no constitutional right to engage in homosexual conduct" (Dronenburg v. Zech, 1984), their concern seems warranted. In 1970, the Supreme Court affirmed in Doe v. Commonwealth's Attorney a lower court's decision to deny a challenge to a state criminal statute prohibiting sodomy "as applied to private consensual homosexual conduct" (Beller v. Middendorf, 1980). A 1984 decision by the District of Columbia Court of Appeals upheld the Navy's discharge of petty officer Dronenburg for homosexual acts, stating that neither the plaintiff's constitutional right to privacy nor that of equal protection had been violated "as unique needs of the military justify determination that homosexual conduct impairs its capacity to carry out its mission" (Dronenburg v. Zech, 1984).

In arguing that homosexual conduct would have a deleterious effect on morale and discipline, the court reasoned that others would be "uncomfortable" and feel "dislike and disapproval" because they "find homosexuality morally offensive." Such "needs" of the military hardly seem "unique." After all, discomfort around homosexuals and "disapproval" of homosexuality are not confined to military esprit de corps.

The opinion also pointed to the possibility of favoritism or seduction, however. At the risk of contributing to the sexist exclusion of women from military service, the question of whether or not these are not problems for heterosexuals in the Navy arises. It would seem that the myth that homosexuality is readily "contagious" may be part of the court's rationale:

> Episodes of this sort are certain to be deleterious to morale and discipline, to call into question the even-handedness of superiors' dealings with lower ranks, to make personal dealings uncomfortable where the relationship is sexually ambiguous, to generate dislike and disapproval among many who find homosexuality offensive, and, it must be said, given the powers of military superiors over their inferiors, to enhance the possibility of homosexual seduction.

The Navy's policy of mandatory discharge was further lauded as serving "legitimate state interests" such as the maintenance of "'discipline, good order and morale[,] . . . mutual trust and confidence among service members . . . and prevent[ing] breaches of security.'" Dronenburg and other gay Naval personnel are responsible not merely for the homophobia of others, but for the fact that it mandates remaining "in the closet," and hence subject to blackmail—leading to "breaches of security" (see also Beller v. Middendorf, 1980).

But the courts have maintained the contradictory premise as well: they have insisted that openly gay employees (as in Gaylord v. Tacoma School District, 1977) threaten the integrity of the public institutions which employ them because their retention implies institutional approval and therefore encourages "imitation." In McConnell v. Anderson (1972), in fact, a court of appeals reversed a ruling in favor of a gay plaintiff, arguing that his gay activism amounted to an attempt to "foist tacit approval of a socially repugnant concept upon his employer." McConnell, who had applied for a license to marry another man, must, in the eyes of the court, have sought to draw public attention to the University of Minnesota's tolerance of gay male employees. This the court construed as a willfully deceitful act, rather than a sincere desire to marry another man or to test statutes governing marriage (quoted and discussed in Hoffman, 1978, p. 340).

LEGAL INTERPRETATIONS: THE HETEROSEXUAL
FAMILY AS NORM

As Altman (1982, p. 64) has observed, in the 1980's "the polite form of homophobia is expressed in terms of safeguarding the family." During the decade of the Family Protection Act, lesbians and gay men remain trapped between two corollaries of the "prevailing social mores" rationale: the one denies them the right to privacy on the grounds that homosexual conduct is not a "family" relationship, the other denies them access to conventional means of achieving family status—marriage—and access to political means for achieving rights similar to those enjoyed by heterosexuals. Dronenburg v. Zech (1984) enumerates the privacy rights listed by the Supreme Court:

> The Court has listed as illustrative of the right of privacy such matters as activities relating to marriage, procreation, contraception, family relationships, and child rearing and education. It need hardly be said that none of these covers a right to homosexual conduct.

Likewise, in Childers v. Dallas Police Department (1981), the defendant's refusing Childers a position on the grounds that he admitted belonging to the Metropolitan Community Church (a church with a predominantly gay and lesbian membership) was upheld by a district court. Its opinion cited McConnell v. Anderson, further declaring that

> The issue of homosexuality is one charged with emotion and anxiety.
> . . . . Such activity will undoubtedly foment controversy and conflict within the department. These considerations, as well as the concern of the police department to protect its public image and to avoid ridicule and embarrassment, are more than sufficient justification for Lochenmeyer's refusal in this instance to hire an admitted homosexual who actively publicized his lifestyle. . . (pp. 141–142)

Denying that Childers' constitutional rights were violated, the court noted that the Supreme Court's decision in another case was "quite capable of being confined by its context, though not by its terms, to private heterosexual contact" (p. 146), a distinction which may well affect future interpretations of the 1986 sodomy ruling.

Heterosexists may draw further comfort from the views on same-sex marriage expressed by Buchanan, a Professor of Law at the University of Houston Law Center. Buchanan's arguments proceed from the assumptions that adult consensual sexual conduct is protected by the right to privacy and that state governments have a "compelling"

interest in protecting and fostering the marriage institution. In artic-
ulating the majority view on the moral wrongness of homosexual
conduct and hence on same-sex marriage, Buchanan (1985, pp. 546–
549) appeals to historical and contemporary proclamations made by
major Jewish and Christian groups. He quotes in detail from the
Roman Catholic Church's 1975 Declaration on Certain Questions
Concerning Sexual Ethics, and it is reproduced here because it contains myths about homosexuality no longer entertained by the psychiatric profession, but affirmed by the Church *ex cathedra:*

> A distinction is drawn, and it seems with some reason, between homo-
> sexuals whose tendency comes from a false education, from a lack of
> normal sexual development, from habit, from bad example, or from
> other similar causes, and is transitory or at least not incurable; and
> homosexuals who are definitively such because of some kind of innate
> instinct or pathological constitution judged to be incurable.
>
> In regard to this second category of subjects, some people conclude
> that their tendency is so natural that it justifies in their case homosex-
> ual relations within a sincere communion of life and love analogous to
> marriage, in so far as homosexuals feel incapable of enduring a solitary
> life.
>
> In the pastoral field, these homosexuals must certainly be treated
> with understanding and sustained in the hope of overcoming their per-
> sonal difficulties and their inability to fit into society. Their culpability
> will be judged with prudence. But no pastoral method can be employed
> which would give moral justification to these acts on the grounds that
> they would be consonant with the condition of such people. For accord-
> ing to the objective moral order, homosexual relations are acts which
> lack an essential and indispensable finality . . . [and] are intrinsically
> disordered and can in no case be approved (Buchanan, 1985, pp. 8–9).

For Buchanan, writing a decade after this declaration, homosexual conduct and same-sex marriage are expressly condemned within
the Judaeo-Christian heritage, just as opposite-sex marriage is expressly affirmed (p. 549). The courts, he concludes, firmly grounded
within this heritage, must protect and foster the institution of heterosexual marriage as it now exists; same-sex marriage would threaten
"the moral climate the majority wishes to preserve" (p. 559).

Buchanan's contention that the majority has the right to use the
legal system to promote its own perception of moral excellence in the
area of marriage pervades his article. It amounts to a defense of
institutionalized heterosexism in the law—particularly interesting in
light of Rich's observations on the role of marriage in oppressing all
women (outlined above). But it is also indicative of a broader normative standard used during the past two decades to justify discrimi-

nation against homosexuals, the fact that homosexual conduct is not constitutionally protected (and presumably unworthy of constitutional protection) because the right to privacy is confined to issues involving marriage and childrearing. The absence of virulent condemnation in such court rulings should provide no consolation to gay activists; appeals to the sanctity of the family and its necessity in the social fabric serve only to signal an increased conservatism which broadens the category of conduct judged at worst immoral and at best irrelevant.

ACQUIRED IMMUNE DEFICIENCY SYNDROME: HYSTERIA AND HETEROSEXISM

Acquired Immune Deficiency Syndrome (AIDS), unnamed until 1981 when it was first diagnosed as a distinct disease entity, has already reached epidemic proportions. "By April, 1985, the United States Center for Disease Control (CDC) had reported almost 10,000 confirmed cases of the most severe form of this condition in the United States" (Leonard, 1985, p. 681). By November 3, 1986, *Time* (Levine, 1986, p. 76) reported that the cumulative death toll from the disease was 15,000 in the United States alone, and a figure of 180,000 was expected in five years.

In the United States, AIDS seemed at first to be confined to the gay community, and was termed the "homosexual plague" or the "gay plague." By 1982, however, CDC identified it among hemophiliacs, intravenous drug users, and Haitian immigrants (Keerdoja, 1982, p. 10). Nonetheless, most AIDS victims are gay men. Despite reassurances by most medical experts that AIDS is transmitted only through intimate sexual contact or blood products, the fear that the disease will spread beyond the current high-risk groups to other segments of the population (fueled by the discovery that AIDS is a "heterosexual disease" in Africa) has already led to a wave of discrimination against both AIDS sufferers and the gay community. One gay activist at a 1985 National Gay/Lesbian Leadership Forum summed up recent AIDS-intensified homophobia: "Fifteen years ago homosexuals were classified as mentally ill. That was a long battle, but we changed that. Now with AIDS, we're a public health threat." (quoted in Leerhsen, 1984, p. 24)

AIDS victims have been refused treatment by nurses, transportation by ambulances, and embalming by morticians (Starr, 1983, p. 20). Two incidents illustrate the extent of public hysteria over the possible risk of contagion. A San Francisco television station producing "Demystifying AIDS," a 1983 special intended to allay AIDS panic, was embarrassed that two AIDS victims "had to be interviewed by telephone when technicians refused to be in the same room with them" (Starr, 1983, p. 21). In a New York trial court the following year, a defendant with AIDS wore a surgical mask, and a City Health Commissioner appeared on request of the judge to assure court personnel and jurors that there was no danger of contagion. Nonetheless, half of the panel of jurors "asked to be excused, and court officers insisted on wearing masks and surgical gloves. The judge denied defense counsel's request that the officers be ordered to remove their protective paraphernalia to avoid prejudicing the jury" (Leonard, 1985, p. 697).

Jerry Falwell and the Moral Majority have seized upon the idea that the "gay plague" is God's punishment for the sin of homosexuality (McQuaid 1983; Krauthammer 1983). On July 4, 1983, Falwell called a press conference to propose ways to protect the nation's blood supply; the Moral Majority Report featured an article entitled "AIDS: Homosexual Diseases Threaten American Families" (Krauthammer, 1983). But, as Ross (1986) indicates in her discussion of the "metaphor of AIDS as punishment" and its role in homophobia, fundamentalist ministers have not been alone in viewing "the gay plague" as divine punishment:

> Two behaviors account for 90 percent of these transmissions in the U.S.: homosexual intercourse and illegal intravenous (IV) drug use. Both these behaviors are regarded as sinful by many and perhaps most people; gay sex is still illegal in half of the United States, and IV drug use without a prescription is illegal in all states. Because behavior that is regarded as sinful has resulted in exposure to disease, it is easy for the disease to become the punishment for sin. (p. 16)

The term "innocent victims," used to describe AIDS victims who are neither gay men nor drug users, implies that the latter are "guilty" victims. This assessment is "translated into action in hospitals, in public agencies, and in the news media, where gay men or drug users with AIDS are treated with less sympathy than 'innocent' AIDS patients" (Ross, 1986, p. 17). So widespread has been the heterosexist backlash that in 1983 a New York City Episcopal bishop felt compelled to state that "AIDS is not God's vengeance on the homosexual community" (Starr, 1983, p. 20). That same year, syndicated columnist Buchanan, later to become White House director of communications, appealing to the belief that homosexuality is "unnatural" (rather than "immoral"), wrote, "The poor homosexuals: they have declared war upon nature, and now nature is exacting an awful retribution" (quoted in Krauthammer, 1983, p. 21).

Those who wish to deny gay men civil liberties on moral grounds have been quick to use the public health issue to do so. Buchanan called for the closing of gay bathhouses and for cancelling gay pride marches; a well-known conservative, he found more of the American public receptive to his feigned concern for gay health than to his often-expressed homophobia. Similarly, "Dallas Doctors Against AIDS" used the epidemic as an excuse to campaign on the recriminalization of homosexuality (Krauthammer, 1983, p. 21) and a legal scholar commenting on the Georgia sodomy statute (prior to the 1986 ruling by the Supreme Court) urged the court to outlaw "potentially lethal" sexual behavior "for every AIDS case prevented will save a human life" (ARIC Press, 1983, p. 74). The threat of AIDS defeated a Houston gay rights bill, after members of the Houston City Council listened to a social psychologist call for the quarantining of all gay men (FitzGerald, 1986).

It has been but a simple leap of illogic to assume that since most AIDS victims are gay men, most gay men are or will be AIDS victims. Attempts to repress homosexuality and suggestions for segregating gay men have been the consequences. In the words of Krauthammer (p. 20): "Just as society was ready to grant that homosexuality is not an illness, it is seized with the idea that homosexuality breeds illness. And that gives those opposed to recent homosexual gains . . . powerful lines of attack for reversing them." At the same time, perceiving AIDS as a gay disease has convinced some liberals outside the gay community that they need not fear contracting the disease, nor feel a sense of responsibility for those who have (Ross, 1986):

> The metaphor of AIDS as otherness permits us to accept lesser treatment for those belonging to that other group than they would demand for themselves. The idea of otherness is possible only as long as "we" are able to isolate ourselves from linguistic connection with people who have the disease or who are at risk for it. By referring in print to AIDS as a "gay disease" or a "gay plague," those in the straight community are encouraged to think of AIDS as something happening beyond their borders, outside the "general population," as something happening to people for whom they have no human responsibility. The metaphor of otherness provides comfort to those who use it because it implies they will be spared harm and responsibility. (p. 18)

DEFINING "LESBIAN": LEXICAL INVISIBILITY

In an article on civil rights for homosexuals, Lasson (1985, p. 648) observes that "In most jurisdictions one has the right to be homosexual, but he or she has no right to participate in homosexual acts." He undermines his use of the pronoun "he or she" with a footnote, however: "The writer notes that in most jurisdictions female homosexuality—lesbianism—is legal," through cautioning us to see a 1974 decision in which the definition of sodomy was found to include cunnilingus.

In 1986 Supreme Court ruling upholding the Georgia sodomy statute supports a very broad ruling of sodomy which includes same-sex acts by lesbians and opposite-sex acts:

> A person commits the offense of sodomy when he performs or submits to any sexual act involving the sex organs of one person and the mouth or anus of another. . . . (cited in Hardwick v. Bowers, 1985)

(The "he" here is intended to be generic, following the usual legal usage. The Virginia statute at issue in Doe v. Commonwealth's Attorney, on the other hand, uses "he or she" to describe the felon guilty of these "crimes against nature" [also cited in Hardwick v. Bowers]). However, the ordinary sense of the word "sodomy" seems to preclude lesbian sexual acts; the dictionary definition implies that a male agent is assumed:

> sodomy n. 1. Anal copulation of one male with another. 2. Anal or oral copulation with a member of the opposite sex. 3. Copulation with an animal. (AHD, 1982)

In addition, "copulation" means "to engage in coitus," and "coitus" the "physical union of male and female sexual organs, leading to orgasm and the ejaculation of semen"; since all interpretations of "sodomy" use the term "copulation," many jurisdictions may well interpret a prohibition against sodomy as male-specific unless involving an act of bestiality involving a woman. (Interestingly enough, some states have provided within an antisodomy statute for the right to privacy within marriage—hence affirming the rightness of the heterosexual family, whatever sexual practices may occur within it—as did a Pennsylvania former statute, prohibiting "all sexual intercourse per os or anus between human beings who are not husband and wife." [see Altman, 1982, p. 109])

Discrepancies in interpretations of the word "sodomy" as a generic (including all contact between the genital organs of one individual and the mouth or anus of another individual) or male-specific (involving the penetration of the mouth or anus of one individual by the penis of another) parallel debates over the inclusiveness of the words "homosexual" and "gay." Boswell (1980, pp. 44–45), in explaining his avoidance of the noun "homosexual," offers two reasons: first, "homosexuality" comprises all same-sex phenomena, while "gay" refers to "persons conscious of erotic inclination toward their own gender as a distinguishing characteristic, and "homosexual" places undue emphasis on the sexuality of gay individuals; second, "homosexual" has become a male-specific noun.

> Moreover, "homosexual" has come to be associated with males more than females. The phrase "lesbians and homosexuals" now appears more frequently in print. . .

Boswell also states that the term "gay people" evokes images of individuals of all age groups, whereas "homosexuals" evokes images of adults, and concludes with the assertion that gay people appear to prefer the term "gay."

If Boswell is skeptical about the inclusiveness of "homosexual," others have been equally skeptical about "gay." Stanley and Robbins (1985, p. 2) provide quotes from Warren which indicate that the noun appears to have male-specific reference:

> The gay who is a good dancer can turn even the foxtrot into an uninhibited celebration of male sexuality (p. 74).

> The lesbians tell us that only a woman knows how to love a woman. The gays will answer that only a man knows how to love a man (p. 120).

Indeed, the recent inclusion of the term "lesbian" within its organization's title by the National Gay Task Force is a recognition of the fact that "gay," like "man," functions as a pseudo-generic, obscuring the existence of lesibans as surely as "man" serves to erase the presence of all women.

Lesbian invisibility in the lexicon reflects the status of lesbians in the world. Lacking the socioeconomic privilege and status of men, according to Rich (1985), lesbians have been denied a political existence, as their experiences have been subsumed under those of gay men:

> Lesbians have historically been deprived of a political existence through "inclusion" as female versions of male homosexuality. To equate lesbian existence with male homosexuality because each is stigmatized is to erase female reality once again. Part of the history of lesbian existence is, obviously, to be found where lesbians, lacking a coherent female community, have shared a kind of social life and common cause with homosexual men. But there are differences: women's lack of economic and cultural privilege relative to men. . . (pp. 52–53)

In some ways, lesbian invisibility may appear to have provided a measure of security for lesbians. Most court cases involving discrimination against lesbians on the basis of their sexuality have been child custody cases; few have involved employment. But a number of factors may have determined the low ratio of cases involving lesbian identity or sexuality as compared with those involving gay men. Lesbians may have had less access to legal avenues of redress, for instance. Or, as de Beauvoir (1952) has suggested, lesbianism may simply be nonthreatening to men as long as it is unaccompanied by assertive behavior or feminist beliefs:

> A man is more annoyed by an active and independent heterosexual woman than by an unaggressive lesbian; only the first assaults the masculine prerogatives; sapphic love affairs by no means run counter to the traditional distinction of the sexes; they involve in most cases an acceptance of femininity, not its denial. (pp. 382–383)

de Beauvoir herself sees nothing unusual in a lesbian affair as a stage in heterosexual development, activities for timid adolescent girls not yet ready for heterosexual relations—she sees only the "exclusive" lesbian, the "invert" who desires no heterosexual activity, as requiring explanation, and some of these may aspire toward the subject role impossible in a male-dominated society.

She explains that men find the gay male "a deadly attack upon the virile ideal" but may views lesbians "with indulgence":

> "I avow," said Count de Tilly, "that it is a rivalry which in no way disturbs me; on the contrary, it amuses me and I am immoral enough to laugh at it." Colette attributes the same amused indifference to Renaud. . .

In a footnote, she observes that lesbianism was not illegal under English law, a legal reflection of the same "amused indifference." The early white settlers of North America seem not to have uniformly shared this indifference; the death penalty was prescribed for lesbians in New Haven, Connecticut in 1656 (Rich, 1986, p. 198).

Nonetheless, it remains true that comparatively few cases involving lesbianism—other than child custody cases—have reached courts in the United States. No findings in such cases correspond to gay male cases in which mere admission of homosexual tendencies has been ruled adequate cause for dismissal, as in Gaylord v. Tacoma School District. In fact, Ben Shalmon v. Secretary of the Navy, a 1980 decision by the United States District Court for Eastern Wisconsin, is notable for Judge Evans' assertion that Ben Shalom's homosexuality "caused no disturbances except in the minds of those who chose to prosecute her" (973). Since there was no evidence of overt homosexual acts on the part of Ben Shalom, Evans concluded that her first amendment rights of association and of expression and her right to privacy had been violated.

In two other cases, one involving a teaching assistant and another a bisexual counselor, the courts denied that sexuality was a determining factor in their decisions. In the former (Naragon v. Wharton, 1984), a graduate teaching assistant sexually involved with a freshman student was relieved of her teaching duties, evidently at the insistence of the freshman's parents. Although the parents' homophobia was evident from the testimony, the court allegedly relied upon the plaintiff's breach of professional ethics in rejecting her claim. (A dissenting judge contended that her lack of "professionalism" and her unacceptability as a role model would not have been issues had she not been involved with another woman, however.) In the case of the bisexual counselor (Rowland v. Mad River Local School District, 1984), the plaintiff informed other teachers and the vice-principal of her bisexuality and stated that she had a female lover. However, she also told a secretary that two of the boys she was counseling were homosexual. She was thus guilty of a breach of confidence; her dismissal was thus held to be proper both because of unsatisfactory job performance and indiscretion. In other words, her revelation of bisexuality rather than her bisexuality alone constituted grounds for her dismissal. If this distinction seems specious (as it did to the dissenting judge), it still provides no evidence that the mere admission of female homosexuality would inevitably have led to Rowland's suspension.

LESBIANS AND ENFORCED HETEROSEXUALITY

Even a brief examination of child custody decisions is capable of disproving the hypothesis that men—or at least male judges—are tolerant of lesbianism. Rivera, in her article "Sexual Preference Law," (1980–81) states that custodial cases are more widely litigated than any other homosexual rights issue, that the bulk of the cases involve lesbian mothers, and that "homosexuality is almost always the deciding factor when gay parents lose their children." Even the "tender years" presumption, through which the courts "almost unfailingly awarded children" to their mothers on the basis of their need for women's nurturance, has carried no weight in the face of the detrimental effects alleged to result from a mother's lesbianism. Lesbians have been regarded as unfit mothers per se (Rivera, 1980–81, pp. 327–328).

Rivera cites DeStefano v. DeStefano as typical. In this case, the appellate court concluded that "The wife's conduct in failing to keep her lesbian relationship . . . separate from her role as a mother has had and predictably will have, a detrimental effect upon the children." Affirming the trial court's change to paternal custody because the wife was sharing a home with a female lover, the court also made her visitation rights conditional upon ensuring that her lover would not be present.

N. K. M. v. L.E.M., a Missouri appellate case, involved removing custody from a lesbian mother who had violated the condition that she sever any relationship with her lover. Seemingly basing its decision on a definition of "gay" as "not straight" (discussed above), the court held that it was reasonable to condition custody on dissociation with "an habitual criminal, or a child abuser, or a sexual pervert, or a known drug pusher." The court contended that the change in custody was intended to remove the child from an "unwholesome" environment (cited from Hitchens & Thomas [1983]). In S. v. S., a Kentucky appellate court reversed the trial court's decision, awarding custody to the father rather than the lesbian mother; in its reasoning, the court accepted the contagion myth advanced by a psychologist, who explained that a child raised by a lesbian mother might find it difficult to achieve heterosexual fulfillment (Hitchens & Thomas, 1983, p. 20).

Numerous gay activists and lesbian feminists have discussed the fallacy inherent in assuming that children raised in gay or lesbian homes will become homosexual. Even before the early development of sexual orientation had been accepted by the mental health establishment, it was patently obvious that most gay men and lesbians came from heterosexual homes; why, then, should it be assumed that heterosexual identity cannot be established in gay or lesbian homes? Underlying this assumption, of course, are the twin assumptions that homosexuality has an intrinsic appeal but that heterosexuality is the normative standard, the goal and measure of fulfilled adulthood.

Goodman (1977) has discussed at length the challenge to institutionalized heterosexuality and motherhood presented by the "anomaly" of the lesbian mother. The function of the heterosexual nuclear family, and particularly of the woman within it, is the maintenance of existing social values, or, in the language of the courts, "prevailing social mores"; any alternative to the model family is the object of "negative social pressure," according to Goodman, but perhaps none more than the home headed by a lesbian mother:

> One of the most isolated, ridiculed and feared of all those who attempt an alternative expression of selfhood is the lesbian mother. As a homosexual she belongs to the only minority group with no support system anywhere in our society. Homosexuals are condemned by law, religion, educational institutions, their own families and, until recently, the entire medical profession for their sexual orientation. Unlike other minority groups, homosexuals were not even available to each other for support until the Gay movement that emerged in 1969. But even within the Gay movement, the lesbian mother remains an anomaly. Her very existence challenges society's assumptions about the proper function of woman and motherhood. Both lesbian and mother, she is regarded as a threat to the very foundation of our civilization. . . (p. 60)

If Goodman identifies the plight of the lesbian mother with that of other homosexuals, the nonetheless distinguishes the intensity of the "otherness" experienced by lesbian mothers. But Rich finds all lesbians doubly oppressed—as women and as homosexuals—attributing their oppression to the enormous social and cultural pressure brought to bear on all women to ensure that they remain available to men sexually and generally. "Lesbian existence comprises both the breaking of a taboo and the rejection of a compulsory way of life. It is also a direct attack on male right of access to women (Rich, 1986, p. 52)."

Rich attacks the notion that women either choose heterosexuality voluntarily or tend naturally towards it. If women are the first source of emotional and physical nurturing for male and female children, she asks "why in fact would women ever redirect that search" for love and tenderness originally directed toward women (p. 35). In response to this question, she enumerates some of the forces brought to bear upon women (some of which have been quoted above) and explains:

> . . . each one I have listed adds to the cluster of forces within which women have been convinced that marriage and sexual orientation toward men are inevitable—even if unsatisfying and oppressive—components of their lives. The chastity belt; child marriage; erasure of lesbian existence (except as erotic and perverse) in art, literature, film; idealization of heterosexual romance and marriage—these are some fairly obvious forms of compulsion, the first two exemplifying physical force, the second two control of consciousness (p. 39).

In naming the lies which have driven many lesbians to remain "in the closet," Rich includes

the Western romantic "ideal" of heterosexuality: the notions that "primary love between the sexes is 'normal'; that women need men as social and economic protectors, for adult sexuality, and for psychological completion; that the heterosexually constituted family is the basic social unit; the women who do not attach their primary intensity to men must be, in functional terms, condemned to an even more devastating outsiderhood than their outsiderhood as women. Small wonder that lesbians are reported to be a more hidden population than male homosexuals (p. 64).

Gearhart (quoted in Altman, 1982, p. 179) explains that the invisibility of lesbians is increased by the supposed "inclusiveness" of the word "gay"; in subsuming lesbians within the general category "gay people," distinctions between the sexual behavior of lesbians and that of gay males are obscured:

In being part of the word "gay" weary lesbians have spent untold hours explaining to Middle America that lesbians do not worry about venereal disease, do not have sex in public bathrooms, do not seduce small boys, do not go to the baths for flings, do not regularly cruise Castro Street, and do not want to go to the barricades fighting for the lowering of the age of consent for sexual acts.

In fact, as Altman mentions, the National Organization for Women resolution to support lesbian issues explicitly excluded pederasty, public sex, sadomasochism, and pornography as matters of sexual exploitation, not sexual orientation. Altman in turn expressly condemns Gearhart for "appealing to a conservative stereotype that sees any sex outside stable, long-lasting relationships as somehow inferior," arguing that there may be as much compulsion within heterosexual marriage as in any of the behaviors she condemns.

However, the gay liberation movement outlined by Altman in his book is inextricably tied to an emphasis on gay male sex, including a wide range of sexual activities, the availability of numerous and often anonymous sexual partners, and (in Altman's own words) a hedonistic glorying in sex for its own sake. Altman correctly observes that not all lesbians would agree with what he evidently regards as Gearhart's prudery. Indeed, it is probably dangerous for lesbians to attack gay male sexual practices, attacks which will undoubtedly buttress the homophobia of the heterosexual public (and, in fact, many of these practices have been severely curtailed by the outbreak of the AIDS epidemic).

Yet as Rich points out, lesbians as a whole are more likely to perceive lesbian existence in terms of a primary intensity among women, an emotional as well as an erotic sharing of female energy. "Woman identification is a source of energy, a potential springhead of female power, curtailed and contained under the institution of heterosexuality (p. 63)."

It is clearly in the interest of heterosexism—or compulsory heterosexuality—that lesbians remain invisible, particularly to women. To preserve heterosexuality as an institution, women must remain available to men, isolated from each other. Obscuring lesbian existence through the sexist bias of the word "gay" serves that end.

When lesbians are visible, all possible social and cultural forces are marshalled in order that heterosexual women may perceive lesbian existence merely as a deviant form of sexual behavior, one which is punishable. Legal institutions deny lesbian mothers access to their children, and lesbians may find themselves rejected by family and community, and even placed in psychiatric wards. At the same time, heterosexist rhetoric terms all same-sex relationships immoral, sick and unnatural; terms them "detrimental" to children; finds them to have a "deleterious" effect on efficiency in the workplace.

Heterosexist rhetoric represents a cultural force, a means of controlling the consciousness of women and men, whether heterosexual, lesbian, or gay. It serves to filter the perceptions not only of those who hear or read it but of those who contribute to it. It serves to monitor and shape the behavior of all of us, with effects which have been outlined above. We continue to employ it at our own risk.

REFERENCES

Altman, D. (1982). *The Homosexualization of America, The Americanization of the Homosexual*. New York: St. Martin's Press.

American Heritage Dictionary of the English Language. (1976). New College Edition. Boston: Houghton Mifflin.

American Heritage Dictionary of the English Language. (1982). Second College Edition. Boston: Houghton Mifflin.

ARIC Press. (1986, April 7). A law that dares not say its name: Sodomy and the court. *Newsweek*, p. 74.

Beller v. Middendorf. (1980). 632 F.2d 788.

Ben Shalom v. Secretary of the Navy. (1980). 489 F. Supp. 964 (E. D. Wisc.)

Boswell, J. (1980). *Christianity, Social Tolerance, and Homosexuality: Gay*

People in Western Europe from the Beginning of the Christian Era to the Fourteenth Century, Chicago: University of Chicago Press.
Bowers v. Hardwick. (1986). 106 S.Ct. 2841.
Buchanan, G. S. (1985). Same-sex marriage: The linchpin issue. *University of Dayton Law Review, 10,* 541–573.
Childers v. Dallas Police Department. (1981). 513 F. Supp. 134.
Daly, M. (1973). *Beyond God the Father: Toward a Philosophy of Women's Liberation.* Boston: Beacon Press.
de Beauvoir, S. (1952). *The Second Sex.* New York: Alfred A. Knopf.
DeStefano v. DeStefano. (1978). 60 A.D.2d 976, 401 N.Y. Supp. 636 (N.Y. Sup. Ct. App. Div.)
Dronenburg v. Zech. (1984). 741 F.2d 1388.
FitzGerald, F. (1986, July 28). A reporter at large: The Castro—II. *The New Yorker,* pp. 44–63.
Gaylord v. Tacoma School District No. 10. (1977). 88 Wash. 2d 286, 559 P.2d 1340 (1977), *cert. denied,* 98 S. Ct. 234.
Goodman, B. (1977). *The Lesbian: A Celebration of Difference,* New York: Out & Out Books.
Hardwick v. Bowers. (1985). 760 F.2d 1202.
Hitchens, D. J., & Thomas, A. G. (1983). *Lesbian Mothers and Their Children: An Annotated Bibliography of Legal and Psychological Materials.* San Francisco: Lesbian Rights Project.
Hoffman, S. C. (1983). An analysis of rationales in homosexual public employment cases. *South Dakota Law Review,* 338–357.
Keerdoja, E. (1982, August 23). 'Homosexual plague' strikes new victims. *Newsweek,* p. 10.
Krauthammer, C. (1983, August 1). The politics of a plague. *The New Republic,* pp. 18–21.
Lasson, K. (1985). Civil liberties for homosexuals: The law in limbo. *University of Dayton Law Review, 10,* 645–679.
Leerhsen, C. (1985, September 23). 'Hard times ahead': Gays brace for a wave of homophobia. *Newsweek,* p. 24.
Leonard, S. (1985). Employment discrimination against persons with AIDS. *University of Dayton Law Review, 10,* 681–703.
Levin, R. (1986, July 14). Two contentious rulings. *MacLean's,* p. 34.
Levine, J. (1986, November 3). The toughest virus of all. *Time,* pp. 76–78.
McConnell v. Anderson. (1972). 451 F.2d 193 (8th Cir. 1971), *cert. denied,* 405 U.S. 1046.
McQuaid, J. (1983, August 1). First AIDS. *The New Republic,* p. 16.
Miller, C., & Swift, K. (1977). *Words and Women: New Language and New Times.* Garden City: Anchor Books.
N.K.M. v. L.E.M. (1980). 606 S.W.2d 179 (Mo. Ct. App.).
Naragon v. Wharton. (1984). 737 F.2d 1403.
National Gay Task Force v. Board of Education of the City of Oklahoma City. (1984). 729 F.2d 1270.
Rich, A. (1986). Compulsory heterosexuality and lesbian existence. *Blood,*

Bread, and Poetry: Selected Prose 1979–1985 (pp. 23–75). New York: Norton.

Rich, A. (1976). *Of Woman Born*. New York: Norton.

Rivera, R. R. (1980–81). Recent developments in sexual preference law. *Drake Law Review, 30*, pp. 311–346.

Rowland v. Mad River Local School District, Montgomery County, Ohio. (1984). 730 F.2d 444.

Ross, J. W. (1986). Ethics and the language of AIDS. *Federation Review: The Journal of the State Humanities Councils, 9.3*, pp. 15–19.

S. v. S. (1981). 608 S.W.2d 64 (Ky. Ct. App.).

Schlegel v. United States. (1969). 416 F.2d 1372 (Ct.Cl.), *cert. denied* (1970) 397 U.S. 1039.

Schulz, M. (1979). The semantic derogation of women. In B. Thorne & N. Henley (Eds.), *Language and Sex: Difference and Dominance* (pp. 64–75). Rowley: Newbury House.

Slovenko, (1985). The homosexual and society: A historical perspective. *University of Dayton Law Review, 10*, pp. 445–457.

Spender, D. (1980). *Man Made Language*. London: Routledge & Kegan Paul.

Stanley, J. P. (1977). Gender-marking in American English: Usage and reference. In A. P. Nilsen et al. (Eds.), *Sexism and Language* (pp. 43–74). Urbana: National Council of Teachers of English.

Stanley, J. P., & Robbins, S. J. (1979). Sexist slang and the Gay Community: Are you one, too? *Michigan Occasional Paper No. XIV*. Ann Arbor: University of Michigan Women's Studies Program.

Starr, M. (1983, July 4). The Panic over AIDS. *Newsweek*, 20–21.

PART IV

Cultural Discourse

CHAPTER 8

It Jus Be's Dat Way Sometime: The Sexual Politics of Women's Blues*

Hazel Carby

English Department
Wesleyan University

This essay considers the sexual politics of women's blues in the 1920's. Their story is part of a larger history of the production of Afro-American culture within the North American culture industry. My research has concentrated almost exclusively on those black women intellectuals who were part of the development of an Afro-American literature culture and reflects the privileged place that we accord to writers in Afro-American Studies (Carby, 1987). Within feminist theory, the cultural production of black women writers has been analyzed in isolation from other forms of women's culture and cultural presence and has neglected to relate particular texts and issues to a larger discourse of culture and cultural politics. I want to show how the representation of black female sexuality in black women's fiction and in women's blues is clearly different. I argue that different cultural forms negotiate and resolve very different sets of social contradictions. However, before considering the particularities of black women's sexual representation, we should consider its marginality within a white-dominated feminist discourse.

---

* This paper was originally a presentation to the conference on "Sexuality, Politics and Power" held at Mount Holyoke College, September 1986. It was reprinted in *Radical America* 20,4 (1986): 9-24. The power of the music can only be fully understood by listening to the songs which should be played as the essay is read.

In 1982, at the Barnard conference on the politics of sexuality, Hortense Spillers condemned the serious absence of consideration of black female sexuality from various public discourses including white feminist theory. She described black women as "the beached whales of the sexual universe, unvoiced, misseen, not doing, awaiting *their* verb." The sexual experiences of black women, she argued, were rarely depicted by themselves in what she referred to as "empowered texts:" discursive feminist texts. Spillers complained of the relative absence of African-American women from the academy and thus from the visionary company of Anglo-American women feminists and their privileged mode of feminist expression.

The collection of the papers from the Barnard conference, the *Pleasure and Danger* (1984) anthology, has become one of these empowered feminist theoretical texts and Spillers' essay continues to stand within it as an important black feminist survey of the ways in which the sexuality of black American women has been unacknowledged in the public/critical discourse of feminist thought (Spillers, 1984). Following Spillers' lead black feminists continued to critique the neglect of issues of black female sexuality within feminist theory and, indeed, I as well as others directed many of our criticisms toward the *Pleasure and Danger* anthology itself (Carby, 1986).

As black women we have provided articulate and politically incisive criticism which is there for the feminist community at large to heed or to ignore—upon that decision lies the future possibility of forging a feminist movement that is not parochial. As the black feminist and educator Anna Julia Cooper stated in 1892, a woman's movement should not be based on the narrow concerns of white middle class women under the name of "women;" neither, she argued, should a woman's movement be formed around the exclusive concerns of either the white woman or the black woman or the red woman but should be able to address the concerns of all the poor and oppressed (Cooper, 1892).

But instead of concentrating upon the domination of a white feminist theoretical discourse which marginalizes non-white women, I focus on the production of a discourse of sexuality by black women. By analyzing the sexual and cultural politics of black women who constructed themselves as sexual subjects through song, in particular the blues, I want to assert an empowered presence. First, I must situate the historical moment of the emergence of women-dominated blues and establish a theoretical framework of interpretation and then I will consider some aspects of the representation of feminism, sexuality, and power in women's blues.

MOVIN' ON

Before World War I the overwhelming majority of black people lived in the South, although the majority of black intellectuals who purported to represent the interests of "the race" lived in the North. At the turn of the century black intellectuals felt they understood and could give voice to the concerns of the black community as a whole. They were able to position themselves as spokespeople for the "race" because they were at a vast physical and metaphorical distance from the majority of those they represented. The mass migration of blacks to urban areas, especially to the cities of the North, forced these traditional intellectuals to question and revise their imaginary vision of "the people" and directly confront the actual displaced rural workers who were, in large numbers, becoming a black working class in front of their eyes. In turn the mass of black workers became aware of the range of possibilities for their representation. No longer were the "Talented Tenth," the practioners of policies of racial uplift, the undisputed "leaders of the race." Intellectuals and their constituencies fragmented, black union organizers, Marcus Garvey and the Universal Negro Improvement Association, radical black activists, the Sanctified Churches, the National Association of Colored Women, the Harlem creative artists, all offered alternative forms of representation and each strove to establish that the experience of their constituency was representative of the experience of the race.

Within the movement of the Harlem cultural renaissance, black women writers established a variety of alternative possibilities for the fictional representation of black female experience. Zora Neale Hurston chose to represent black people as the rural folk; the folk were represented as being both the source of Afro-American cultural and linguistic forms and the means for its continued existence. Hurston's exploration of sexual and power relations was embedded in this "folk" experience and avoided the cultural transitions and confrontations of the urban displacement. As Hurston is frequently situated as the foremother of contemporary black women writers, the tendency of feminist literary criticism has been to valorize black women as "folk" heroines at the expense of those texts which explored black female sexuality within the context of urban social relations. Put simply, a line of descent is drawn from *Their Eyes Were Watching God* to *The Color Purple*. But to establish the black "folk" as representative of the black community at large was and still is a convenient method for ignoring the specific contradictions of an urban existence in which most of us live. The culture industry, through its valorization in print and in film of *The Color Purple,* for example, can *appear* to comfortably address issues of black female sexuality within a past history and rural context while completely avoiding the crucial issues of black sexual and cultural politics that stem from an urban crisis.

"THERE'S NO EARTHLY USE IN BEIN TOO-GA-THA IF IT DON'T PUT SOME JOY IN YO LIFE." (Williams, 1981.)

However, two other women writers of the Harlem Renaissance, Jessie Fauset and Nella Larsen, did figure an urban class confrontation in their fiction, though in distinctly different ways. Jessie Fauset became an ideologue for a new black bourgeoisie; her novels represented the manners and morals that distinguished the emergent middle class from the working class. She wanted public recognition for the existence of a black elite that was urbane, sophisticated, and civilized but her representation of this elite implicitly defined its manners against the behavior of the new black proletariat. While it must be acknowledged that Fauset did explore the limitations of a middle-class existence for women, ultimately each of her novels depict independent women who surrender their independence to become suitable wives for the new black professional men.

Nella Larsen, on the other hand, offers us a more sophisticated dissection of the rural/urban confrontation. Larsen was extremely critical of the Harlem intellectuals who glorified the values of a black folk culture while being ashamed of and ridiculing the behavior of the new black migrant to the city. Her novel, *Quicksand* (1928), contains the first explicitly sexual black heroine in black women's fiction. Larsen explores questions of sexuality and power within both a rural and an urban landscape; in both contexts she condemns the ways in which female sexuality is confined and compromised as the object of male desire. In the city Larsen's heroine, Helga, has to recognize the ways in which her sexuality has an exchange value within capitalist social relations while in the country Helga is trapped by the consequences of woman's reproductive capacity. In the final pages of *Quicksand* Helga echoes the plight of the slave woman who could not escape to freedom and the cities of the North because she could not abandon her children and, at the same time, represents how a woman's life is drained through constant childbirth.

But Larsen also reproduces in her novel the dilemma of a black woman who tries to counter the dominant white cultural definitions of her sexuality: ideologies that define black female sexuality as a primitive and exotic. However the response of Larsen's heroine to such objectification is also the response of many black women writers: the denial of desire and the repression of sexuality. Indeed, *Quicksand* is symbolic of the tension in nineteenth and early twentieth-century black women's fiction in which black female sexuality was frequently displaced onto the terrain of the political responsibility of the black woman. The duty of the black heroine toward the black community was made coterminous with her desire as a woman, a desire which was expressed as a dedication to uplift the race. This displacement from female desire to female duty enabled the negotiation of racist constructions of black female sexuality but denied sensuality and in this denial lies the class character of its cultural politics.

It has been a mistake of much black feminist theory to concentrate almost exclusively on the visions of black women as represented by black women writers without indicating the limitations of their middle-class response to black women's sexuality. These writers faced a very real contradiction for they felt that they would publicly compromise themselves if they acknowledged their sexuality and sensuality within a racist sexual discourse thus providing evidence that indeed they were primitive and exotic creatures. But because black feminist theory has concentrated upon the literate forms of black women's intellectual activity the dilemma of the place of sexuality within a literary discourse has appeared as if it were the dilemma of most black women. On the other hand, what a consideration of women's blues allows us to see is an alternative form of representation, an oral and musical women's culture that explicity addresses the contradictions of feminism, sexuality, and power. What has been called the "Classic Blues" the women's blues of the twenties and early thirties is a discourse that articulates a cultural and political struggle over sexual relations: a struggle that is directed against the objectification of female sexuality within a patriarchal order but which also tries to reclaim women's bodies as the sexual and sensuous subjects of women's song.

TESTIFYIN'

Within black culture the figure of the female blues singer has been reconstructed in poetry, drama, fiction, and art and used to meditate upon conventional and unconventional sexuality. A variety of narratives, both fictional and biographical, have mythologized the woman blues singer and these mythologies become texts about sexuality.

Women blues singers frequently appear as liminal figures that play
out and explore the various possibilities of a sexual existence; they
are representations of women who attempt to manipulate and control
their construction as sexual subjects. In Afro-American fiction and
poetry, the blues singer has a strong physical and sensuous presence.
Shirley Anne Williams wrote about Bessie Smith:

> the thick triangular
> nose wedged
> in the deep brown
> face nostrils
> flared on a last hummmmmmmmm.
>
> Bessie singing
> just behind the beat
> that sweet sweet
> voice throwing
> its light on me
>
> I looked in her face
> and seed the woman
> I'd become. A big
> boned face already
> lined and the first line
> in her fo'head was
> black and the next line
> was sex cept I didn't
> know to call it that
> then and the brackets
> round her mouth stood fo
> the chi'ren she teared
> from out her womb. . . . (Williams, 1982)

Williams has argued that the early blues singers and their songs
"helped to solidify community values and heighten community morale in the late nineteenth and early twentieth centuries." The blues
singer, she says, uses song to create reflection and creates an atmosphere for analysis to take place. The blues were certainly a commu-
nal expression of black experience which had developed out of the
call and response patterns of work songs from the nineteenth century
and have been described as a "complex interweaving of the general
and the specific" and of individual and group experience. John Col-
trane has described how the audience heard "we" even if the singer
said "I." Of course the singers were entertainers but the blues was
not an entertainment of escape or fantasy and sometimes directly
represented historical events (Williams, 1979).

Sterling Brown has testified to the physical presence and power of Ma Rainey who would draw crowds from remote rural areas to see her "smilin' gold-toofed smiles" and to feel like participants in her performance which articulated the conditions of their social existence. Brown in his poem "Ma Rainey" remembers the emotion of her performance of "Back Water Blues" which described the devastation of the Mississippi flood of 1927. Rainey's original performance becomes in Brown's text a vocalization of the popular memory of the flood and Brown's text constructs itself as a part of the popular memory of the "Mother of the Blues." (Brown, 1981.)

Ma Rainey never recorded·"Backwater Blues" although Bessie Smith did but local songsters would hear the blues performed in the tent shows or on record and transmit them throughout the community. Ma Rainey and Bessie Smith were among the first women blues singers to be recorded and with Clara Smith, Ethel Waters, Alberta Hunter, Ida Cox, Rosa Henderson, Victoria Spivey, and Lucille Hegamin they dominated the blues-recording industry throughout the twenties. It has often been asserted that this recording of the blues compromised and adulterated a pure folk form of the blues but the combination of the vaudeville, carnival, and minstrel shows and the phonograph meant that the "folk-blues" and the culture industry product were inextricably mixed in the twenties. By 1928 the blues sung by blacks were only secondarily of folk origin and the primary source for the group transmission of the blues was by phonograph which was then joined by the radio.

Bessie Smith, Ma Rainey, Ethel Waters, and the other women blues singers travelled in carnivals and vaudevilles which included acts with animals, acrobats and other circus performers. Often the main carnival played principally for white audiences but would have black sideshows with black entertainers for black audiences. In this way black entertainers reached black audiences in even the remotest rural areas. The records of the women blues singers were likewise directed at a black audience through the establishment of "race records" a section of the recording industry which recorded both religious and secular black singers and black muscians and distributed these recordings through stores in black areas: they were rarely available in white neighborhoods.

WHEN A WOMAN GETS THE BLUES . . .

This then is the framework within which I interpret the women blues singers of the twenties. To fully understand the ways in which their performance and their songs were part of a discourse of sexual relations within the black community, it is necessary to consider how the social conditions of black women were dramatically affected by migration, for migration had distinctively different meanings for black men and women. The music and song of the women blues singers embodied the social relations and contradictions of black displacement: of rural migration and the urban flux. In this sense, as singers these women were organic intellectuals; not only were they a part of the community that was the subject of their song but they were also a product of the rural-to-urban movement.

Migration for women often meant being left behind: "Bye Bye Baby" and "Sorry I can't take you" were the common refrains of male blues. In women's blues the response is complex: regret and pain expressed as "My sweet man done gone and left me dead," or "My daddy left me standing in the door," or "The sound of the train fills my heart with misery." There was also an explicit recognition that if the journey were to be made by women it held particular dangers for them. It was not as easy for women as it was for men to hop freight trains and if money was saved for tickets it was men who were usually sent. And yet the women who were singing the songs had made it North and recorded from the "promised land" of Chicago and New York. So, what the women blues singers were able to articulate were the possibilities of movement for the women who "have ramblin on their minds" and who intended to "ease on down the line" for they had made it—the power of movement was theirs. The train, which had symbolized freedom and mobility for men in male blues songs became a contested symbol. The sound of the train whistle, a mournful signal of imminent desertion and future loneliness was reclaimed as a sign that women too were on the move. In 1924, both Trixie Smith and Clara Smith recorded "Freight Train Blues." These are the words Clara Smith sang:

> I hate to hear that engine blow, boo hoo.
> I hate to hear that engine blow, boo hoo.
> Everytime I hear it blowin, I feel like ridin too.

> That's the freight train blues, I got box cars on my mind.
> I got the freight train blues, I got box cars on my mind.
> Gonna leave this town, cause my man is so unkind.

> I'm goin away just to wear you off my mind.
> I'm goin away just to wear you off my mind.
> And I may be gone for a doggone long long time.

> I'll ask the brakeman to let me ride the blind.
> I'll ask the brakeman to please let me ride the blind.
> The brakeman say, "Clara, you know this train ain't mine."

When a woman gets the blues she goes to her room and hides.
When a woman gets the blues she goes to her room and hides.
When a man gets the blues he catch the freight train and rides.

The music moves from echoing the moaning, mournful sound of
the train whistle to the syncopated activity of the sound of the wheels
in movement as Clara Smith determines to ride. The final opposition
between women hiding and men riding is counterpointed by this
musical activity and the determination in Clara Smith's voice.
"Freight Train Blues" and then "Chicago Bound Blues," which was
recorded by Bessie Smith and Ida Cox, were very popular so Para-
mount and Victor encouraged more "railroad blues". In 1925 Trixie
Smith recorded "Railroad Blues" which directly responded to the
line "had the blues for Chicago and I just can't be satisfied" from
"Chicago Bound Blues" with "If you ride that train it'll satisfy your
mind." "Railroad Blues" encapsulated the ambivalent position of the
blues singer caught between the contradictory impulses of needing to
migrate North and the need to be able to return for the "Railroad
Blues" were headed not for the North but for Alabama. Being able to
move both North and South the women blues singer occupied a privileged space: she could speak the desires of rural women to migrate
and voice the nostalgic desires of urban women for home which was
both a recognition and a warning that the city was not, in fact, the
"promised land."

Men's and women's blues shared the language and experience of
the railroad and migration but what that meant was different for
each sex. The language of the blues carries this conflict of interests
and is the cultural terrain in which these differences were fought
over and redefined. Women's blues were the popular cultural embodiment of the way in which the differing interests of black men and
women were a struggle of power relations. The sign of the train is one
example of the way in which the blues were a struggle within language itself to define the differing material conditions of black wom-
en and black men.

BAAAD SISTA

The differing interests of women and men in the domestic sphere was
clearly articulated by Bessie Smith in "In House Blues," a popular
song from the mid-twenties which she wrote herself but didn't record
until 1931. Although the man gets up and leaves, the woman remains,
trapped in the house like a caged animal pacing up and down. But at

the same time Bessie's voice vibrates with tremendous power which implies the eruption that is to come. The woman in the house is only barely restrained from creating havoc; her capacity for violence has been exercised before and resulted in her arrest. The music, which provides an oppositional counterpoint to Bessie's voice, is a parody of the supposed weakness of women. A vibrating cornet contrasts with the words that ultimately cannot be contained and roll out the front door.

Sitting in the house with everything on my mind.
Sitting in the house with everything on my mind.
Looking at the clock and can't even tell the time.

Walking to my window and looking outa my door.
Walking to my window and looking outa my door.
Wishin that my man would come home once more.

Can't eat, can't sleep, so weak I can't walk my floor.
Can't eat, can't sleep, so weak I can't walk my floor.
Feel like calling "murder" let the police squad get me once more.

They woke me up before day with trouble on my mind.
They woke me up before day with trouble on my mind.
Wringing my hands and screamin, walking the floor hollerin an
    crying.

Hey, don't let them blues in here.
Hey, don't let them blues in here.
They shakes me in my bed and sits down in my chair.

Oh, the blues has got me on the go.
They've got me on the go.
They roll around my house, in and out of my front door.

The way in which Bessie growls "so weak" contradicts the supposed weakness and helplessness of the woman in the song and grants authority to her thoughts of "murder."

The rage of women against male infidelity and desertion is evident in many of the blues. Ma Rainey threatened violence when she sang that she was "gonna catch" her man "with his britches down," in the act of infidelity, in "Black Eye Blues." Exacting revenge against mistreatment also appears as taking another lover as in "Oh Papa Blues" or taunting a lover who has been thrown out with "I won't worry when you're gone, another brown has got your water on" in "Titanic Man Blues." But Ma Rainey is perhaps best known for the rejection of a lover in "Don't Fish in My Sea" which is also a resolution to give up men altogether. She sang:

If you don't like my ocean, don't fish in my sea,
If you don't like my ocean, don't fish in my sea,
Stay out of my valley, and let my mountain be.

Ain't had no lovin' since God knows when,
Ain't had no lovin' since God knows when,
That's the reason I'm through with these no good triflin' men.

The total rejection of men as in this blues and in other songs such as "Trust No Man" stand in direct contrast to the blues that concentrate upon the bewildered, often half-crazed and even paralyzed response of women to male violence.

Sandra Leib (1981) has described the masochism of "Sweet Rough Man," in which a man abuses a helpless and passive woman, and she argues that a distinction must be made between reactions to male violence against women in male and female authored blues. "Sweet Rough Man," though recorded by Ma Rainey, was composed by a man and is the most explicit description of sexual brutality in her repertoire. The articulation of the possibility that women could leave a condition of sexual and financial dependency, reject male violence, and end sexual exploitation was embodied in Ma Rainey's recording of "Hustlin Blues," composed jointly by a man and a woman, which narrates the story of a prostitute who ends her brutal treatment by turning in her pimp to a judge. Ma Rainey sang:

I ain't made no money, and he dared me to go home.
Judge, I told him he better leave me alone.

He followed me up and he grabbed me for a fight.
He followed me up and he grabbed me for a fight.
He said, "Girl, do you know you ain't made no money tonight.

Oh Judge, tell him I'm through.
Oh Judge, tell him I'm through.
I'm tired of this life, that's why I brought him to you.

However, Ma Rainey's strongest assertion of female sexual autonomy is a song she composed herself, "Prove it on Me Blues," which isn't technically a blues song which she sang accompanied by a Tub Jug Washboard Band. "Prove it on Me Blues" was an assertion and an affirmation of lesbianism. Though condemned by society for her sexual preference the singer wants the whole world to know that she choses women rather than men. The language of "Prove it on Me Blues" engages directly in defining issues of sexual preference as a contradictory struggle of social relations. Both Ma Rainey and Bessie

Smith had lesbian relationships and "Prove it on Me Blues" vacillates between the subversive hidden activity of women loving women with a public declaration of lesbianism. The words express a contempt for a society that rejected lesbians. "They say I do it, ain't nobody caught me, They sure got to prove it on me." But at the same time the song is a reclamation of lesbianism as long as the woman publicly names her sexual preference for herself in the repetition of lines about the friends who "must've been women, cause I don't like no men." (Leib, 1981.)

But most of the songs that asserted a woman's sexual independence did so in relation to men, not women. One of the most joyous is a recording by Ethel Waters in 1925 called "No Man's Mamma Now." It is the celebration of a divorce that ended a marriage defined as a five year "war." Unlike Bessie Smith, Ethel Waters didn't usually growl, although she could; rather her voice, which is called "sweet-toned," gained authority from its stylistic enunciation and the way in which she almost recited the words. As Waters (1951) said, she tried to be "refined" even when she was being her most outrageous.

> You may wonder what's the reason for this crazy smile,
> Say I haven't been so happy in a long while
> Got a big load off my mind, here's the paper sealed and signed,
> And the judge was nice and kind all through the trial.
> This ends a five year war, I'm sweet Miss Was once more.
>
> I can come when I please, I can go when I please.
> I can flit, fly and flutter like the birds in the trees.
> Because, I'm no man's mamma now. Hey, hey.
>
> I can say what I like, I can do what I like.
> I'm a girl who is on a matrimonial strike;
> Which means, I'm no man's mamma now.
>
> I'm screaming bail
> I know how a fella feels getting out of jail
> I got twin beds, I take pleasure in announcing one for sale.
>
> Am I making it plain, I will never again,
> Drag around another ball and chain.
> I'm through, because I'm no man's mamma now.
>
> I can smile, I can wink, I can go take a drink,
> And I don't have to worry what my hubby will think.
> Because, I'm no man's mamma now.
>
> I can spend if I choose, I can play and sing the blues.
> There's nobody messin with my one's and my twos.
> Because, I'm no man's mamma now.

You know there was a time,
I used to think that men were grand.
But no more for mine,
I'm gonna label my apartment "No Man's Land."

I got rid of my cat cause the cat's name was Pat,
Won't even have a male fox in my flat,
Because, I'm no man's mamma now.

Waters' sheer exuberance is infectious. The vitality and energy of the performance celebrates the unfettered sexuality of the singer. The self-conscious and self-referential lines "I can play and sing the blues" situates the singer at the center of a subversive and liberatory activity. Many of the men who were married to blues singers disapproved of their careers, some felt threatened, others, like Edith Johnson's husband, eventually applied enough pressure to force her to stop singing. Most, like Bessie Smith, Ethel Waters, Ma Rainey, and Ida Cox did not stop singing the blues but their public presence, their stardom, their overwhelming popularity, and their insistence on doing what they wanted caused frequent conflict with the men in their personal lives.

FUNKY AND SINFUL STUFF

The figure of the woman blues singer has become a cultural embodiment of social and sexual conflict from Gayl Jones' novel *Corregidora* to Alice Walker's *The Color Purple*. The women blues singers occupied a privileged space; they had broken out of the boundaries of the home and taken their sensuality and sexuality out of the private into the public sphere. For these singers were gorgeous and their physical presence elevated them to being referred to as Goddesses, as the high priestesses of the blues, or like Bessie Smith, as the Empress of the blues. Their physical presence was a crucial aspect of their power; the visual display of spangled dresses, of furs, of gold teeth, of diamonds, of all the sumptuous and desirable aspects of their body reclaimed female sexuality from being an objectification of male desire to a representation of female desire.

Bessie Smith wrote about the social criticism that women faced if they broke social convention. "Young Woman's Blues" threads together many of the issues of power and sexuality that have been addressed so far. "Young Woman's Blues" sought possibilities, possibilites that arose from women being on the move and confidently asserting their own sexual desirability.

Woke up this morning when chickens were crowing for day.
Felt on the right side of my pillow, my man had gone away.
On his pillow he left a note, reading I'm sorry you've got my goat.
No time to marry, no time to settle down.

I'm a young woman and ain't done running around.
I'm a young woman and ain't done running around.
Some people call me a hobo, some call me a bum,
Nobody know my name, nobody knows what I've done.
I'm as good as any woman in your town,
I ain't no high yella, I'm a deep killa brown.

I ain't gonna marry, ain't gonna settle down.
I'm gonna drink good moonshine and run these browns down.
See that long lonesome road, cause you know its got a end.
And I'm a good woman and I can get plenty men.

The women blues singers have become our cultural icons of sexual power but what is often forgotten is that they could be great comic entertainers. In "One Hour Mama" Ida Cox used comedy to intensify an irreverent attack on male sexual prowess. The comic does not mellow the assertive voice but on the contrary undermines mythologies of phallic power and establishes a series of woman-centered heterosexual demands.

I've always heard that haste makes waste,
So, I believe in taking my time
The highest mountain can't be raced
Its something you must slowly climb.

I want a slow and easy man,
He needn't ever take the lead,
Cause I work on that long time plan
And I ain't a looking for no speed.

I'm a one hour mama, so no one minute papa
Ain't the kind of man for me.
Set your alarm clock papa, one hour that's proper
Then love me like I like to be.

I don't want no lame excuses bout my lovin being so good,
That you couldn't wait no longer, now I hope I'm understood.
I'm a one hour mama, so no one minute papa
Ain't the kind of man for me.

I can't stand no green horn lover, like a rookie goin to war,
With a load of big artillery, but don't know what its for.
He's got to bring me reference with a great long pedigree
And must prove he's got endurance, or he don't mean snap to me.

I can't stand no crowin rooster, what just likes a hit or two,
Action is the only booster of just what my man can do.
I don't want no imitation, my requirements ain't no joke,
Cause I got pure indignation for a guy whats lost his stroke.

I'm a one hour mama, so no one minute papa
Ain't the kind of man for me.
Set your alarm clock papa, one hour that's proper,
Then love me like I like to be.

I may want love for one hour, then decide to make it two.
Takes an hour 'fore I get started, maybe three before I'm through.
I'm a one hour mama, so no one minute papa,
Ain't the kind of man for me.

But this moment of optimism, of the blues as the exercise of power and control over sexuality, was short lived. The space occupied by these blues singers was opened up by race records but race records did not survive the depression. Some of these blues women, like Ethel Waters and Hattie McDaniels, broke through the racial boundaries of Hollywood film and were inserted into a different aspect of the culture industry where they occupied not a privileged but a subordinate space and articulated not the possibilities of black female sexual power but the "Yes, Ma'ams" of the black maid. The power of the blues singer was resurrected in a different moment of black power; re-emerging in Gayl Jones' *Corregidora;* and the woman blues singer remains an important part of our 20th century black cultural reconstruction. The blues singers had assertive and demanding voices; they had no respect for sexual taboos or for breaking through the boundaries of respectability and convention, and we hear the "we" when they say "I."

REFERENCES

Brown, S. (1980). Ma Rainey. *The Collected Poems of Sterling A. Brown.* New York: Harper and Row.

Carby, H. V. (1986). On the threshold of woman's era: Lynching, empire and sexuality in black feminist theory. In H. L. Gates, Jr. (Ed.), *'Race,' Writing and Difference* (pp. 301–316). Chicago: University of Chicago Press.

Carby, H. V. (1987). *Reconstructing Womanhood: The Emergence of the Afro-American Woman Novelist.* New York: Oxford University Press.

Cooper, A. J. (1892). *A Voice from the South.* Xenia, OH: Aldine Publishing House.

Cox, I. (1980). One hour mama. *Mean Mothers.* Rosetta Records, RR 1300.

Leib, S. (1981). *Mother of the Blues: A Study of Ma Rainey.* Amherst: University of Massachusetts Press.

Rainey, G. (1974). *Ma Rainey.* Milestone Records, M47021.

Smith, B. (n.d.). In house blues. *The World's Greatest Blues Singer.* Columbia Records, CG33.

Smith, B. (1972). Young woman's blues. *Nobody's Blues But Mine.* Columbia Records, CG 31093.

Smith, C. (1980). Freight train blues. *Women's Railroad Blues.* Rosetta Records, RR 1301.

Spillers, H. (1984). Interstices: A small drama of words. In C. Vance (Ed.), *Pleasure and Danger: Exploring Female Sexuality* (pp. 73–100). London: Routledge and Kegan Paul.

Waters, E. (1951). *His Eye is on the Sparrow.* New York: Doubleday & Co., Inc.

Waters, E. (1982). No man's mama. *Big Mamas.* Rosetta Records, RR 1306.

Williams, S. A. (1979). The blues roots of contemporary Afro-American poetry. In M. S. Harper & R. B. Stepto (Eds.), *Chant of Saints* (pp. 123–135). Chicago: University of Illinois Press.

Williams, S. A. (1981). The house of desire. In E. Stetson (Ed.), *Black Sister: Poetry by Black American Women, 1746–1980.* Bloomington: Indiana University Press.

Williams, S. A. (1982). Fifteen. *Some One Sweet Angel Chile.* New York: William Morrow and Co., Inc.

CHAPTER 9

Censorship of Women's Voices on Radio

Cheris Kramarae

Dept. of Speech Communication
University of Illinois at Urbana-Champaign

Some radio news directors who employ a woman as part of a news announcing team encourage the woman to sound "feminine." Other directors advise the woman to work on a "masculine," "hard edge" sound. Some directors say that before they employ any woman or any more women as announcers they need market research to ask listeners, "Do you find female announcers pleasing to the ear?" Whatever the specific action of the directors, chances are slim that listeners will hear women consequently on radio airshifts, or two women working on the same airshifts (Learner, 1982). Now that they know that various agencies occasionally make counts of the number of women and minority staff members, many station managers do hire a few women for the news staff. But not too many; meanwhile station managers do not seem to worry about the pervasive presence of male voices and themes on air.

Women's "undesirable" voices are said to be the reason why radio announcing remains primarily a man's job. A close listening and reading finds the problem in another location, however, and suggests the following analysis: (a) Radio (and TV) broadcasting processes in English-speaking countries developed as a product of women's and men's relationship and women's relative lack of power. Women have been excluded from decision making positions and their voices have been systematically silenced on air. (b) Radio broadcasting, both in its voice and in the message the voice conveys, functions to keep women in their social, and non-broadcasting place. "Women's voices" and the troubles associated with them were not, of course, invented by male radio managers; they have just elaborated on the concept. (c) Women's life experiences are different from men's in many everyday ways, and in these differences lies the special opportunity for radio to enhance the interaction of women and between men and women. The potential existed at the beginning days of broadcasting when women lived a more "shut-in" traditional life, and today when more women live a "double day." Yet, instead, much broadcasting seems designed to make women more isolated. What follows is an account of some of the causes and results of men's anxiety about, and control of, women's voices on radio.

A review of the efforts made to restrict women's participation in reporting the news can give valuable information about the widespread, strong prejudices against women's public speaking.

To keep this account short, I will focus on radio here, giving examples from what was initially the British Broadcasting Company and soon became the British Broadcasting Corporation (BBC). The story of women's announcing voices on television broadcasting has some strong similarities to that of radio. While I deal primarily with the manner in which the BBC officials have censored women's voices, my collection of related material indicates that chronological studies of women as radio and television newsreporters in the United States will reveal similar patterns to that reported here. The history of broadcasting and public speaking is different for the U.S. and Great Britain; however, in both countries employment of a woman in a male-dominated media job often receives much attention in the media along with predictions of major gains in the number of or influence of women involved in the mass communication industry. Repeatedly through the years, predictions that women have finally broken down barriers have proved incorrect. The news that the barriers are (slightly) broken receives more attention than does their repair. Little attention is given to the often subsequent hiring of a man for that woman's job. Additionally, minimal representation of women on broadcasting staffs often means "presence without power" and no significant employment gains for women (United States Commission on Civil Rights 1977, 108, pp. 126–127; *Media Report to Women,* beginning with vol. 1, 1972). I mention this because some people might assume, now that they can hear *some* women hired as announcers, that the general exclusion of women is no longer common. As one radio news manager declared, "If you have two on—it sounds a lot" (Ross, 1977, p. 24).

Raymond Williams (1974), in his short, very useful (but masculist) social history of British broadcasting, suggests that while radio and television were initially systems of transmission without a driving content, they were established during a time when "new relations between men, and between men and things, was being intensely experienced" (p. 22). The broadcasting systems became a product, Williams argues, of the increased urban industrial living—with, paradoxically, more mobility *and* the seemingly self-sufficient family home, with larger settlements and industrial organizations *and* the dispersal of extended families. He calls this a "mobile privatisation" (p. 26). The broadcasting systems were not just the outgrowth of technical knowledge of cathode ray tubes and such, but also the outgrowth of specific organizational development. He stresses the importance of considering the interrelationship of factors which produce technological processes, cautioning us about the dangers of assuming technological determinism. Right. But what were those increased needs for communication created by the more complex urban life and the privatized family life? Williams, like most other male social historians, shies away from any discussion of women as they may have different urban and family lives from the "we" and "people" mentioned in the histories. However, if we listen a while to the programming of radio and television, we hear a strange tale regarding the communication among women and men.

During the first two decades of the 20th century, many women in the U.K. had been publicly and politically active. Women aligned with the various feminist organizations were writing and distributing flyers and articles, and lecturing in public squares and halls, as well as engaging in less literary activities such as breaking storefront windows, and setting fire to boat houses at exclusive men's clubs—in an effort to win the legal right to vote. During the war years, women were encouraged to become involved in publicly recognizable ways in the fight for preservation of the home land. After the war, the community kitchens organized by the government and many other supports for women's activities outside the home were shut down. While women's work toward equal rights and work in public service projects certainly did not end in the 1920s (see Dale Spender, 1983), many women moved, or were moved, into more domestic activities.

Here is certainly a group of people who could make good use of radio, as broadcasting systems developed in the 1920s. Many women were restricted to the home during much of the day, had more limited access to automobiles then men had, and were responsible for much repetitive household work which left ears and mind free for listening. Logically, radio should have become a medium for interaction among women, a way of exchanging questions and information. If women were to have a central role in deciding what was said by whom on radio then they would need to be policymakers, program planners, and have access to the microphones. As we all know, this didn't happen. The basic controlling decisions about what was to be broad-casted and by whom were made by directors who limited the pro-grams directed to women to continuing lessons on how to take care of family and home. Women have been the majority of the listeners of radio, but not the organizers or speakers of radio programming.

The policy makers and producers have been recruited from a nar-row range of university graduates with backgrounds which pre-dispose them to follow establishment standards (Garnham, 1978, p. 31). In fact, the governing body of the BBC in general has been mostly older and male. In 1926 the new five-member Board of Governors included one woman, Mrs. Snowden, who, the *Wireless Magazine* explained, "will look after women's interests in broadcasting" (Dec. 26, 1926, p. 406). What the four men would be looking after isn't mentioned. Already, women's interests were separated from the un-labelled concerns of the supposedly ungendered, universal group, men. During the first 50 years there were 67 men and 18 women serving on BBC's Board of Governors (Briggs, 1979, p. 14). A mid-1980s BBC report lists 159 men and 6 women in top-ranked positions, and 263 men and 27 women as heads of departments. (A summary of Monica Sim's report *Women in BBC Management* is contained in Commission of European Communities, 1986.) Asa Briggs, the historian who has written several volumes about the BBC, did reserve a little space for discussion of the women. One Governor, Lady Reading, who Briggs said had been called "the most remarkable woman alive," was mentioned only a few times. Her remarkable qualities were not explained. In Briggs' book on the governing bodies of the BBC (1979), several other women are mentioned as having been forceful advocates, but of what is not made clear. While Briggs (1965) states that "no history of the BBC would be complete without refer-ence to the key part [women] played in the daily running of the organization," this "let us not forget the ladies" phrasing suggests that they *were* almost forgotten. He mentions several women: the first archivist; the person who played a key role in the development of overseas broadcasting; others who moved from secretarial work to "positions of responsibility"; and Miss G. M. Freeman, the Women Staff Administrator. As he indicates, there have been women in a few important positions—but the BBC has basically been a male domain with males hiring mostly males. One of those men, hired as an Outside Broadcasts Assistant, said that joining the BBC in 1936 "was rather like becoming a novice in a Jesuit seminary." He changed the figure of speech a paragraph later to describe the Director-General as "the captain on the bridge, guiding his great ship towards the wide horizon of art, music, religion, indeed towards all the higher things of the mind" (Vaughan-Thomas, 1980, pp. 124–125). Seminary and ship— not places associated with women's presence or influence.

Those unnatural voices. Early managers made the decision that women were not to be announcers. The BBC managers have, in fact, been very particular about who does the announcing. For example, in 1924 the Director directed that announcers should be men of culture and knowledge, with good articulation and accurate pronunciation (memo in BBC archives). In practice this meant that announcers were men who had Oxford or Cambridge degrees. Men with regional dialects (as opposed to the "good university" dialects) were not employed at the BBC Broadcasting House until the 1940s. The largest part of the radio audience was working class (Briggs, 1965). The men speaking to them were "gentlemen" (unnamed on the air since the BBC officials wanted them to be thought of as the BBC, not as individual men) who actually wore morning jackets or dinner jackets as they spoke (Briggs, 1965; Vaughan-Thomas, 1980). Broadcasting served as an invasive transmission of middle-class male ideology and control.

While only a few males with proper ruling class voices were hired to be the Voice of the BBC, no females were wanted as announcers in the 1920s and 1930s. During WWII, women *were* hired (what alternatives did the officials have with so many of the men in the armed forces?) for many jobs at the BBC, including some announcing work—although not the reading of war news. On January 24, 1942, *The Evening News* reported, "The old prejudice against women announcers has disappeared since the war, and listeners, as well as the B.B.C. have decided that announcing—as distinct from news reading—is a job that women can handle with ability and charm." The women were assured that that they had proved themselves fine announcers, acceptable to the public. Yet, within a few years after the war the job advertisements for BBC announcers indicated that, once again, only men were wanted. I have collected (with the help of archivists at the BBC in London and Reading and at the Fawcett Library in London) thousands of broadcasting in-house memos, listener research surveys, job advertisements, press releases, and newspaper clippings dealing with broadcasting policies regarding women's voices on the air.[1] They tell a saga with a repetitive plot. BBC offi-

---

[1] I thank BBC archivists in Reading and London for the valuable assistance they gave me during my research work, and I thank the librarians at the Fawcett Library for the help they provided me during the months I worked there.

cials did not want women as regular announcers although some women were hired to do some announcing of women's and children's programs.

Some women's groups, newspaper columnists, and hundreds of individual women applying for jobs questioned the BBC on the policies regarding women announcers; they were likely responsible for pushing the BBC to what officials called "experiments." The experiments usually consisted of male officials putting *one* woman on the air to read news while arguing (in interviews reported in newspapers) that these experiments do not work and while setting forth reasons that women should not be made news announcers. Ironically, one of the reasons given by the officials for "failed experiments" was that women experimentees appeared too self-conscious. Other reasons officials gave were that other women did not want to hear women's voices reading the news, that women were too frail (one BBC official said he feared that they would not be able to make the run sometimes required from one studio to another), that women's voices were unsuitable, or that the broadcasting equipment carried male voices better than female voices (Kramarae, 1984). A telescoping review of BBC policy on women announcers makes clear that during most of the BBC history, the officials have not allowed women to speak publicly on matters and places which are considered important by men.

The U.S. radio managers had similar policies and motives. During WWII, many women were hired for announcing jobs while the "regular" announcers were in the armed services. The women were "not retained" after the war because, according to the authors of *The Announcers Headbook,* "the higher-pitched female voices could not hold listeners' attention for any length of time, while the lower-pitched voices were frequently vehicles for an overly polished, ultra-sophisticated delivery that sounded phoney." Women's voices are not absolutely good for nothing, however. The authors continue: "Women's delivery, that in general is lacking in the authority needed for a convincing newscast, is frequently just right for commercials demonstrating household items and fashion trends" (Hennecke & Dumit, 1959, p. 19).

The mission position of the BBC. The charter of the BBC declares it is to "provide . . . broadcasting services . . . for general reception . . . disseminating information, education and entertainment."[2]

---

[2] Another stated objective of the BBC was to develop "an informed democracy" (Paulu, 1956, p. 228)—the information to be provided, of course, primarily by correctly educated, middle-class males. One broadcasting historian excuses the non-democratic policies of the BBC this way: "Whatever it does, the BBC always takes its assignments

This is a very general directive since almost anything broadcasted would likely be thought to have one of those functions by some programmers or listeners. Over the years, this mission of the BBC has changed somewhat. Initially the emphasis was supposedly on providing solace—comfort particularly for the lonely. (The programming was not, however, designed to let the lonely talk with each other about the causes of or solutions for their loneliness.) Later, according to social historians, the people in charge of broadcasting thought they could use their influence and equipment to develop or transform the "taste" of the audience—to (in middle-class accents) inform and inspire the country. The even more expansive Empire Service, begun in 1932, included an annual Christmas message to the Empire from the King, news bulletins, and many programs drawn from the BBC's domestic services. These programs included entertainment shows and sports with, as one historian assures us, "particular emphasis on sport classics of interest to the British Empire, such as inter-Empire cricket and football matches" (Paulu, 1956, p. 375). I can find no indication of, for example, how many women in India had access to short wave broadcasting or what they thought of the classic cricket matches. It is possible that they didn't know that the BBC was "an accepted and essential part of the machinery of civilization" as judged by Lord Gainford in *Radio Times* (December 1926).

Today, while there is, fortunately, more explicit discussion within the BBC of the importance of broadcasting to satisfy a pluralistic society, these discussions have not led to major changes. The BBC voice and message is still very white and male, supported by many women clerical staff members who are supposed to use their verbal skills only to process the men's themes, and the men's language. And to do this with appreciation, offering little criticism for fear their voices also might be found displeasing.

Whatever the ideological positions of the governing bodies, what have been the implications for women? Through the years the BBC officials have known that women are the primary audience for sound broadcasting. And certainly many of these women have heard much of interest in the broadcasts. (During my years of teaching and researching in the U.K., I have listened, with appreciation, to many hours of music and drama broadcasted by the BBC, and the listener reports indicate that many others have enjoyed many of the programs.) But instead of radio serving as a communication link for the many women who listen in their homes, radio broadcasting seems

---

seriously: some critics have called it authoritarian, but friends and foes alike agree that it is entirely responsible" (Paulu, 1956, p. 229).

planned to making women more isolated. In a review of some of the sexist practices on BBC radio, Mileva Ross (1977) quotes from a newspaper interview with David Hamilton, a BBC disc jockey:

> I try to talk to one person. I've got this picture of a woman, a housewife, young or young at heart. She's probably on her own virtually all day. She's bored with the routine of housework and with her own company and just for her I'm the chatty, slightly cheeky romantic visitor. (*Daily Mail*, April 12, 1973)

The jingle which introduced the daily beauty advice spot on that disc jockey's show went "Keep young and beautiful if you want to be loved." Does such talk fall in the category of information, education, or entertainment (the functions listed by the BBC charter)? Or should it more accurately be labelled patronizing, paternalistic patter to keep women at home and/or responsible for the home? The pattern for this type of program was set in 1946 when the first edition of "Woman's House" opened with a talk on "Mother's Midday Meal," followed by hints on "Putting Your Best Face Forward." The broadcasting officials' image of the listener (as a bored housewife, uninterested in work or events beyond her home and family, waiting for advice and company from a man) has effectively kept women from peak-time presenting. One radio critic points out that female presenters would change the topics *and* style of presentation. A woman presenter would be unlikely to respond to a male caller requesting information or music in this way:

"All on your own then? I pass your house on my way home, I'll nip in for a cup of tea. Ho, ho." The critic continues: "She could not, she would not. Men can, men do" (Gillian Reynolds, quoted in Baehr & Ryan, 1984, p. 33).

The situation was much the same in the U.S. In a 1947 special edition of *Life* magazine, the editors explore "The American Woman's Dilemma," mentioning the radio in a discussion of the problem of underemployment and boredom experienced by "nearly half of the adult female Americans ". . . [who] do not have children under 18, . . . do not work on farms, nor are . . . aged or infirm." These women's "props for idle hours" include such ineffective items as "jewels, pretty clothes, sleeping pills, perfume, small pets, sexy fiction"—and the radio over which "women may hear anything from *When A Girl Marries* to *Life Can be Beautiful*" (June 16, p. 109). (Such criticism had little impact on radio programming or on subsequent TV programming; in 1959 TV programs "especially for women . . . range from cooking shows to interviews with visiting celebrities or the local Community Chest representative" [Hennecke &

Dumit, 1959, p. 19].) These programs might well be of interest to some listeners. But clearly, only very traditional aspects of women's lives were being discussed; the topics and announcers address women only as wives, homemakers, mothers, sex objects, and caretakers of others' needs.

Holding very limited conceptions of women's interests and individuality, and ignoring the fact that women's "political issues" are more comprehensive (including the concerns and lives of women as well as of men), some critics have complained about women's lack of attention to "public issues." One historian of broadcasting (and Director of Talks for the BBC in the '30s) wrote of American women:

> From a democratic point of view, it appears . . . that women are a serious liability, and from a psychological and social point of view, they constitute a major problem . . . If ignorance and indifference to public affairs are threats to the successful functioning of democracy, women, as compared with men, are a menace. (Siepmann, 1950, p. 105)

Women, he wrote, were not listening to public issue radio programs in the same numbers as the men were. Also, they were lagging behind the men in their knowledge of the broadcasting system. Further, they were showing an obsession with daytime serials. (He said nothing about men's obsession with listening to men's politics or sports.)

Topics worth an airing. What might programming sound like if women were considered major users of broadcasting rather than as a special interest group which needs occasional, paternalistic help with its homework?[3] Some producers have more daringly dealt with such topics as the Pill, homosexuality, frigidity, and impotence. There are other possibilities: call-in programs about vaginal thrush or the unemployment of older women; women's work and salaries in the labor force; discussions of relationships including marriage; information on basic technical skills to demystify household plumbing, electricity and appliances, hygiene and medical self-help, menopause, sexuality and sexual techniques and problems, and the pol-

---

[3] One broadcasting textbook used in many U.S. university journalism courses includes a section on the special interest programming for "ethnic groups, as well as for other groups, such as women, farmers, and country music fans" (Smith, 1985, p. 166). Should we have to point out the several basic problems with this labelling and categorizing?. Certainly we want broadcasting to serve people with varying interests in various occupations and activities. But to label women a special interest group ignores the fact that women have been more than half the listening audience. It is revealing that women rather than men are listed as a special interest group.

itics of child care (see Helen Roberts' suggestions in *The Guardian*, July 15, 1976).

Additional suggestions for daytime programming for women (and men) are listed by Helen Baehr and Michele Ryan (1984): tranquilizers and other medication frequently prescribed for women; "compulsive eating"; well-women clinics; ante-natal services; changes in family life; pressures on family life; new technology and its relationship to women's lives (as discussed by women); complexities, dissatisfactions, and satisfactions of daily activities; the history and events of international Woman's Day, for example. Baehr and Ryan also write of the importance of radio courses for women, courses which can be used by, for example, working-class women (with poor job possibilities, social security problems, and poor housing) to produce programs on these problems, presenting the problems as politically, not personally, produced.

In some European countries it has taken illegal action by women to get their concerns aired. Birgitte Jallov ("Birgitte Jallov Report," 1983) reports that Radio Donna in Italy was a pirate broadcasting system by a group of homemakers sending discussions every morning on issues taboo on the state radio. She also reports they were shot at and their studio was burned by a rightist, fascist undergound group in 1979.

In Sweden, several women of a local radio station have produced a 40-minute three-times-a-week program which deals with medical problems, work, women's everyday problems, leisure time, relationships, falling in love, dance, sport, children, politics, and other issues that are of particular concern to their listeners, who call and express appreciation for serious and regular attention to what traditional broadcasting managers would consider "petty problems" ("Birgitte Jallov Report," 1983). Some of the women producing these broadcasts report that in order to be successful the programs are planned through collectives. In these instances, women's voices are used in the preparation and in the production—places where women's voices are usually not audible. In most cases, however, even the "women's programs" are framed by men who set broadcasting policy, budgets, and hiring policies.

Radio broadcasting could have been (and could be) a wonderful innovation for women, who have needed such a linking innovation more than do men. But it has been governed and transmitted primarily by men. Because of the great publicity given the relatively few women in radio and television broadcasting, we might forget that they have not been there long and that they are there at the whim of male officials. Their voices and their concerns are not yet built into the broadcasting system. The gender politics of broadcasting managers systematically exclude women from decision-making positions, and silence their voices so that female listeners remain private consumers, listening to the public pronouncements and voices of men. These are policies, not openly arrived at and not regularly reviewed, which perpetuate traditional roles for women.

Men's restrictions on women's radio voices are not isolated policy and events. The admission of women's voices and themes in any public situation involving men is always more than a matter of adding a higher pitch and a few additional topics. Allowing women the same speaking rights as men would be allowing a change in the relationships between women and men. Our analyses of men's and women's evaluation of women's voices in *any* situation needs to include the discussion of continuing power asymmetries, and the continuing evaluation of *men's* voices.

REFERENCES

Baehr, H., & Ryan, M. (1984). *Shut Up and Listen!* London: Comedia Publishing.

Birgitte Jallov Report. (1983, November/December). *Media Report to Women*, p. 14.

Briggs, A. (1961). *The Birth of Broadcasting*. London: Oxford University Press.

Briggs, A. (1965). *The Golden Age of Wireless*. London: Oxford University Press.

Briggs, A. (1979). *Governing the BBC*. London: British Broadcasting Corporation.

Commission of European Communities. (1986, May 15). Directorate-General Information. *Women of Europe*. Communication Women's Information Service, Rue de la Loo 200, B-1049 Brussels, Belgium.

Garnham, N. (1978). *Structures of Television*. London: British Film Institute.

Hennecke, B. G., & Dumit, E. (1959). *The Announcers Handbook*. New York: Rinehart and Winston.

Kramarae, C. (1984). Nachrichten zu sprechen gestatte ich der Frau nicht. In S. Trömel-Plötz (Ed.), *Gewalt durch Sprache* (pp. 203–228). Frankfurt: Fischer Taschenbuch Verlag.

Learner, B. (1982, July 19). Women struggling for newsroom equality. *Earshot, The Newspaper for the Radio Newsroom*.

Media Report to Women. Women's Institute for Freedom of the Press. 3306 Ross, N.W., Washington, D.C. 20008.

Paulu, B. (1956). *British Broadcasting: Radio and Television in the United Kingdom*. Minneapolis: University of Minnesota Press.

Ross, M. (1977). Radio. In J. King & M. Stott (Eds.). *Is This Your Life? Images of Women in the Media* (pp. 9–35). London: Virago.

Siepmann, C. A. (1950). *Radio, Television and Society.* New York: Oxford University Press.

Smith, F. L. (1985). *Perspectives on Radio and Television.* New York: Harper & Row.

Spender, D. (1983). *There's Always Been a Women's Movement.* London: Routledge & Kegan Paul, Pandora Press.

U.S. Commission on Civil Rights. (1977). *Women Dressing on the Set: Women and Minorities in Television.* Washington, D.C.

Vaughan-Thomas, W. (1980). *Trust to Talk.* London: Hutchinson.

Williams, R. (1974). *Television: Technology and Cultural Form.* London: Fontana/Collins.

Wireless Magazine. (1926, December 26, p. 406).

CHAPTER 10

Interpretive Strategies and Sex-marked Comparative Constructions*

Julia Penelope

INTRODUCTION

Text linguistics is a relatively new critical approach with an ambitious, if naïve, research program. Among the stated goals of the text linguist is the identification of the pragmatic rules that govern "the systematic use of utterances" and specification of the ways in which "lexical meaning and general meaningfulness" are determined by world knowledge (van Dijk, 1977, pp. 2–4). These aims are held to be essential to the explication of such phenomena as meaningfulness, interpretation, informativity, cohesion, and coherence. A corollary assumption requires that pragmatic rules and world knowledge be shared by both writer and reader. That is, the writer must accurately gauge the ability and willingness of readers to interpret the use of specific words and constructions and supply additional information from "real world" knowledge when it is not explicit in a text. As a result, discussions of meaningfulness, interpretation, informativity, and coherence assume the complicity of readers. Using as data sex-specific similes and comparative constructions collected from several different prose genres in the popular media (book reviews, science fiction novels, recipe books, essays, and Letters to the Editor), I will argue that text analysis requires a distinction between critical and

---

* Different versions of this research and analysis have been presented at the annual conventions of the Popular Culture Association, Wichita, Kansas, April 23–26, 1983, and the Western Division of the American Philosophical Association, Chicago, Illinois, April 28–30, 1983, and to a linguistics colloquium at New Mexico State University, Las Cruces, New Mexico, December 8, 1983.

complicitous readers, and that the failure of text linguists to make such a distinction invalidates their theoretical framework and the terminology they have developed from it. In particular, I will use my examples to discuss the inadequacies of the text linguists' formulations of redundant information, pragmatic knowledge, and congruence between the "real world" models of writers and readers.

READING AND THE CREATION OF TEXTS

Up to a point, the assumption of reader complicity seems to be both reasonable and obvious. It is, by now, virtually a truism that readers actively participate in the construction of texts. Even in the simplest cases, such as pronominalization or deletion, we make connections among sentences and supply information that is only implicit in the surface structure of texts, and we use that information, as well as what is explicit, to construe our interpretations. Although we are limited in the range of possible interpretations by the syntactic and lexical choices of an author, our cooperation in the creation of the text is necessary. One fairly innocuous example will illustrate the various kinds of pragmatic knowledge readers supply during the interpretive process.

> (1) In times past there lived a king and queen who said to each other every day of their lives, 'Would that we had a child!' and yet they had none. But one day when the queen was bathing, a frog jumped out of the water and said, 'Thy wish shall be fulfilled.' (Beginning of *The Sleeping Beauty*," from *The Universe Within* by Morton Hunt, p. 21)

Our awareness of the quantity of information our minds supply as we read such passages is marginal, at best. As Hunt points out in his discussion of the opening lines from *Sleeping Beauty*, the words, *per se*, are not the message; they act as linguistic cues to our brains, and we then make several inferences based on previous experience and knowledge. "In times past," for example, indicates that we are about to be told a fairy tale, and we align our expectations accordingly. When the frog appears and speaks to the queen, we know that the structure of the story itself is about to unfold. More subtly, however, we know, as soon as we're told that there lived "a king and a queen," that these characters are a male and a female, respectively, that at least the king, and perhaps the queen (but not necessarily), wields great power over most of the people who live in the kingdom, and that the two are probably married to each other. Without the first and third assumptions, the rest of the opening sentence wouldn't make sense to an acculturated modern reader. But Hunt doesn't mention additional kinds of information we supply. We also know, for example that the indefinite pronoun *none* refers back to *a child,* and we read the rest of that sentence as "and yet they had no child." Furthermore, we may initially assume that the queen was taking a bath in much the same way that we do; that is, we might think that she was inside a castle, in a bathtub, in a room specifically designated for that activity. When we are told that a frog has leaped out of the water, we revise our assumptions, erase the bathtub in the bathroom in the castle, and move the queen outside into, perhaps, a pond, a lake, or a river.

The ability of our minds to make connections between items in discourse, to correctly infer information that is not overtly available, and to construct multiple possible interpretations all at once is amazing. But not all discourse is equally amenable to successful interpretation, and syntactic rules can be manipulated to force the reader/hearer to provide spurious information, in the absence of help from the writer, or to make the reader think that s/he has read in the text what s/he has, in fact, supplied out of her/his own linguistic experience. In order for a text to be judged as *coherent, informative,* and *cohesive,* according to text linguists, the "real world" models of the writer and reader must match, or be congruent, for the most part. This postulate entails several conditions. The reader must agree with what the writer posits as "pragmatically relevant:" the underlying concepts and relations of the text must be mutually accessible and relevant to both the writer and the readers. "Continuity of sense" is possible only if the writer and the reader share the socially accepted model of the "real world;" a minimally informative text is to be preferred because "ordinariness supports easy processing;" the most successful text is one that is highly noncontroversial. This framework, and its attendant assumptions, rules out the possibility that we might find a text that is both coherent and highly informative, because, supposedly, its readers would judge it to be "nonsense" if the frame and presuppositions of the writer didn't match theirs. The excerpt in example (2), from an article which appeared under Ronald Reagan's name, illustrates the quantity of inferential work that some writers require of their readers:

(2) Over the years, I have learned that one key to exercise is to find something that you enjoy. The other key is to keep the exercise varied. Using those two principles, let me explain my fitness plan, and perhaps you can see ways in which this could help you in your own exercising. (R. Reagan, "How to Stay Fit," *Parade Magazine,* December 4, 1983, p. 4)

During his presidency, Reagan has made something of a name for himself as a folk orator; with the help of his speechwriters, he has cultivated a casual, conversational style. The conversational style requires the most cooperation from its audience because the speaker assumes the kind of intimacy with an audience that permits vast inferential gaps, gaps which must be filled with information from the hearers' real-world knowledge. In the first sentence of this excerpt, the "key to exercise" lies in the infinitive clause, "to find something that you enjoy." As cooperating readers, we know perfectly well that Reagan has used the indefinite pronoun, *something,* to refer to "exercise." But, some of his readers, perhaps less generous or less enthusiastic about exercise, might interpret *something* more broadly, given the verb *enjoy,* and decide that "exercise" can include drinking a six-pack of beer or soda pop with one's feet propped up in front of a TV set, or going out to see a movie, or cooking oneself a gourmet feast. Reagan's encouragement "to find something" that we enjoy leaves many of us with the kind of latitude of interpretation that defeats communicative efforts. His third sentence is even more unfortunate. He begins with a dangling participle, "Using those two principles," and we assume that the deleted agent of *using* will be a first person pronoun, referring to the writer. But the following imperative construction, *let me,* requires a second person pronoun, *you,* and we revise our interpretation of *using* to mean that we are supposed to use the two principles. Surely, however, Reagan meant to say that *he* will use those principles as part of his explanation about his exercise plan. How would his readers use them? Within that participial phrase, why did he use *those* instead of *these* to refer back to the preceding principles? *Those* implies that there is more textual distance between his statement of the principles and his remention of them. Another example of confusing reference occurs toward the end of the sentence, Reagan's use of *this,* which, apparently, he intended to refer backward to his mention of his "fitness plan" or forward to the explanation itself, the remainder of the article. However we decide to interpret *this,* Reagan's casual style forces us to work overly hard for very little information. By choosing a conversational stance, Reagan can leave most of the writer's work to his readers. If they like him, they'll readily trade off substance for intimacy. Those of us who don't like him will use the text to figure out how he's using the language. Much then seems to depend upon the cooperative principle, which, in turn, depends upon a pre-existing friendly relationship between writer and readers. If readers are unwilling to supply the implicit information or pragmatic knowledge necessary to textual coherence, the text would, presumably, fail. But this cannot be the case.

In order to talk about what we do when we say we "read," we assume as given terms like "meaningfulness," "interpretation," "informativity," "cohesion," and "coherence"; we assume that they refer to abstract properties of texts that could be described if we only knew what we were looking for and, then, how to characterize them. As I've tried to suggest with the Reagan excerpt, much depends upon the reader's disposition toward the writer and the text in question. With respect to the assumptions writers make about their audiences, it seems clear that properties such as meaningfulness, interpretability, informativity, and coherence must be relative rather than absolute. One example of the relativity of these properties can be found in sex-specific descriptions, descriptions in which the focal term of a comparison is sex-marked as +FEMALE or +MALE.

CHARACTERIZING GENDERIZATION

In her 1975 article, "Referential Genderization," Elizabeth Beardsley defines *genderization* as the requirement that a sex distinction be made linguistically. By "requirement," she means that in those instances where the speaker fails to make the sex distinction, the resulting utterance will be judged to be "incorrect" or "inappropriate" by the hearer. She points out for example that most speakers of English would say either "There is a woman waiting to see you" or "There is a man waiting to see you," but not "There is a person waiting to see you," a possibility in the language that has not yet been colloquialized. "Referential Genderization" is, then, the linguistic habit of requiring sex-specific terms for referring to human beings. "Characterizing Genderization," which she discusses elsewhere (Beardsley, 1973), is the use of sex distinctions to characterize human beings. Characterizing Genderization, in contrast to Referential Genderization, is an act of attribution rather than reference.

The vocabulary of English is rich in its potential for "Characterizing Genderization," and provides speakers with numerous antonymous sets of sex-specific adjectives and nouns for describing people solely in terms of attributed behaviors, e.g., *womanly/manly, womanish/mannish, feminine/masculine, effeminate/virile, tomboy/sissy*. The dictionary definitions for such terms show that their putative "information value" consists only of cultural stereotypes, prescribed behaviors; if such stereotypes didn't exist and weren't valued by speakers, no occasions would arise for their use. As Sarah Hoagland (1977) has observed, these terms aren't empirical because they can't be disconfirmed; they are, rather, evaluative terms. In fact, the cultural load of pairs like *womanly/manly* and *womanish/mannish* is so great that they can be used to refer to individuals of either sex, and the import of a specific term depends on the biological sex of the individual so characterized. The examples in (3) show the contrastive value of sex-marked descriptions.

(3)(a)   It snowed every day now, . . . sometimes for real, the low whistle of the wind cranking up to a *womanish shriek* that made the old hotel rock and groan alarmingly . . . (Stephen King, *The Shining*, p. 212)

   (b)   Difficult as the master's role may be, it is even more disquieting to admit to *masochistic tendencies, since they involve dependence and helplessness, those 'feminine' traits.* (Richard Goldstein, "S & M: The Dark Side of Gay Liberation," *Village Voice*, July 7, 1975, p. 10)

   (c)   She seemed *smaller, softer, more feminine and compliant than the Amazon who had fired arrows* into a beast a hundred times her size less than two hours before. (Robert A. Heinlein, *Glory Road*, p. 175)

   (d)   Ignorant, in the Handdarn sense: to ignore the abstraction, to hold fast to the thing. There was in this attitude something *feminine, a refusal of the abstract, the ideal, a submissiveness to the given,* which rather displeased me. (Ursula K. LeGuin, *The Left Hand of Darkness*, pp. 202–203)

In each example, stereotypical behaviors attributed to females are implicitly contrasted with behaviors attributed to males. That is, of course, the purpose of such terms: Opposition facilitates contrast, and contrast perpetuates opposition. It is a semantic-conceptual loop. Is there, for example, such a thing as a "mannish shriek"? Why did King use the adjective *womanish*? What sort of contribution to his text did that adjective make? Is it somehow more "colorful," or "vivid," or "creative"? I can rule out "creative" immediately because the phrase is trite, and I doubt that claiming colorfulness or vividness will rescue the usage. *Womanish,* after all, refers only to an abstract collection of cultural attributions; there's nothing "concrete" or "visual" or "tangible" in that description. King's use of *womanish* to describe the wind's howling has meaning only if the reader believes that the stereotype is accurate; as a cliché, the phrase requires no interpretation. Our minds don't contemplate the description. If we consider it in terms of the entire novel, however, one could argue that this particular phrase, and countless others, do provide information concerning the protagonist and are, therefore, cohesive elements in the novel. Such descriptions are used by the male protagonist so frequently that King may have intended for them to function as cues to signal the character's misogyny, and, therefore, doomed to seek his own destruction. This interpretation, however, requires a particular kind of reader, one who finds such descriptions distasteful and unnecessary.

Examples (3)(b) and (d), unlike (c), explicitly use the adjective *feminine* as part of a negative characterization that includes typical attributes associated with female behaviors, dependence, help-lessness, submissiveness, a mistrust of abstraction, and a penchant for the concrete. In both cases, as readers, we are asked to accept the idea that such traits are negatively valued and to be judged as in-ferior characteristics when set against the positive attributes of maleness and masculinity. It may seem incongruous, then, when we find *feminine* being used in a complimentary way, in example (3)(c), but the comparison with an Amazon makes it clear that the female character is now behaving in an appropriate, therefore "good" way. The associated adjectives in this description reveal more about the perceptions of his male character than Heinlein might have intended. *Smaller,* for example, tells us something about the male's desire for dominance, and the use of *compliant,* rather than *submissive,* spec-ifies the positive value we are expected to associate with such behav-iors in women. To the extent that we are willing to grant that such descriptions are meaningful in some loose sense, that is, that writers use them in texts for some identifiable reason, our interpretation of their function depends upon whether or not we believe that sex-role stereotypes are accurate.

The examples in (3) emphasize that sex-marked words in English require the cooperative reader to accept the premise of such terms, supply the cultural stereotypes those words allude to, and interpret the character so described as though the words were meaningful. This is a lot to ask of one's readers, especially when we take into consideration that, although sex-specific terms are semantically symmetrical, they are pragmatically asymmetrical. To say that a woman is *mannish* is a pejorative attribution because the charac-terization assumes that the woman so described has exhibited behav-iors that she isn't supposed to have. To say that a woman is *manly,* however, is ambiguous; the context of the utterance will determine whether or not the attribution is favorable or pejorative. The adjec-tive *manly* points to positively-valued behaviors attributed to men, e.g., strength, honesty, courage, self-confidence, etc., in our society. Only the speaker's intentions determine whether these attributes are valued or devalued when a woman exhibits them. In contrast, the use of *womanly* or *womanish* to characterize a man is always pejorative, never ambiguous, because female-specific adjectives applied to males are intended as insults. Those attributes positively valued for women, passivity, tenderness, weakness, dependence, are regarded as abnormalities in the male sex. For one boy to say of another "He throws just like a girl" is one of the worst insults available to male speakers, and the pejorative force of female-specific descriptions is a staple of military training in the U. S. The asymmetry of such sex-specific attributions exposes the relative social status of women and men: describing a woman with [+MALE] terms is interpretively ambiguous because male attributes are higher on the social scale and have, therefore, the potential to move the woman "up." [+FEMALE] terms, however, used to describe a man, can only be interpreted as pejoratives because female attributes are low on the scale of social values; being described as female lowers a man socially and semantically because the "semantic priority" of his maleness has been negated. Applying a devalued attribute to a valued referent can only move that referent "down."

The English language also provides us with a wide range of syntactic constructions in which sex-specific terms ascribe behavior to people, events, objects, and abstractions; these constructions include similes, with *like* or *as,* and the various comparatives, *-er . . . than, as . . . as,* etc. In such syntactic structures, the sex-specific terms establish the basis of the comparison, defining the particular features of behaviors as they are embodied in cultural stereotypes. Although some linguists have discussed comparative constructions and their function in texts, Levin (1971) and Halliday and Hasan (1976), no one has examined the kind of information they require readers to supply or their descriptive effects in popular kinds of prose.

Comparative constructions assert a similarity relation between unlike objects, events, or individuals; consequently, they provide an opportunity to examine closely the usefulness of basic notions in text linguistics: coherence, recoverability, pragmatic knowledge, and how congruence, or the lack of it, between writers' and readers' real world models affects informativity. The writer's assertion of a similarity relation between two events, people, or objects creates a structural redundancy that is deleted syntactically in both similes and comparatives, e.g., *Mary is taller than Sue* < *Mary is taller than Sue is tall.* When we encounter such structures in a text, we provide the deleted information on the basis of our knowledge of English syntactic rules. These constructions exemplify the ways in which specific types of rules remove "redundant" material from texts. Yet, even material that we may regard as clearly redundant, and therefore something to be deleted of necessity, can turn out to be more complicated interpretively than the examples frequently used in linguistics texts. Indeed, readers are asked to provide some kinds of information that, while redundant syntactically, nevertheless require extra-linguistic information for adequate interpretation. Example (4) is one such instance.

(4) Dear Bill [Allen], write about the Super Bowl. I'd like an in-depth analysis of the game. (What, another one?) Signed, Mary Beth, sophomore, beanbag stuffing. P. S. *Your picture is better than Ann Landers'*.

After we have supplied those portions of the sentence removed by redundancy rules, the italicized P.S. reads something like "Your picture is better than Ann Landers' picture is good," and we can be rightfully grateful that the syntactic rules of English discourage the articulation of such an unlovely comparison. Even so, the recovery of the redundant information is still inadequate for those readers who don't know that both Bill Allen and Ann Landers are newspaper columnists, and that both run pictures of themselves with their columns. Without this extralinguistic information, readers are likely to miss the intended humor altogether.

When the focal term of comparatives is a sex-specific word, the necessary interpretive processes are more complicated, and the examples I will discuss from this point on raise questions about exactly what it is we do when we are asked by a writer to be "cooperative readers" and the textual functions, if any, of such constructions in English prose. It is fair, after all, to ask what is to be regarded as "information" in a text when the resulting surface structures turn out to be "informative" only in a pernicious sense because what the author requires us to provide as "pragmatic" knowledge is nothing more than prevailing cultural stereotypes. That is, when sex-specific terms function as the "informative" focus of similes and comparisons, the writer forces us to supply Characterizing Genderization. The examples in (5) illustrate the cultural information we are supposed to read in when female-specific terms are the referential ground of similes.

(5)(a) Runners talk obsessively, *like little old ladies,* about their injuries and illnesses and bowel movements and mineral deficiencies. (P. N. Warren, *The Frontrunner,* pp. 18–19)

(b) *Like a woman* who needs a dot of make-up to accent her best features, the egg needs and deserves more attention than it gets. (Mel Marshall, *The Delectable Egg*)

(c) Vladimir Nabokov spreads his hands around the bulge of his stomach *like a pregnant woman who, long past the time for such things, cannot quite believe what God and man have done to her.* (Gerald Clarke, "Checking in with Vladimir Nabokov," *Esquire,* July 1975, p. 67)

(d) This [care] might have given them an air of assimilation and repose, had they not been the kind of houses which, *like some women,* reward care and attention by becoming smug. (M. Renault, *The Middle Mist,* p. 18)

(e) It [the perfect knife] would be stainless and rustproof. It would be *like a woman,* as one maker puts it, and have 'warmth, character, and a good shape.' (J. McClintock, "Blades with Class," *Esquire,* July 1975, p. 140)

(f) *Like a woman telling a joke,* Miss Waugh starts with the punch line and asks us to be patient while she fills in. (G. Davenport, review of *Mirror Mirror* in *New York Times Book Review,* June 8, 1975, p. 6)

If one is willing to accept some functional relationship between metaphors and similes (Miller, 1979), then one would also expect the feature transfer in similes to work as it does in metaphorical expressions. As Searle (1979, p. 102) has observed, in the statement "Richard is a gorilla," nothing in the specification of the term *gorilla* changes. We *map* our cultural stereotype of gorillas, their appearance, and their attributed behaviors *onto* the term *Richard,* reinterpret the human qualities imputed by the proper name, and assign to Richard our assumptions about gorillas. (Those assumptions cannot be equated with "real-world knowledge.") In this instance, the term *gorilla* has no semantic value. It is merely a token of certain attributes that the speaker (and perhaps the listener) finds repulsive or reprehensible.

Likewise, sex-specific terms that occur in similes are empty categories that ask the reader to supply extra-linguistic, extra-textual stereotypes *as a substitute* for explicit description on the part of the author. That such descriptors are largely gratuitous can be seen in examples (5)(a), (c), and (d), in which the similes are nonrestrictive clauses, as in (a) and (d), or contain embedded nonrestrictive clauses within them, as in (c). Such similes apparently violate hypotheses about textual structure as it is understood by text linguists. In examples (5)(a), (c), and (d), readers are given explicit information that is irrelevant to textual coherence; furthermore, we are asked to use these elements to provide stereotypes compatible with the writers' models of the world (*not,* I want to emphasize, anything so innocuous as "our knowledge of the world"). As we supply the implicit information for each of the quotations in example (5), we are simultaneously accepting both the ground of the comparison and the presuppositions of that ground carried by the predication. For example, as we read example (5)(a), we must accept the propositions about "little old ladies," i.e., "Little old ladies talk obsessively about their injuries and illnesses and bowel movements and mineral deficiencies." The sex-specific term *ladies* restricts such obsession only to females, while it excludes the possibility that little old men might also indulge in that behavior. (The ageism and sizeism in this quote are equally unfortunate. Note that, in order to keep the sex-specific terms parallel, I had to retain both of the adjectives *little* and *old*.) In example (5)(b) we must accept the assertion that "A woman needs a dot of make-up to accent her best features" before we can go on to the problems of the egg. (How the egg's need and merit for more attention than it gets has anything to do with a woman using make-up is, mercifully, left to our imaginations.) The simile in (5)(c) is, at least, explicit, but no less pernicious. In order to understand the author's intentions, we must accept the propositions about pregnant women, recognize the exaggerated credulity and naïveté attributed to the delay and the wonderment of the woman, accept the idea that this is meant to be funny, and then transfer the implied insult as a description of Nabokov's pose. As in example (5)(b), the sense of the analogy depends entirely upon the sex-specific term. The next two examples in this group, (5)(d) and (e), require us to supply the deleted predications ("Some women reward care and attention by becoming smug," and "A woman has warmth, character, and a good figure"); the sex-marked terms restrict the attributed behaviors to women, and exclude the possibility that males or people in general might behave in such ways. Yet, recasting the simile to read "Some people reward care and attention by becoming smug" would not change its import, and it is only the last phrase, "and a good figure," that blocks both the generic and male-specific terms as possibilities. The widespread use of such similes and the type of reading they necessitate force us to question seemingly self-apparent assertions, such as van Dijk's (1977) acknowledgement that every text is ontologically incomplete because writers include, as *explicit* signals, "only those facts which are *pragmatically relevant*," and his assertion that we aren't likely to find full descriptions in texts because such information "would be redundant or irrelevant." The occurrence of sex-specific comparisons poses difficult problems for text linguists who wish to treat texts as abstract entities.

As I've said, these similes don't give us substantial information; by forcing us to provide and accept stereotypes of women, the authors force us to understand runners, knives, houses, and Nabokov only in the terms specified by those similes, and a majority of them are pejorative. What a text linguist would call "pragmatic" or "real-world" knowledge turns out to be nothing more than culturally-promulgated prejudice. In these cases, it becomes clear that what are said to be deletions of material on the grounds of redundancy are structures that coerce readers to accept extraneous, unnecessary propositions about the behavior of women that are irrelevant to the text itself.

In contrast, consider the group of similes in example (6), in which the terms are male-specific:

(6)(a) 'Come out and fight *like a man!*"
        (R. Heinlein, *Glory Road,* p. 265)
   (b) They treated him *like a brother,* they did all they could to make
        him feel not lost, not alien, but at home.
        (U. LeGuin, *The Dispossessed,* p. 62)
   (c) Shevek belonged to them like an old friend, *like an elder
        brother.*
        (U. LeGuin, *The Dispossessed,* p. 157)
   (d) 'Of course, I have known highly intelligent women, women who
        could think *just like a man, . . .'*
        (U. LeGuin, *The Dispossessed,* p. 14)

These similes exemplify what Malkiel has called a "hierarchy of semantic preference" (Lyons, 1977: p. 276). Within this hierarchy, *female* and *male* are, respectively, the negative and positive terms of a bipolar opposition. Thus, although one might be able to think of alternatives for expressing the same propositional content, e.g., "Come out and fight as though you were serious!", "I have known highly intelligent women, women who reasoned impeccably," etc., the effect is not the same on the reader, and one whould be, perhaps, expecting too much originality on the part of writers. The examples in (6)(a) and (d) require us to supply the deleted verbs *fights* and *thinks,* respectively. Both of these similes assert that men fight and think in ways that are different, and therefore, better than the ways women fight and think. And, if men and women do think differently, that doesn't mean that women are less intelligent than men. The male terms have a "privileged" status in our vocabulary that is reflected in such comparisons; they are the positive, standard terms of the constructions, and in example (6)(d) the ability of a woman to "think just like a man" is intended as a compliment, to emphasize through the male term how intelligent such women are. But the assertion also implies that only men in general are "highly intelligent," that most women aren't "highly intelligent," that an intelligent woman is an exception to some "rule," a freak, and that the possession of high intelligence is inherently a male attribute. Examples (6)(b) and (c), because the similes are intended to describe men, might seem unexceptionable, but I wonder, nevertheless, why the term *brother* was chosen to convey warmth and caring rather than a sex-neutral term. The restriction seems especially strange in example (6)(c) because "like an elder brother" glosses a preceding simile, "like an old friend," which one might think was sufficient in and of itself. Perhaps the privileged status of brothers, as opposed to sisters, cousins, parents, grandparents, or friends, can be explained by reference to the popular usage of *brother* in other instances where it is intended to convey some pseudo-generic type of caring, e.g., *brotherhood, brotherly love*. Yet, we also talk about *motherly love, fatherly love, sisterly love*. It is only, I think, the narrow range of behaviors attributed to such socially-defined roles that makes *brother* seem a likely candidate for generic status, because all of these descriptions explicitly negate the possibility of *sexual* associations with respect to the love being so characterized. As a result, the use of *brother* in examples (6)(b) and (c) must have been chosen to assure the reader that sexuality was *not* a factor in the treatment given to the men. Such reassurances are only meaningful in a homophobic culture.

The cognitive importance of the cultural assumption that females represent the negative pole of contrast and that males represent the positive pole is clear in the examples in (7).

(7)(a) A good evening's work; a good friend, too, *as straight as a man.*
(Mary Renault, *The Middle Mist,* p. 244)

  (b) This must be a good life, she thought; hard, but good. Working at something you know beyond doubt to be useful, under *a boss who's your boss because he's a better man.*
(Mary Renault, *The Middle Mist,* p. 182)

Both descriptions, which are intended to convey some sense of satisfaction, a positive response of some kind, compare a female to a male. The comparison requires the reader to accept the hypothesis that only male terms can be used for positive denotation, even when the individual being compared to a male is a female! Apparently, a female term cannot function in such descriptions in the way that conjuring a male similitude does. If we supply the deleted information in these comparisons, the absurdity is clear, especially for example (7)(b). Example (7)(a) asks us to accept the premise that only men are "straight," that is, honest, explicitly, forthright, i.e., "as straight as a man is straight." Women, children, sisters, and artichokes need not apply. Supplying the deleted phrase of (7)(b), the "redundant" information, reveals that "he's a better man than you are a man" amounts to a tautology. Because the character being referred to in the comparison is a woman, it would stand to reason that *any* man might "better" fulfill the criteria of male biology. But, of course, I'm being purposely obtuse! Renault isn't invoking biology, she's referring to cultural traits attributed to men that makes some "better" than others, i.e., honesty, loyalty, strength, and the right hair tonic.

What textual function do such comparisons serve? Because they do not affect, one way or another, either the coherence or informativity of a text, we must look elsewhere for an explanation of their use and frequency. Ted Cohen (1979) has suggested that one of the functions of metaphorical usage is the cultivation of intimacy with one's readers. If metaphors (and similes) require extra work by the reader (or listener), they must serve some purpose other than aesthetics. As Cohen puts it,

> There is a unique way in which the maker and the appreciator of a metaphor are drawn closer to one another. Three aspects are involved: (1) the speaker issues a kind of concealed invitation; (2) the hearer expends a special effort to accept the invitation; and (3) this transaction constitutes the acknowledgement of a community (p. 6).

What he concludes from this is extremely interesting: "In general, and with some obvious qualifications, it must be true that all literal use of language is accessible to all whose language it is. But a figurative use can be inaccessible to all but those who share information about one another's knowledge, beliefs, intentions, and attitudes" (p. 7). I think his notion of acknowledging a community bond between the reader and writer is plausible, for it accounts for the comparisons in example (8).

(8)(a) 'No one who does what these people do, and sees what they see, could go on taking the human body seriously all their spare time. . . .' 'The women particularly. On top of their own troubles, they've got several generations of hush-hush and brooding in corners, and then all that nervous frank-and-fearless stuff in the twenties, to get off their chests. Personally, it makes me feel good to see them. *Healthy as your mother sweeping house.* (M. Renault, *The Middle Mist,* p. 133)

   (b) No need to fool with taps, just move one way or the other for the temperature that you like—or move down-stream where it evened out to temperature *as gently warm as a mother's kiss.* (R. Heinlein, *Glory Road,* p. 63)

> (c)   I soon realized that Star wore my designs because they were my
> gift, *just as mama pins up the kindergarten drawings that sonny*
> *brings home.*
> (R. Heinlein, *Glory Road,* p. 235)

Such examples, especially (a) and (b), which contain sex-specific
terms designating familial relationships, do not tell us anything substantive. Instead, they assume that the reader belonged to a family,
had a mother, spent time relating to that woman in a specific cultural
context, and that that context was Western. In (a) and (b), the term
mother is used to call up for the reader feelings of security, warmth,
and lovingness. Renault, for example, uses the "wifely" stereotype to
encourage her readers to think of the somewhat unconventional lifestyle of her characters as "healthy" in the traditional model she assumes they have. In that model, only women sweep house, and only a
woman who is also a mother would be living in that house. (Why
sweeping a house is to be thought of as "healthy" is beyond my
imaginative ability.) Heinlein's comparison asks us to experience a
certain temperature of water by transferring our experience of being
kissed by our mothers to immersion in pleasantly warm water. Likewise, in (8)(d), he assumes that only *sonny* brings home drawings
from kindergarten, that only mothers (here, the familiar form *mama*)
willingly make the gesture of displaying them in the home. This example further implies that there is a certain diffidence in the act,
perhaps pretense, and it is this implication that we are supposed to
transfer to our interpretation of Star's actions. Such comparisons,
while they may seem harmless, nevertheless assume a specific homelife is available to readers (at least as a cultural stereotype), that
readers have had that kind of homelife and that women, specifically
mothers, behave in uniform ways and perform identical functions.
But some people are orphans; others live in foster homes; others live
in single-parent families, some without a female parent. Substituting
generic or indefinite terms for the sex-specific terms in the examples
will illustrate exactly how much information is lost and the kind of
information it is.

> (9)(a)   Healthy as someone sweeping house.
>   (b)   . . . as gently warm as a loving kiss.
>   (c)   . . . just as parents pin up the kindergarten drawings their chil-
>   dren bring home.

Such alternatives (and they are simply more general expressions of
attribution) do not add to or detract from the content of the com-

parisons, and they are certainly among the many possibilities available to the authors quoted. Moreover, they expand the rather narrow models actually incorporated by the comparative structures to reflect the fact that anyone can sweep a house, behave lovingly, or pretend pride in a child's accomplishments. They also emphasize, by contrast, the impoverishment of so-called "creative imaginations." If such choices are among the possible ones that can be made by writers, then forcing one's readers to provide cultural stereotypes merely invites us to an intimacy based on false premises; the willing reader won't notice and the unwilling reader (like me) will stop reading (or use the offending assertion for data).

Examples like those in (8) raise additional questions concerning the function of comparatives and similes in prose, however. Because comparatives and similes can be used to introduce cultural stereotypes, do we interpret them figuratively or literally? Similes are typically regarded as figurative structures implying partial transfers of features, whereas comparative constructions are interpreted as literal statements about gradable or non-gradable terms. Thus, for example, one would not want to argue that comparatives generally have figurative import e.g., *Mary is taller than a bear,* which suggests that the determining factor (or factors) is to be discovered in the semantic features of the specific words used in similes and comparisons. Cohen (1979: p. 73), addressing the problem of literal and figurative interpretations, has suggested that

> most metaphorical cancellation, like all nonmetaphorical cancellation, begins at the lower end of the scale. Rather general features like +ANIMATE or +METALLIC are highly eligible for cancellation because they are semantically unimportant; whereas features representing specific peculiarities of appearance or behavior are considerably less eligible for cancellation because they are semantically much more important.

But this description will not lead us to an understanding of the difference between literal and nonliteral expressions because the features +FEMALE/+MALE, although they are the most important distinguishing features for +COMMON, +COUNT, +HUMAN nouns (*mother/father, aunt/uncle, sister/brother*), aren't sufficient to force a figurative rather than a literal reading of a construction, as the quotations in example (10) illustrate.

(10)(a)   [George Steiner] describes the translator's task as a sequence of four movements: trust that there is something to be trans-

ferred; then aggression, or *an appropriated act similar to breaking a code and even to sexual possession;* . . .
(Review of *After Babel* by George Steiner, *New York Times Book Review,* June 8, 1975, p. 23)

(b)   In the broad, non-technical sense of the term *critic,* we are all critics when we judge *the quality of a steak or the beauty of a woman.*
(Alice Kaminsky, *Chaucer's Troilus and Crisede and the Critics,* 1980, p. 8)

(c)   It is a far cry from the unfortunate days when slaps and kicks were exchanged, *weak sisters exploded in tears,* and *strong men staged walkouts.*
(Judith Crist, *New York,* January 20, 1975, p. 50)

(d)   Anyone who has studied math knows that the inside does not have to be smaller than the outside, in theory, and anyone who has had the doubtful privilege of seeing *a fat woman get in or out of a tight girdle* knows that this is true in practice, too.
(R. Heinlein, *Glory Road,* p. 53)

(e)   In government hands, the simplest tasks become dilatory, labyrinthine, outrageously expensive exercises in frustration, *guaranteed to produce tears in strong men.*
(Letters, Sgt. James D. Bramlett, *TV Guide,* August 23–August 29, 1975, p. A-6)

Although each of the underlined phrases or clauses is intended to function as an additional, clarifying description of some event or action, and, in spite of the fact that the clarification is intended to be carried by the comparative force of each description, I cannot read any of them as figurative or metaphorical. These are clearly intended to be *literal* comparisons, and, while they may lack explicit claims to factualness, the authors assert them as though we are to accept them as "true" descriptions of some world. The reviewer in example (10)(a) compares translation to breaking a code and to rape; in (b), the act of criticism is compared to judging the quality of two types of "meat," steaks and women; the contrasted, explanatory conjunct clauses of (c) merely "describe" a previous state of affairs, but we understand them to also functionally exclude their opposite assertions, that men might "explode in tears" or that "women staged walkouts." Indeed, in this example, so contrastive are these two clauses that the adjectives *strong* and *weak* appear to be superfluous. The mention of "a fat woman" (not, mind you, just any woman) getting in or out of a girdle fails to explicate the mathematical theory it purports to describe, and is apparently intended by Heinlein as a "humorous" bid for intimacy with his readers. I can see the jocular, good-ole-boy-elbow-in-the-ribs heh heh. "Hey! Just us guys here, heh heh." Finally, Sgt. Bramlett's usage of "guaranteed to produce tears in strong men" is meant to convey, by hyperbole (!), the extremity of frustration one experiences when dealing with government bureaucracy, and it's safe to observe that the exaggerated force of his description would fail if one were to compare that frustration to the production of "tears in *weak* men" or "in women." Such comparisons emphasize two of my central concerns in this paper: First, sex-specific comparisons are ploys used by writers to coerce readers into accepting their model of the real world; second, these writers intend such assertions of similarity to be accepted by their readers as factual descriptions of some state of affairs. If my analysis of their functions is accurate, we are also supposed to read them as literal assertions of similarity, not figurative ones.

CONCLUSIONS

The frequency of comparative constructions in which the focal term of the comparison is sex-specific in both fiction and nonfiction indicates that writers (a) like to use them, (b) believe that they serve some function in texts, and (c) assume that they are noncontroversial. However, readers who refuse to accept the real world model assumed by the writer are likely to find such comparisons unenlightening, presumptuous, and offensive. Do they, perhaps, serve some "aesthetic" function? Is their appearance in a text intended to give pleasure to readers? If, as I have suggested, such comparisons are minimally figurative, and writers seem to intend them to be interpreted as more literal than figurative, we are left with Cohen's suggestion that some uses of language are "covert" invitations to readers to acknowledge identification as members of the same "community." We may accept or refuse the writer's invitation, and our decision will be based on the degree of mismatch between our real world model and that implied in the textual world by the writer. My analysis suggests that only unimaginative writers and text linguists require complicity on the part of readers, and that such an assumption leads to minimally illuminating descriptions of texts and the function of specific elements within texts. The real world models of socially dominant groups favor stereotypes that degrade and dehumanize those people who do not belong to the dominant group, whether by choice or not. To construct a theoretical analysis of texts that assumes an utterly complicitous reader goes beyond vacuity very quickly and becomes yet another theory that promulgates white male supremacy in the guise of dispassionate inquiry. Accepting the diction and syntax of texts without question, without trying to discover the functions of writers' choices, defeats the purpose of text linguistics: figuring out how texts are created and identifying those elements that make them work for readers.

CHAPTER 11

Making Sense of "The Woman Who Becomes A Man"

Susan E. Chase

Department of Sociology
University of Tulsa

I

No woman speaks about herself as "the woman who becomes a man," unless she is speaking ironically.

Nonetheless, this expression, and others like it—"the manly woman," "the woman who acts like a man"—persist as familiar and uni-ironic phrases in everyday speech.

Although no woman would describe herself as "the woman who becomes a man," there have been women who have taken on the disguise of a man—in the form of manly clothing or a male pseudonym—as a self-conscious and calculated action designed to ensure that their work is evaluated according to the same standards as a man's work. Yet, even when the intention of their disguise is clear, even when their disguise of a man is just that—a concealment of the fact that they are women—writers such as Virginia Woolf (1977), and Sandra Gilbert and Susan Gubar (1979), who have studied the phenomenon of the male pseudonym, detected signs that the women experienced "inner strife" and "anxiety" about the relation between their gender identity and their work. The disguise may have had practical advantages, but the conventions which made the disguise necessary troubled them anyway.

But the contemporary usage of the expression "the woman who becomes a man" is not a description of a woman disguised as a man. It refers to a woman who, for some reason, can no longer claim to *be* womanly. Her identity as a woman is at stake. In one sense, her identity is more at stake because she can not or does not claim to be wearing a disguise. The expression is, of course, metaphoric; it is not about a woman who undergoes a sex change operation, but is about a woman who, supposedly, acts like a man, and hence is problematic interactionally because she no longer deserves to be treated as a woman. She *is* no longer womanly. The metaphoric character of the expression increases rather than decreases its power: identity as a woman cannot be taken for granted as "natural" or as "inscribed" in the body, but is subject to standards for action and speech.

That no woman would describe herself as becoming a man means that the description is external to the one it describes; it does not represent the way she thinks about herself or her actions. My first aim in this essay is to explicate the point of view of the woman who is *deemed* to be one who "becomes a man." What is the desire of the woman who is described as becoming a man? What is her experience of the world? What does the world look like from her point of view? These questions assume that we can imagine the one to whom the expression refers, but they do not assume that the charge inherent in the description is justified. My second aim is to address how a woman could be described as becoming a man. I will argue that the charge is sometimes meaningful, but not in the ways that it is commonsensically used.[1]

While my overt task is the explication of the meanings and situations which are taken for granted in the everyday uses of this expression, my deeper aim is to explore how acute questions about gender are inherent in everyday life and speech.

Who, then, is the woman described as becoming a man? She is a familiar image in popular culture: an aggressive woman, unsoftened by "feminine" attributes such as graciousness, modesty, and a concern for attractiveness; or an executive woman, dressing for success, calculating, using her femininity (she does not look manly) to manipulate interactions to get what she wants in the boardroom. The protagonist in Caryl Churchill's play *Top Girls* (1984) is one example of such a woman. Marlene has just been promoted to managing director of Top Girls Employment agency. She has been promoted over a co-

---

[1] One caveat: in its spurious form, the expression is used to undermine a woman's confidence in her work or in herself. For example, Joanna Russ (1984) shows that statements such as "She writes like a man" demean a woman in the guise of complimenting her writing. Although I wish to examine the meanings and uses of the expression "the woman who becomes a man," I do not intend to support the demeaning use of the expression.

worker, a man whose wife comes to Marlene to discuss her husband's humiliation and the possibility that Marlene might give up the job to the husband. This is the end of their exchange:

Mrs. Kidd: It's not that easy, a man of Howard's age. He's been here longer than you have. You don't care. I thought he was going too far in what he said about you but he's right. You're one of those ballbreakers, that's what you are. You'll end up miserable and lonely. You're not natural.

Marlene: I'm sorry but I do have some work to do.

Mrs. Kidd: I'll stand by him, I've got feelings.

Marlene: Could you please piss off?

(Churchill, 1984, p. 30)

It is impossible to capture Churchill's layers of caustic irony in this short excerpt. The wife defends her husband, but her real concern is that she "bears the brunt" of his humiliation. Marlene is sympathetic to *that* complaint but not to the husband's. The wife's defense itself takes on the form of "shitwork:" why can't he speak for himself? It is with reference to private concerns—his psyche, his need to support his family—that the wife claims her husband deserves the job, yet she does not wonder about Marlene's private concerns. In fact, Marlene has made difficult decisions in her private life—her sister raises her child who does not know that her "aunt" is her mother—in order to be the ambitious woman she is. And finally, unlike his, Marlene's private concerns (although they represent the difficult decisions any woman faces concerning public and private life) are of the skeleton-in-the-closet type, which means she cannot speak about them publicly or use them to defend herself.

This brief scrutiny of a "woman who becomes a man" shows us one important thing. The expression does not refer merely to certain behaviors such as aggressiveness or callousness in speech ("Could you please piss off?"). The behavior begs for explanation, and the explanation (barely hinted at here) promises to show us a woman attempting to solve a particular problem in a particular kind of situation.

The expression "the woman who becomes a man" also arises in discussions among feminist theorists. In this context it is even clearer that the expression is not used to describe behavior alone, but refers to a certain orientation to the self and to the world.

For example, Xaviere Gauthier criticizes the idea that women will advance and perform as well as men in all fields as soon as their conditions are equal to men's. She reveals the image of woman embodied in this idea: "woman (though slightly retarded) is considered to 'like' a man or is in-the-process of becoming a man" (Gauthier, 1981, p. 162).

Gauthier's criticism is echoed in other contemporary feminists' objections to the early feminist analyses of women's situation. Mary O'Brien, for example, though appreciative of de Beauvoir's arguments, claims that the world de Beauvoir holds out to women is a world in which women must imitate men: "There is no way of escape, except by an undignified catch-up scramble along the paths which men have beaten" (O'Brien, 1981, p. 71). And Jean Elshtain writes about Friedan's analysis: "Her book is a paean of praise to what Americans themselves call the 'rat race': she just wants women to join it" (Elshtain, 1981, p. 251).

It is fair to say that according to both de Beauvoir's *The Second Sex* (1974) and Friedan's *The Feminine Mystique* (1963), women start out "slightly retarded" due to the unequal conditions they have suffered historically—being confined to the suburban domicile, or being treated as "the other." And in these accounts they progress only when their conditions are equal to men's.

Both de Beauvoir and Friedan find their model for what is desirable for women in the relation to the world which men seem to possess. Neither writer is defensive about this. Friedan, for example, writes of the Seneca Falls generation of feminists:

> Of course they envied man. Some of the early feminists cut their hair short and wore bloomers, and tried to be like men. From the lives they saw their mothers lead, from their own experience, those passionate women had good reason to reject the conventional image of woman. (Friedan, 1963, p. 317)

De Beauvoir, in a more sophisticated way, analyzes the disjunction between the world women live in and the world to which women should have access. Women have been stuck in the domestic world of brute conditions—of "immanence"—which gives them no opportunity for self-development. In contrast, the world of "transcendence" is a world in which one reaches out to explore what is beyond the self, in which one participates in creating the ideas and institutions which guide social life. The opportunity for self-expansiveness and creative work which this world makes possible is presented by de Beauvoir as radically attractive in comparison to the domestic world in which the greatest task is "the war against dust."

The argument between feminist theorists about "the woman who becomes a man" concerns the difference between "being" and "having," or between "becoming a man" and "acquiring what men have." Some feminists claim that the ambitious woman wants no more than the opportunities which men have always had. Others claim that in acquiring what men have always had, she imitates the way men are in the world, and thus threatens her identity as a woman.

To make this distinction is not to have reached a stalemate; rather the distinction frees me to understand and develop the different points of view. What is the perspective of the woman who conceives of herself (or of the theorist who conceives of women) as interested in acquiring the opportunities men have had? And where does the boundary lie between seeking an opportunity for self-expression and acting in the world in a way that threatens one's identity as a woman? Most importantly, how could it be said that the public world poses such a threat to gender identity in the first place?

II

Women who become professionals are a good example of a group of women who seek opportunities that conventionally have been more open to men.[2] In order to develop their perspective, I will look at some examples of how women who have entered the male professional world talk about the situations they face there, and at the sociologists' analyses of their situations.

In "Making it: Marginality and Obstacles to Minority Consciousness," Hochschild (1974) discusses "not what makes a woman successful but rather, how being successful makes her feel less like other women" (p. 194). Hochschild analyzes autobiographical accounts given by twelve successful women at a conference on women and success (Kundsin, 1974). She makes a curious observation: although they give examples of incidents in which they have experienced discouragement and/or discrimination in their fields because they are women, their concluding statements often include a denial that they

---

[2] To get the facts straight:

Although there have been clear increases in the numbers of women in male-dominated professions over the past decade, the increases still reflect that, except in academe, women are, for the most part, statistical rarities in the elite professions. (Kaufman, 1984, p. 354)

Kaufman's statistics show that from 1970 to 1980, the percentage of doctors who are women increased from 9% to 13%, lawyers and judges from 5% to 13%, clergy from 3% to 6%, professors from 29% to 37% (p. 355).

have suffered any discrimination at all. To give one of several examples, one woman stated that

> her thesis adviser was "totally unsympathetic to career women" and left her to do her thesis work alone; but she also notes "I cannot say that I face any unique problems in the profession because of my sex." (Hochschild, 1974, p. 195)

What interests Hochschild is the denial of discrimination: what compels these successful women to resist identifying themselves as women and making a collective issue of being in a minority group in the professional world?

Hochschild understands the problem this way: as part of a marginal group, professional women suffer two kinds of rejection. "Defeminization"—"She writes clearly; she writes like a man" (p. 196) —accepts her as a professional but rejects her as a woman. "Deprofessionalization"—"She used her sex to get a promotion" (p. 196) —accepts her as a woman but rejects her as a professional.

Hochschild argues that in terms of her identity as a professional, the specific problem a woman faces is not that she must prove herself to her employers, for men must do this too, *but that she must work against a negative stereotype of women in general*. In order to establish herself as a professional, she must prove that she is more independent and productive than people expect women in general to be.

The professional woman needs and wants to prove that expectations about women who work professionally aren't necessarily true. She is different from those women who quit work to have babies, who can't think analytically, who are not wholly committed to work, who move when their husbands move, *and* from those professional women who make life difficult for colleagues by acting like men. Thus, according to Hochschild, she distances herself from other women: "she does her own subtle 'defeminization'" (p. 196). One successful architect declared:

> now, unwillingly, I seem to be part of the Women's Liberation Movement, a fact that I resent because I refuse to be bunched up under the heading 'women' . . . (Minnhaar, 1974, p. 31)

This statement shows the speaker's resentment toward others who focus on the fact that she is a woman. Being classified with women in general inhibits her sense of herself. She needs to separate herself from the group "women," and particularly from a group of women who directly identify themselves as women, in order to think of herself as a professional.

My question is this: what obfuscated desire underlies the resentment to being "bunched up under the heading 'women'"? If she is working against negative stereotypes of women in general, how would she like to think of herself, and to be thought of by others? A successful physicist stated: "I should like to be known, if I'm known at all, for my contributions to physics research and teaching, and not for being "a woman in physics" (Ancker-Johnson, 1974, p. 44). This statement unveils the frustrated desire of the previous quote: the women want merit to count (as Hochschild says, "reasonably enough"). But what is required of a woman who wants merit to count?

As a professional, she wants her work to be evaluated seriously on its own merits. But the very fact that she must *assert* that desire implies that there is an obstacle to her desire which she must fight to overcome. When a man says he wants merit to count or that he wants to be treated seriously, he may be fighting various expectations or assumptions, for example, that he is riding on a family name, or wealth, or connections. Or he may be fighting an impression others have that he has never been serious about his work, that he is lazy, or concerned only with status, etc. But notice that none of these qualifications concern the fact that he is a man. A man would never say, "I would like to be known for my contributions to physics research, and not for being 'a man in physics'." Even less would one hear a man say, "I resent being bunched up under the heading 'men'."

Similarly, Rosabeth Moss Kanter writes about the problem faced by the few women at the management level in corporations: "The token does not have to work hard to have her presence noticed, but she does have to work hard to have her achievements noticed" (Kanter, 1977, p. 216).

Ironically, this can be true even on occasions which purportedly recognize her achievements. One woman, for example, describes her experience of an event at which "outstanding women in business" were celebrated; she felt as though she were being

"taken on a date. It was more like a senior prom than a business event." She expressed resentment at being singled out in such a fashion, "just for being a woman at Indsco, not for any real achievement." (Kanter, 1977, p. 213–14)

This woman experiences the very celebration of her success as deeply failing to appreciate her achievement. The senior prom metaphor, besides being embodied in practice—a corsage, a vice-president for an escort, his name rather than hers being listed in the program—represents her feeling that she was "displayed as a showpiece."

In her study of professional women, Cynthia Epstein writes: "the woman's sex status may create enough 'noise' to drown out what she has to say." For example, "patients don't believe they are seeing 'the doctor' when they see a woman" (Epstein, 1970, pp. 181–182).

One woman's remark shows how the "noise" of sex status interferes when work is being evaluated:

> if you're a woman, you have to make less mistakes . . . a woman must put greater effort into her work . . . because if you make a fool of yourself, you're a damn fool woman instead of just a damn fool. (Epstein, 1970, p. 191)

Interestingly, the architect previously quoted expressed what seems to be the opposite sentiment: "It seems that so very little is expected from us that our level of 'success' is achieved with little effort (Minnhaar, 1974, p. 29).

But rather than contradicting each other, both statements show that the "noise" created by the salient fact of being a woman is louder than the standard for judging her work, or rather, the quality of her work is understood to be determined by the fact that she is a woman.

The professional woman does not want to be singled out as a *woman* professional because she wants her work and achievement to be attended to in themselves. She would argue that gender plays no part in the quality of her professional work, because gender has nothing to do with the content of her work.

The obstacle to the woman's desire is that the fact of being a woman both distracts attention away from her work, and interferes in the attention given to her work. Her resentment stems from her impotence to redirect others' attention to her work. The argument that merit alone should count is reasonable but has no weight.

The problem becomes more complex when we look at another side of it: "woman" is not merely a negative and noisy status, it is also part of the professional woman's identity; being a woman is part of who she is. If being singled out as a woman makes her feel like she is being escorted to a senior prom rather than to a business event, or if being "bunched up under the heading 'women'" deprofessionalizes her, it is also true that the professional woman does not see herself as becoming like a man. She wants to dissociate herself from the negative connotations of "woman," but she does not want to be defeminized.

The same woman who asserted that she does not want to be bunched up under the heading "women" also stated:

> In my work I wear tailored clothing, but always very feminine. I find that it's not necessary to shout or to sprinkle my order with foul language, which is used constantly during our meetings. (Minnhaar, 1974, p. 30)

And Muriel Siebert, "the first woman to buy a seat on the N.Y. Stock Exchange" stated: "If a woman displays the same aggressiveness as a man, they say: 'Is she an aggressive thing!' . . . and no woman wants to be regarded as a tough person" (Chesler & Goodman, 1976, p. 190).

What the professional woman wants is complex and apparently contradictory: while she does not want to be treated as a *woman* professional, she also does not want to be denied the fact that she is a woman. She resists both "deprofessionalization" and "defeminization" in Hochschild's terms, and according to Kanter, tries to live up to two contradictory standards.

> In the men's informal conversations, women were often measured by two yardsticks: how *as women* they carried out the sales or management role; and how *as managers* they lived up to images of womanhood. (Kanter, 1977, p. 214)

One woman expressed the problem thusly:

> I do research and management for fun, but nevertheless I compete vigorously. And here again a woman is in trouble. She's damned if she does and damned if she doesn't. If she does not compete, it proves women can't do physics; if she does compete, she isn't feminine and hence, presumably, is some sort of a freak. (Ancker-Johnson, 1974, p. 48)

And, the same contradictory tension is expressed, sarcastically, in the title of a "how to" success book for women in business: *Think Like a Man, Act Like a Lady, and Work Like a Dog.*[3]

Furthermore, Kanter demonstrates that conventional images of woman are used (by both men and women) to routinize interaction between men and women in an unconventional setting; the reliance

---

[3] This and similar books are discussed by Koester, 1982.

on these conventional images gives the women the "security of a 'place'" but at the same time "constrains their areas of permissible or rewarded action" (Kanter, 1977, p. 231). Thus a woman may become the "mother" whose task is to offer emotional support to colleagues; or the "seductress" who attaches herself to one protector in order to avoid the label of "whore;" or the "pet" who serves as cheerleader for the men in exchange for her own competencies being fussed over as special.

In terms of her identity as a woman, then, the specific problem a professional woman faces is that she must embody one of the conventional images of woman in order to maintain securely in the professional world a place as a woman, and to claim for herself a secure identity as a woman. This is a way of minimizing the noise that being a woman makes in the professional setting.

The alternative to submitting to this pressure is to risk being cast in the image of the "iron maiden," the "role into which strong women are placed." This role arises from the woman's refusal to use or trade on her femininity to gain the security of a place.

> If a token insisted on full rights in the group, if she displayed competence in a forthright manner, or if she cut off sexual innuendoes, she could be asked, "You're not one of those women's libbers, are you?" Regardless of the answer, she was henceforth regarded with suspicion, undue and exaggerated shows of politeness . . . and with distance, for she was demanding treatment as an equal in a setting in which no person of her kind had previously been an equal. Women inducted into the "iron maiden" role were stereotyped as tougher than they are . . . and trapped in a more militant stance that they might otherwise take. Whereas seductresses and pets, especially, incurred protective responses, iron maidens faced abandonment. . . . (Kanter, 1977, p. 236)

Unlike the "mother," the "seductress," and the "pet," the "iron maiden" is not a feminine image: the "iron maiden" is an expression like "the woman who becomes a man." It is possible to speculate[4] that the "iron maiden" refuses to acquiesce to a rigid image of woman and refuses to construct through interaction with others an acceptable (unnoisy because conventional) presence as a woman. Her refusal to work interactionally to reduce the distraction to herself and others of being a woman in the professional world means that she is a particularly distracting, irritating, and noisy (perhaps both literally and metaphorically) woman. The demeanor of the iron

---

[4] I recognize that this speculation imputes something different, or something more, to the "iron maiden" than Kanter intended.

maiden is, of course, suicidal in the context of the organization. She makes trouble for others and hence is left without support. Furthermore, in her very attempt to resist stereotypes, she is stereotyped.

Finally, Kanter suggests that rather than "fear of success" (Horner, 1974), women in a minority situation suffer from a "fear of visibility."

> The token must often choose between trying to limit visibility—and being overlooked—or taking advantage of the publicity—and being labeled a "troublemaker." (Kanter, 1977, p. 221)

Yet there is a course that a woman—an extraordinary woman—can chart between notoriety and complete social invisibility, (or between deprofessionalization and defeminization):

> to over-achieve and carefully construct a public performance that minimized organizational and peer concerns. . . . [This] means that the tokens involved are already outstanding and exceptional, able to perform well under close observation where others are ready to notice first and to attribute any problems to the characteristics that set them apart—but also able to develop skills in impressions management that permit them to retain control over the extra consequences loaded onto their acts. (Kanter, 1977, p. 219)

What is extraordinary about this woman is that she manages to be both secure in her work and secure in her identity as a woman. What interests me is the nature of the *invisible work*—Kanter calls it a delicate balance—that she must do in order to live up to the contradictory standards. She must insist on her professional work being considered on its own merits, but she must do this graciously rather than aggressively; she must demonstrate that she is not in any way obsessed with the fact of being a woman, yet be womanly in a recognizable way; she must make sure she does not jeopardize her femininity by acting like a man; and she must act so as to make others comfortable with her presence and her achievements.

This, then, is the portrait of what the professional woman in general desires, and of what the extraordinary woman achieves through her invisible work: a neutralization of the gender issue in relation to the world of professional work. She desires a relation to that world which is unencumbered by what seems to be inessential to her work: her own and others' concerns about gender. She wants her work to be judged on its own merits *and* she wants her womanliness to be taken for granted as secure.

In short, *she desires to make the fact of being a woman unnoticeable or invisible or silent or neutral without casting doubt upon it.*

From her perspective, man's luxury, or what appears to be man's luxury, is the freedom to take gender identity for granted as unproblematic and insignificant vis-à-vis participating in the world of professional work. From her point of view, what she wants is a luxury men seem to have; it would be unfair to say she wants to become a man.

The extraordinary professional woman who is successful in achieving this balance will probably escape being called "a woman who becomes a man" because that is the kind of notoriety and visibility that she works so hard to avoid.

III

Where do the sociologists stand in relation to the professional woman's desire for a gender-neutral relation to work? We can infer from their analyses that both Kanter and Hochschild would defend the idea that merit alone should be the measure of work. Both would support the ideas that gender identity should not need to be secured through rigid images of woman, and should be inconsequential in relation to work. Further, both would assert that a secure place in the public world should not be a matter of extraordinary work, achievable only by an extraordinary woman.

In particular, Kanter proposes a structural analysis in relation to gender issues. It is not the fact that they are women that is problematic from Kanter's structural perspective, but the fact that women tend to end up in positions that lack power and opportunity, and in which they are tokens. In this analysis, gender issues are subsumed under the issues of power, opportunity, and tokenism. What appears to be a focus on women as women will disappear as soon as women are not in the minority, and when they acquire power and opportunities equal to men's. Kanter's idea is that it is not really gender at all—it is not ideas about or expectations for women—that are most problematic. They are the ostensible problem that hides the deeper structural problem of distribution of power and opportunities. When women are participating equally, the expression "a woman in physics" will be as meaningless as "a man in physics."

According to Kanter, gender neutrality will be achieved—concerns about gender will disappear—when women share power and opportunities equally with men.

For example, in a discussion about how attitudes toward women as leaders are determined by the power the woman possesses rather than by her personal characteristics as a woman, Kanter writes:

But power wipes out sex. A woman who does acquire power stops arousing the same level of concern about whether or not she will be wanted as a leader. People who want to attach themselves to power may not even notice sex. On one occasion, a senior Indsco salesman told a long story to colleagues about a problem with a "very, very smart, tough-minded" president of a small company . . . It took a long time for the audience to this story to realize that the salesman was saying "she." Some even interjected comments using "he." The salesman presented the story with such awe of the powerful customer that sex made no difference. He said later that she was someone he would eagerly work for. (Kanter, 1977, p. 200)

Kanter's point is that if a person has power, is powerful, is successful, etc., then gender ceases to be a factor in evaluating the person or her performance: gender is not noticed.

But something is certainly amiss here. This story shows a glaring paradox: when gender is not noticed, when gender is neutralized, when gender seems not to be an issue, when sex status ceases to be noisy, the person talked about is assumed to be male. To be mistaken for a man (either in the abstract as in this story, or worse, in person) is something that any woman would be compelled to resist. Kanter might say that the woman would not have been thought to be a man if the numbers of men and women executives were equal. This may be true. However, as long as gender is not a matter of indifference to individuals' self-identities, gender will not become a neutral or invisible or taken for granted aspect of social life in the workplace.

What underlies Kanter's analysis are *the problematic assumptions that the culture of the public world is gender neutral and that men do enjoy a gender-neutral relation to that world.* Although the desire for a gender-neutral relation to the world can be understood from the woman's perspective as an interest in an opportunity men have rather than an interest in "becoming a man," the desire for gender neutrality and the idea of gender neutrality itself need to be examined. The question is whether the desire for gender neutrality masks some deeper cultural problem concerning gender.

IV

The questions that need to be asked of the professional woman's desire for gender neutrality are these: what is being desired in the desire for a relation to the world in which gender is unproblematic or insignificant? And, how do men accomplish a gender-neutral relation to the world?

We have seen that the woman who seeks to be taken seriously as a professional is engaged in a contradictory project when she attempts to direct attention away from the fact that she belongs to the group "women," and yet simultaneously attempts to secure her identity as a woman.

But the problem is deeper: she cannot dissociate herself from the noise "woman" makes because the noise is not simply a matter of negative stereotypes about women, lower or higher expectations for women, and criticisms of "damn fool women."

In *The Second Sex,* de Beauvoir writes:

> In the midst of an abstract discussion it is vexing to hear a man say, "you think thus and so because you are a woman:" but I know that my only defense is to reply, "I think thus and so because it is true," thereby removing my subjective self from the argument. It would be out of the question to reply: "and you think the contrary because you are a man," for it is understood that the fact of being a man is no peculiarity. (de Beauvoir, 1974, p. xviii)

The luxury that men have is that no distinction is made between speaking as a man and speaking as a person. That is, no distinction is made between speaking as a man and *speaking*. To speak as a man is not a qualification of his subjectivity. This means that *all* of the connotations of gender—practical, literal, and metaphoric connotations—sexuality, desire, eros, passion, lust, reproduction, consequentiality, responsibility, vulnerability, etc.—are not visible when the term "man" is used. Women, on the other hand, are always vulnerable to their visibility as women; women embody the gender-specific gender. Hence, the word, the image, or the presence of women makes visible the same connotations of gender that are absent in the case of men. Man's relation to the world is gender neutral; woman's relation to the world is gender specific and gender oriented.

Thus, women who aspire to a gender-neutral relation to the world can be understood as resisting something deeper than negative stereotypes about women and rigid images of woman. What they resist is not only that women are seen through their relationships to men, or that women are expected to stay at home, or that when they work they are expected to do women's jobs. The more general cultural problem is that a woman, unlike a man, is seen through her relationship to being a woman. It is assumed that *being a woman* is what mediates her relation to the world.[5] Thus, the noise created by sex

---

[5] Georg Simmel's essays in *Georg Simmel: On Women, Sexuality, and Love* exemplify this idea in a provocative and complex way. To give one example:

status can *not* be overcome by dissociating herself from negative stereotypes about women.

Because the fact of being a woman is conceived as mediating her relation to the world, her work is subject to a standard which holds her accountable to the fact of her gender—and more specifically, to the quality of her womanliness.

A particularly invidious application of this standard is found in Norman Podhoretz' comments about Susan Sontag, whom he claims has taken Mary McCarthy's "place" as the "Dark Lady of American Letters."

> The next Dark Lady would have to be, like her, clever, learned, good-looking, capable of writing family-type criticism as well as fiction with a strong trace of naughtiness. But . . . by the 1960's, it was not nearly enough to confess to having slept with The Man in the Brooks Brothers Shirt . . . hints of perversions and orgies had to be there . . . her figure mystically resembled that of the young Mary McCarthy and she had the same rich black hair. (cited in Russ, 1984, p. 34)

That Podhoretz singles out the fact that Sontag is a woman under-states and euphemizes the impact of his statements, to say the least. Susan Brownmiller could easily find something to say about this quote in every chapter of her book *Femininity* (1984) which details such aspects of being a woman as hair, body, skin, clothes, move-ment, and emotion.

To desire the luxury that men have—a gender-neutral relation to the world—is more than a desire for freedom from the extra baggage of insidious comments imposed by such speakers as Podhoretz. What is desired is mastery of one's relation to the world, rather than one's relation to the world being determined or mediated by gender—the fact of being a women. In short, women want to master their own subjectivity. De Beauvoir (1974) suggests that women "forget them-selves" (p. 781) in order to transcend the world of immanence and "engage in freely chosen projects" (p. xxxiii). What they need to forget is the treatment of women as merely gendered beings.

While no one would argue against de Beauvoir's idea that women need to free themselves from a passive relation to the world, deter-mined by the mediation of gender, some feminist theorists (for exam-ple, O'Brien, 1981) criticize her complete rejection of gender as an element in woman's (and man's) relations to the world. De Beauvoir's

---

The woman [unlike the man] lives in the most profound identity of being and being-a-woman, in the absoluteness of immanently defined sexuality . . . (Sim-mel, 1984, p. 107)

idea can be used to deepen Kanter's structural perspective on gender neutrality, but she ultimately shares Kanter's unexamined assumptions that gender neutrality can be achieved through transcending gender altogether, and that men do achieve gender neutrality.[6]

The question remains: how have men achieved this gender-neutral (gender-transcendent) relation to the world? How do men as subjects speak "neutrally"?

It is true that being a man is not noticeable, and does not qualify or limit subjectivity. We don't speak of "men writers" the way we speak of "women writers." No one speaks of a "man professional" the way one might speak of a "woman professional." And no one writes books about how being a man affected the work of a great thinker such as Hegel or Shakespeare. But what kind of work goes into achieving this equation of being a man and being human? On what kind of work does the luxury of moving freely in the gender-neutral world depend?

Interestingly, men who want to take jobs that women usually do, suffer more discrimination than women seeking jobs that are usually done by men (Levinson, 1982). While the expression, "the woman who becomes a man" is troublesome, it at least represents a culturally conceivable aspiration: women want the opportunities that men have in the public world. But what opportunities do women have (in the public world) that men could want? To speak of a "man who becomes a woman" is not to have in mind a culturally conceivable aspiration, but is to evoke the image of a transsexual.

The image evoked by "the man who becomes a woman"—the image of a man literally being transformed into a woman—demonstrates what we have already shown: women embody gender specificity. But it also shows that *the fact of being a man as a fact of gender neutrality is an invisible social accomplishment* which carries with it severe sanctions in the case of its violation. Behind what appears to be gender neutrality in speech, and gender neutrality in the public world, are standards for the achievement of masculinity.

On a concrete level this is hardly news. Men who are not am-

---

[6] Feminist theorists raise the question of how gender influences subjectivity: if the subject or speaker has conventionally been male, then how does woman as subject speak? (This question is raised in the context of different practices, for example, in the field of cinema, by Theresa de Lauretis, 1984.) Further, how does the idea of woman as subject influence the idea of subjectivity itself? Julia Kristeva writes:

In a culture where the speaking subjects are conceived of as masters of their speech, they have what is called a "phallic" position. The fragmentation of language in a text calls into question the very posture of this mastery. (Kristeva, 1981, p. 165)

bitious, driven, and competitive may find their masculinity suspect. And Barbara Ehrenreich's study (1983) shows how deeply masculinity has been tied up with the breadwinning ethic. She documents the "male revolt" against the "masculine" responsibility of breadwinning and the subsequent struggle not to simultaneously sacrifice masculinity.

On a theoretical level as well, feminists have taken great strides in uncovering the specifically masculine character of what Western culture has taken for granted as "human."[7]

But somewhere between theoretical and empirical approaches to masculinity as a particular way of being in the world, is the problem that in everyday life, and in the studies of professional women's experiences, men are treated by our culture as enjoying the luxury of gender neutrality.

The idea that gender neutrality is a luxurious relation to the world needs to be challenged. Men must *work* to achieve the appearance of gender neutrality in their relation to the world. Kanter notes that a "masculine ethic" has been part of the image of a good manager. This ethic

> elevates the traits assumed to belong to some men to necessities for effective management: a tough-minded approach to problems; analytic abilities to abstract and plan; a capacity to set aside personal, emotional considerations in the interests of task accomplishment. . . . These characteristics supposedly belonged to men; but then, practically all managers were men from the beginning. However, when women tried to enter management jobs, the "masculine ethic" was invoked as an exclusionary principle. (Kanter, 1977, pp. 22–23)

The conflation of masculinity with neutrality works in two directions: "masculine" characteristics are used as the standard for what a good manager should be, and these characteristics which may be gender-neutral characteristics are assumed to belong to men. Hence the practical problem which concerns Kanter—women are excluded. But the conflation of masculinity and the general or neutral is also a theoretical problem: from whence comes the drive to make a specific principle into a general standard? How do men make the claim that they represent neutrality?

Could it be that the interest in transcending gender concerns is a conventionally masculine pursuit? I want to suggest that the lux-

---

[7] To name only two of many works that have contributed to this project: in literary criticism, Gilbert and Gubar's *The Madwoman in the Attic* (1979), and in sociology, Jessie Bernard's *The Female World* (1981).

urious appearance of gender neutrality conceals that the striving for gender neutrality is an essential element in what it (conventionally) means to be a man. This conflation of gender neutrality and masculinity is *more* taken for granted and is *more* invisible than the fact that gender specificity mediates a woman's relation to the world.

This puts men in a tough bind. The cost to a man of exposing that the appearance of gender neutrality is an achievement of masculinity, is great. To care about gender issues, for example, to question the relation between gender identity and work, is something that only certain women do (under the rubric of women's studies or feminism). To raise such issues appears to be women's work.

To sum up: The treatment of women as gender specific is a taken-for-granted social fact; the visibility of women as women is both socially sanctioned and conventionally unnoticed. It is a perfect example of what Garfinkel (1967) means by a "seen but unnoticed background expectanc[y]" (p. 37). Yet rather than making visible and making an issue of this unrecognized social fact—and hence formulating this treatment as something women have in common—(some) women aspire to be less noticed as women. They want gender to be treated as a neutral fact in the professional world, without having to do the work of examining how womanliness and specificity are conflated, and how manliness and neutrality are conflated in the first place.

Returning to Hochschild's analysis is helpful here. In the context of the frustrated desire that merit alone should count, we can understand how a woman could conceive of the issues of sex discrimination, of how women are treated differently than men, and of what women have in common, as distracting her from concentrating on her work. These questions foist upon her a completely different set of problems. From her point of view, these questions draw her even further away from her work, toward an even more direct focus on the fact that she is a woman. The best interpretation of resistance to dealing with these problems is that they subject women to yet another double work load.

But Hochschild implies that the resistance is deeper; these questions have political implications and consequences. When "woman" is used to describe the professional woman, she feels she is characterized as being like women in general, and as being different from professionals in general. Thus, while the woman resists the corporate or professional culture's focus on the fact that she is a woman professional, we can infer from Hochschild's analysis that the woman herself shares and reinforces that culture's assumption that women in general are different from professionals in general. Hochschild argues (implicitly) that women should fight that assumption, rather than reinforce it by dissociating themselves from women in general, and from gender issues in particular. From Hochschild's perspective, when a woman does not address questions about what women have in common, she resists "minority consciousness." Rather than recognizing that the noise "woman" makes needs to be deconstructed, the woman distances *herself* from that noise.

To refuse minority consciousness is to sabotage the possibility of equal participation for women in general and to prolong their marginality, because it reinforces the dissociation of "woman" from "professional." It is the professional woman's refusal to see the problem in these broad terms, as a problem that does concern women in general, as a structural (and I would add, a cultural) problem, that Hochschild rejects. In this sense, Hochschild would applaud the disruption that the "iron maiden" (as I have constructed her) represents.

If it is true that gender neutrality is a social achievement which masks its masculine character and hides concerns about masculinity, then the desire for a gender-neutral relation to the world, as it is expressed by the professional woman, is a desire to reproduce this masking of concerns about gender, both masculine and feminine. In this context, the desire for gender neutrality is a desire to *avoid* gender issues, particularly the question of the relation between gender and work.

The professional woman who aspires to a gender-neutral relation to the world either fails or refuses to recognize that underneath what appears to be the luxury of gender neutrality is the work of making gender *appear* neutral. The conflation of masculinity and neutrality is not effortless, and only appears to be a luxury.

Although we can understand the extraordinary woman's invisible work as a solution to the problem of contradictory expectations for women, what is problematic about her achievement of a balance between contradictory expectations is not just that she has to be extraordinary to achieve this. What is also problematic, on another level, is that her achievement conceals rather than exposes the gender conflations and allows for their reproduction in the everyday work setting. My complaint is that her invisible interactional work makes more invisible the problematic conflations which need to be made visible.

I have asserted that the professional woman's desire for a gender-neutral relation to work is the desire for an opportunity or luxury that men enjoy, and is not a desire to become a man. I further developed her desire as the desire to mediate her relation to the world, rather than to submit to the mediation of gender. But, this *does not free women from the need to mediate their relation to gender itself.* If the desire for a gender-neutral relation to work is the desire to avoid deliberating over gender issues, then the desire for a gender-neutral relation *is* like the desire to become a man. For it is men who conventionally have a stake in not addressing how gender neutrality is achieved.

If there is such an orientation to the self and to the world which can genuinely be called gender neutral, if transcending gender concerns is in some sense both desirable and possible, the model is not to be found in the invisible conflation of masculinity and neutrality. Both the conflation of masculinity and neutrality, and the conflation of femininity and specificity would have to be examined and deconstructed, before such a notion would be possible.

The "iron maiden" seems to earn her name from her attitude and demeanor: she does not allow herself or others to be comfortable with the conventions of gender relations. She forces gender to become an issue in everyday interactions. But in terms of my analysis, she is not manly at all, for she refuses to let gender be taken for granted.

From the point of view of my analysis, the woman who is metaphorically masculine, the woman to whom the expression "the woman who becomes a man" justly refers, is a woman who does not acknowledge, let alone appreciate, both the importance of and the luxury in the project of gender questions. Women have the opportunity, the power, and perhaps the responsibility to demonstrate to men that any reflective self needs to mediate and to deliberate about the relation of gender to one's participation not only in professional work, but in all worldly activities.

REFERENCES

Ancker-Johnson, B. (1974). Physicist. In R. Kundsin (Ed.), *Women and Success*. New York: William Morrow & Co., Inc.

de Beauvoir, S. (1974). *The Second Sex*. New York: Vintage Books.

Bernard, J. (1981). *The Female World*. New York: The Free Press.

Brownmiller, S. (1984). *Femininity*. New York: Simon & Schuster.

Chesler, P., & Goodman, E. J. (1976). *Women, Money, and Power*. New York: William Morrow & Co., Inc.

Churchill, C. (1984). *Top Girls*. Methuen, Inc.

Ehrenreich, B. (1983). *The Hearts of Men*. New York: Anchor Books.

Elshtain, J. B. (1981). *Public Man, Private Woman: Women in Social and Political Thought*. Princeton: Princeton University Press.

Epstein, C. F. (1970). *Women's Place: Options and Limits in Professional Careers*. Berkeley: University of California Press.

Friedan, B. (1963). *The Feminine Mystique.* New York: W. W. Norton & Co., Inc.

Garfinkel, H. (1967). *Studies in Ethnomethodology.* Englewood Cliffs, NJ: Prentice-Hall.

Gauthier, X. (1981). Is there such a thing as women's writing? In E. Marks & I. de Courtivron (Eds.), *New French Feminisms.* New York: Schocken Books.

Gilbert, S., & Gubar, S. (1979). *The Madwoman in the Attic.* New Haven: Yale University Press.

Hochschild, A. (1974). Making it: marginality and obstacles to minority consciousness. In R. Kundsin (Ed.), *Woman & Success.* New York: William Morrow & Co., Inc.

Horner, M. (1974). Achievement-related conflicts in women. In J. Stacey et al. (Eds.), *And Jill Came Tumbling After.* Dell Publishing Co., Inc.

Kanter, R. M. (1977). *Men and Women of the Corporation.* New York: Basic Books, Inc.

Kaufman, D. R. (1984). Professional women: How real are the recent gains? In J. Freeman (Ed.), *Women: A Feminist Perspective.* Palo Alto, CA: Mayfield Publishing Co.

Koester, J. (1982). The woman as manager: Competing views of organizational reality in popular self-help books. Unpublished paper, University of Missouri.

Kristeva, J. (1981). Oscillation between power and denial. In E. Marks & I. de Courtivron (Eds.), *New French Feminisms.* New York: Schocken Books.

Kundsin, R. (Ed.) (1974). *Women and Success: The Anatomy of Achievement.* New York: William Morrow & Co., Inc.

de Lauretis, T. (1984). *Alice Doesn't: Feminism, Semiotics, Cinema.* Bloomington: Indiana University Press.

Levinson, R. (1982). Sex discrimination and employment practices. In R. Kahn-hut (Ed.), *Women and Work.* Oxford University Press.

McIntosh, M. C. (1974). Educator. In R. Kundsin (Ed.), *Women and Success.* New York: William Morrow & Co., Inc.

Minnhaar, G. (1974). Architect. In R. Kundsin (Ed.), *Women and Success.* New York: William Morrow & Co., Inc.

O'Brien, M. (1981). *The Politics of Reproduction.* Boston: Routledge & Kegan Paul.

Russ, J. (1984). *How to Suppress Women's Writing.* London: The Women's Press.

Simmel, G. (1984). *Georg Simmel: On Women, Sexuality, and Love.* (G. Oaks, Trans.) New Haven: Yale University Press.

Woolf, V. (1977). *A Room of One's Own.* London: Granada Publishing Limited.

Author Index

A

Agar, M., 157, 165, *172*
Althusser, L., 126n, *148*
Altman, D., 200, 210, 215, 221, *222*
Ancker-Johnson, B., 281, 283, *294*
Andersen, E.S., 58, 79, *91*
Apfel, R.J., 98, 99, *121*
ARIC Press, 214, *222*
Arms, S., 178, *195*
Arney, W.R., 193n, *196*
Aschenbrenner, J., 78n, *91*
Austin, J.L., 56, *91*

B

Baehr, H., 250, 252, *253*
Barker-Benfield, G.J., 193n, *196*
Barrett, M., 21, 49, *51*, 126, 126n, 127n, *148*
Bart, P., 4, *15*, 21, *54*
Bartz, K.W., 77n, *91*
Baumrind, D., 77n, *91*
Beardsley, E., 259
Becker, J., 58, 60, *91*
Beels, C., 177n, *196*
Bell, S.E., 101, 112, *121*, 152
Bellinger, D.C., 78n, *91*
Belsey, K., 126n, *148*
Bergman, G.E., 23, 23n, *54*
Berliner, H.S., 40n, *52*
Bern, H.A., 98, 119, *121*
Bernard, J., *172*, 291n, *294*
Birgitte Jallov Report, 252, *253*
Bleier, R., 49, *52*
Bloch, J.H., 179, *196*
Bloch, M., 179, *196*
Blum-Kulka, S., 69, 69n, *91*
Bonilla, F., 164, *172*
Borker, R.A., 55, 89, *93*

Boswell, J., 215, 216, *222*
Bourne, G., 195, *196*
Bramlett, Sgt. J., *271*, 272
Briggs, A., 246, 247, *253*
Brook, D., 177n, *196*
Brown, P., 55, 70, *91*
Brown, S., 233, *241*
Browne, T.D.O., 181, 188n, *196*
Brownmiller, S., 289, *194*
Buchanan, G.S., 210, 211, *223*
Buckley, J., 99, *123*

C

Campos, R., 164, *172*
Carby,, H.V., 227, 228, *241*
Cazden, C., 58, 62, *91*, 152, 160, *172, 173*
Chance, M.R.A., 64, *91*
Chesler, P., 283, *294*
Chodorow, N., 3, 11, *15*
Churchill, C., 276, 277, *294*
Churchill, F., 185n, *196*
Cicourel, A., 2, *15*, 51n, *53*
Clarke, G., *264*
Cloward, R.A., 21, 49, *52*
Cohen, T., 268, 270
Connell, K.H., 182n, *196*
Connolly, S.J., 182n, *196*
Conrad, P., 40n, 47, *52*
Cook-Gumperz, J., 58, *91, 92*
Cooley, C.H., 2, *15*
Cooper, A.J., 228, *241*
Cooperstock, R., 21, *52*
Corsaro, W., 58, 79, 80n, 81, *92*
Coward, R.S., 8, 9, 10, *15*, 130, *148*
Cox, I., 240, *241*
Cox, M., 58, 62, *91*
Crist, J., *271*
Cullen, L., 181n, *196*

Subject Index

DATE